The Joy
of
Learning

BOOKS BY AARON STERN

Ethnic Minorities in Poland - 1937
Nazi Atrocities in Europe
The Making of a Genius
The Joy of Learning
Principles of the Total Educational
    Submersion Method

The Joy
of
Learning

By

AARON STERN

RENAISSANCE
PUBLISHERS
2485 N.E. 214th Street
North Miami Beach
Florida 33180
Phone (305) 931-3392

Library of Congress Cataloging in Publication Data.
Stern, Aaron.
     The joy of learning.
     Bibliography: p.
     Includes index.
   1. Education-Philosophy. 2. Education of
children. 3. Genius--Case studies. 4. Stern,
Edith, 1952—I. Title.
LB885.S786 370.1 76-15510
ISBN 0-916560-01-5

Renaissance Publishers
2485 N.E. 214th Street
North Miami Beach, Florida 33180
(305) 931-3392

Manufactured in the United States of America.

To the memory of
my dear friend and colleague,
Dr. Benjamin Fine,
who devoted his life to the
advancement of education,
this book is dedicated.

"Education is not preparation for life;
education is life itself."

John Dewey

Contents

A Word from the Author

This book encompasses a broad and perhaps unusual range of experiences, constantly focusing on the vital significance of knowledge. The primary objective of my work is an in-depth analysis of the Total Educational Submersion Method, one which develops to the fullest, a youngster's intellectual potential. However, its significance in broadening the cultural horizons of adults will hopefully not be underestimated. Because of the complexities of our industrial society abounding in glorious promise as well as in dire peril, only an enlightened citizen can charter his course successfully.

A society which above all worships material attainments must be sternly reminded about the supremacy of moral values. It is against this background that the scope and contents of the *Joy of Learning* will, I trust, be appreciated.

Foreword

John M. Flynn, Ed. D.
Professor,
Nova University

The Joy of Learning is a book about education, struggle, and life. It is an inspiring and dramatic story of a Jewish refugee from Hitler's Europe and his stark determination to mold his children into what he has called "superior human beigns" using his "total educational submersion" approach to education. But of course, it is more than that for it also is a penetrating analysis of a revolutionary pedagogic methodology as well as an indictment of the inequities and ills of American society, in particular of our educational system.

Aaron Stern has a commitment to honesty and justice and he has high standards of conduct and performance to which he would like to see the world adhere. For a man who has survived beatings at the hands of the Nazis, two years of living in a forest as an animal, cancer of the jaw, and a persistent heart condition, he displays a refreshing disbelief in the injustices of life. While he cannot be considered naive, he is as shocked by the corruption of people and their complacency about life as might be the proverbial farm boy visiting the big city for the first time.

Aaron Stern's daughter, Edith, was molded into a genius, not only as demonstrated by her intelligence quotient, but also as repeatedly shown by her academic performance. Further, both of his children show an impressive ability to cope with life and to interact with other people without fear. How was this accomplished? By Stern's own efforts in which his children were totally submerged in educational experiences.

The entire world of Edith, and probably to a lesser extent of David, has been involved with learning and the acquisition of knowledge. These two children were born into an environment where such activities were as much a part of life as are eating and sleeping in most homes. Education was a normal way of life and they took to it just as any child is aculturated into the ways of the society of which he is a member. It is not unusual that Edith Stern progressed so far; it would have been more unusual if she had not.

What then was the basis of his method? Psychologists have found that the behavior of people can be shaped and strengthened by the careful use of praise and rewards. When the person is well motivated, merely telling him how well he is doing will suffice. Stern seemed to be quite proficient in such methods, making extensive use of spontaneous expressions of love and affection following good performances by the children. Also he would frequently buy them ice cream cones or some other small items as a reward. Occasionally, he would require them to complete a learning task before they could do something which they wanted to do. This is another kind of reward. Even when there was no praise or reward given, he would frequently tell them how well they were doing. This is applied psychology at its best, and he was a master at it.

Other aspects of his method are also important. By working with one child at a time, he was able to achieve the optimal in individualized instruction, a one-to-one relationship. His methods have also illustrated that the tools of education can be austere and Spartan. He used the materials at hand and the materials that a poor man could afford such as old travel posters, an abacus, and most often, the world itself.

It is also important to mention the content of the Stern children's education. They, of course, learned the basics of reading and arithmetic, both being able to read before the age of two. Once they learned to read, there was no limit, for reading became the key to the wisdom of mankind. The curriculum was not pre-determined. If it seemed apropos to delve into history, or biology, or religion, that is the direction their learning went. Stern's objectives were the global, amorphous kind which permitted the children to go where their interests took them.

Aaron Stern strove hard to instill into his children commitments to social justice and the brotherhood of man. He taught them that religion is serving God by helping mankind, that war is never just, that all races and creeds are equals, and especially that women are equal to men. He opposed the Vietnam war long before it became fashionable to do so. It would be easy to describe him as a liberal, but that term is too often misunderstood. Rather, he is a humanitarian and a seeker of justice, and if his educational methods have all bordered on being indoctrination, it is in this realm that they have.

He also taught his children that at the root of all education, there must be ethics and morality as patterned after the teachings and examples of gentle men such as Gandhi, who devoted his life to his countrymen. Stern argues that a mathematician, such as Edith, cannot be a good mathematician unless she or he is also an ethical person. This is the problem that gripped the atomic scientists whose work contributed to the Bomb.

Parents wishing to duplicate Stern's work with their own children should keep in mind that because he was frequently ill and unable to be employed, he had a tremendous amount of time on his hands which he could devote to his children. Most of us do not have such large amounts of time and even if we did it is unlikely that we would be willing to devote it to our children. However, even the partial implementation of his methods would be very beneficial to the intellectual growth of most children.

On the other hand, it is pathetic that parents, if they want their children to achieve full potential and to be well educated, have to resort to educating their children in lieu of the schools doing the job. The purpose of the schools, and the justification for their existence, is to educate the children, and if schools were succeeding, no one would have to educate his own children.

There is yet another aspect to this story. Not only did Aaron Stern give his daughter and son educations superior to those which the schools provided, but when he tried to interest the professional educators in his methods, they sneered. He had asked for a chance to demonstrate his approach to education at local, state, and federal levels, not with middle-class children, but with impoverished, underprivileged ones. No one would give him that opportunity. This is a tragic commentary on those who teach our young, particularly since American education is badly in need of help.

This is a book which should be read by all Americans — parents, teachers, taxpayers, and even the children toward whom education is directed. America and the rest of the world must pin its hopes for the future on quality education, for education is the closest to a panacea for the world's problems as we will probably ever attain. *The Joy of Learning* is a vivid portrayal of the power and potential of education. It shows dramatically that man need not be mired in the mud of mediocrity. Given the right opportunities and experiences, his mind can be unleashed to attain great heights of intellectuality. This book should be an important contribution to the national debate on education.

Introduction

Benjamin Fine, Ph.D.

Former Education Editor,
North American Newspaper Alliance
Education Editor, The New York Times

The Joy of Learning is both a scientific document, to be used as a textbook in child psychology courses, and a moving and fascinating story of the dedication of one man to make a genius of his daughter, and do it with love and compassion. Unlike B. F. Skinner, Aaron Stern undertook to raise his daughter into a genius in face of poverty, ridicule, harassment, serious disease, internal strife, and miraculously succeeded in his endeavor. Needless to say this is a breakthrough in educational process, challenging existing school systems to abandon their traditional obstructionism towards progress. Education can be joyful, it can be total, Aaron Stern shows us. For that we are indebted.

That learning can be a way of life in its totality is not generally recognized; (John Dewey knew this, as does Stern). Too many students and their teachers look upon school and college as a prison sentence, to be completed before they can begin their real life away from books, tests, exams, quizzes, themes, papers and the other trappings of a formal education.

Too often today, as Aaron Stern found, education is barren, boring, stilted, irrelevant and theoretical. Many times teachers find themselves in a straitjacket, controlled by officials more concerned with administrative details than genuine learning. Innovative teachers are often not wanted in the school system.

If you want to succeed, obey the rules, conform to set patterns, don't stick your neck out. In his *No Easy Victories*, John Gardner writes: "Even excellent institutions run by excellent human beings are inherently sluggish, not hungry for innovation, not quick to respond to human need, not eager to reshape themselves to meet the challenge of our times. . . A system that is not innovating is a system that is dying."

xiii

Lord Snow put it this way: "A society which does not encourage excellence will not be a decent society for long."

This philosophy may be the very heart of Aaron Stern's book, *The Joy of Learning*. During his checkered lifetime, which includes more adventure, more suffering, more humiliation, and finally more triumphs than is given to most of us to experience, Aaron Stern has worked for a "decent society." He did not bow to the edict of school officials who said: "We cannot permit your child to go at her own pace. She must travel the path that all others travel."

We owe an overwhelming debt of gratitude to Aaron Stern who refused to accept this verdict, but single-handed fought for his principles and won against incredible odds.

The Joy of Learning is the story of Aaron Stern, but more than that, it is the story of his fight to give his daughter Edith a challenging education. When Edith was born, her father told the hospital nurses:

"I'm going to create a genius."

Oh, yes, they agreed, a kind-hearted, enthusiastic father, just like all other fathers - expecting the world wrapped in a lovely red ribbon for their first-born. But when Aaron followed his prediction with actual accomplishments, he could no longer be ignored.

During the first year of Edith's life, before she could sit in her crib or crawl about, the determined father, who spent two incredible years of suffering, hiding from the Nazi storm troopers and their police dogs, living on berries, existing on handfuls of snow in a Polish forest, somehow able to survive, devoted his time, energy and strength to Edith. He developed the Total Educational Submersion Method as a result.

Education was not a sometime thing with Aaron Stern. From the time she left the hospital and entered their small, unimposing apartment, until she entered school and college, Aaron provided his daughter with educational experiences. Before she could talk, he spoke to her in complete sentences, on a level reserved for mature adults. When she was barely two weeks old she had a radio by her crib, listening to soft, classical music. Before she could walk, he wheeled her to art museums, neighborhood stores, the subway and to the city parks.

Being seeped in the writings of John Dewey, Aaron successfully adapted the sage advice given by the nation's foremost educational philosopher: "Education is not preparation for life; education is life itself." Stern was an early and devoted follower of the Dewey method.

That Aaron succeeded is now well known. At 12 years of age, Edith entered college, graduated at 15 and was an instructor in mathematics at Michigan State University at that age, the youngest college teacher in the country. In fact, she was the youngest person in the classroom!

Now that she has attained her maturity, she has fully justified her father's promise that he would create a "genius." She has an important scientific post with one of the world's largest computer companies. But the traditional public or private school could not offer Edith the type of education for which her father had prepared her. At nine, Edith was spry, enthusiastic, her eyes a-sparkle with love of learning. She was not the slightest bit interested in learning that 75 x 82 equals 6,150 or that 7/10 of 1 percent is an imperfect fraction. She was already studying vectors and sets of her own, knew the difference between cardinal numbers and infinity, and had mastered difficult algebraic and geometric equations.

"Whoever heard of a nine year old child talking such gibberish?" one of the teachers, who admitted she always hated math in school, wanted to know. "Edith is in the third grade and she must learn how to add, multiply, divide and subtract just like all the other children. Who does she think she is, anyhow?"

I'll tell you. She thought she was ready to explore the universe. Although her teachers did not know that, Edith's father did; she fell into the category known as the gifted child. There are, according to a recent United States Office of Education study, between 3 and 6 million gifted children in this country. And their education is being woefully neglected. They are academically and culturally shortchanged. Here is a tragic waste of human potential.

Why are we neglecting these children, Aaron wanted to know. "They can take care of themselves," is a common reply.

However, the U.S. Education report has this to say:

"Intellectual and creative talent cannot survive educational neglect and apathy."

Education should go beyond the basic three R's. We know that what they get at home or early in school life will remain with them always. Unless it brings with it a sense of integrity, a feeling of responsibility, high moral and social values, education will not prove meaningful. Too many talented or gifted persons are found among the despoilers of our country, or the selfish knaves who think only of themselves.

Children who are not taught the meaning of responsibility, of education, of honesty, become a menace to society, rather than a blessing. It is sad to find that in the United States, the richest nation in the world, our most precious natural resources -- our brain power -- is dissipated and lost. We hear a great deal about ecology today, the saving of our streams, lakes, forests and oceans, from pollution and destruction. That is all to the good. But we should also turn to our most precious resources -- our children. They, too, need to be saved.

If they are neglected, as they are in so many schools and by so many unyielding principals or school boards, their brains too, will be wasted, just assuredly as we are despoiling our air or destroying our streams and forests.

One major step towards achieving our goal of giving each child an opportunity to grow and develop at his own pace would be to abolish the chronological age straitjacket now used to admit children. Virtually every public school today has rigid, unbreakable regulations concerning age. No matter how bright a child may be, no matter what his capabilities are, no matter how much spcial training he has received at home through the Stern Total Education Submersion Method, a child must be five at a certain date to enter kindergarten, six to enter first grade. "My child can read and write, but the schools won't admit him," a mother complained bitterly to Aaron Stern, seeking his help.

"How old is he?" Stern asked.

"He'll be four next month," the mother replied.

"I'll see if I can help," he volunteered.

So, Stern called the principal's office, even the Superintendent of Schools. The answer in each case was simple, blunt and sharp: "Our rules and regulations say that a child must be five by December 1st to get into kindergarten, and six by December 15th to enter first grade."

"But," Stern interjected in despair, "here is a child who can read at the fourth grade level. He knows his numbers. He can write. He has a high I.Q. What more is needed?"

"Not old enough, sorry," came the dull reply. It might have been a recorder, so mechanical and impersonal was the tone. "Rules are rules. They can't be broken. If we did it for David or Edith we'd have to do it for the others, too."

Well, why not? Stern wanted to know. If Edith has an I.Q. of 202 why shouldn't she be permitted to go from first grade to fourth from grades five to eight, and then skip high school altogether and enter college, which in fact is what she did.

In addition to eliminating the age barrier, schools should develop a non-graded curriculum to meet the needs of children such as Edith. Children who are ready for a higher grade, or a mixed class, should be permitted to advance as they are able, without prejudice or restraint. Bright children are aware of their limitation. They know they have much to learn and recognize, that they will master only a fraction of the world's available knowledge. *The Joy of Learning* shows us how Edith eagerly absorbed everything she could get, read voraciously, completed the Encyclopaedia Brittanica before she entered first grade, and was not satiated no matter how far she advanced. There is no limit to what the human mind can produce, if stimulated enough.

Our nation needs intellectual leaders in this nuclear age. Democracy must have educated men and women if it is to remain a power for good in our troubled world. We should permit children of all races, colors, creeds, economic status or intellectual ability to get an education consistent with their desires and abilities. In this, we can build an educational and intellectual program that has not been in existence since the golden days of Socrates, Plato and Aristotle.

Democracy can only be built on the solid foundation of brainpower -- the Ediths and Davids of our land.

We have the weapons with which to commit cosmic suicide. Both the United States and Soviets have stockpiled atomic weapons that can provide an overkill of 500 times -- although once would be sufficient for total destruction. We need compassion, devotion, warmth, an understanding heart. We need the ability to live one with another, to keep ourselves and our planet alive.

Our youth are our finest and final hope. Schools must provide educational statesmanship to help restore our sanity, our visions, our dreams, our imagination, our courage, our foresight, our democratic ideals.

We need moral education, but as Lord Whitehead, said, "moral education is impossible without the habitual vision of greatness." Too many of us have forgotten that a democratic society needs the cement of human love and understanding to hold it in place. We can put up a thousand bricks and still not have a building -- the bricks will scatter with a dull crash in the first windstorm.

Educational statesmanship must help rebuild the basic human decency found in man, a common belief in each other, the right to walk the streets of our cities without fear, the end of violence and prejudice, of racial strife, of fear and conflict. Always in the past and so must it be today, the wide gap that exists among us should be met with reason, not rifles, with books, not bullets, with open discussions in the classroom, not secret agents on the campus.

Our schools have a moral obligation, an unending responsibility, to stress quality education, an education that can, hopefully, eliminate the dangerous, polluted, poisonous strife that has burdened the world for decades. Only as we train qualified, top level scientists, mathematicians, physicians, physicists, economists and teachers shall we continue to maintain our civilization.

How can we give our children a sense of vision, faith, responsibility, integrity, service? Aaron Stern shows us how in *The Joy of Learning*. His answer is an education that promotes the highest ideals of democracy. He found that our schools are not doing that now. If we are to retain our freedoms, we must educate all youth to their fullest potential. Aaron found that this is difficult if not impossible under existing public school bureaucracy.

Education is the lifeblood of our civilization. It is the sinews, the muscles, the fiber of free living men and women. Quality education must become our nations's main passion and concern. Through quality education we can acquire the basis for cooperative living, harmony, peace and lasting justice. Education can give our youth a sense of security, a sense of peace, a sense of belonging, a sense of vision.

Unfortunately, mediocrity has often replaced excellence in education. This is plainly shown in *The Joy of Learning*. The majority of our school children are not working to capacity. Many children are not challenged, stimulated or motivated to better work. Edith was. They develop indolent habits of study and are satisfied to go through school with a minimum of effort.

Frequently schools insist that children conform to a preconceived norm. The creative, the high I.Q. child, the nonconformist, the below average youngster, is either forced into the traditional school mold, or breaks his traces and becomes a troubled child, a potential school dropout. A more informal atmosphere is needed in the classroom, permitting children, such as Edith, to develop at their own rate. Schools need not remain grim, joyless or oppressive.

Education begins at an early age. That is the message that Aaron Stern gives us in *The Joy of Learning*. You have heard the cliche: "You are never too old to learn." Now Aaron has added a new dimension: "You are never too YOUNG to learn." It is a message of vital importance to all who are interested in our youth, in the development of a better society, in the utilization of our nation's brainpower.

Aaron Stern's position has now been fully vindicated by psychologists who have studied the effect of early home training on children. They have found that the first three years of a child's life may be the most important of all. Dr. Burton White, eminent Harvard University psychologist, has found that children who at birth get good training are superior, have higher I.Q.'s and do better work when they enter first grade than those who are neglected. Unless the child receives proper, sympathetic understanding and attention while yet in his mother's arms, he will be handicapped not only in school but throughout his lifetime.

Dr. White, as well as other equally distinguished educators and psychologists, has found what Aaron Stern discovered pragmatically two decades ago -- total educational submersion works. It is important and can help the child improve his intellectual emotional and physical well-being.

This is indeed a major breakthrough in our educational world. But Stern had to struggle against almost insurmountable odds to prove to the world that a child of two years, or two months, or even two weeks is not too young to be totally immersed in an educational program.

Aaron Stern created a genius. But some ask, what is a genius? Is it some one with a high I.Q.? Then Edith is a genius. Her I.Q. rates with such intellectual giants as Albert Einstein, John Dewey and Socrates. Is it someone who has achieved professional success? Then Edith qualifies as a genius. She was a university instructor at the age of 15. Is it someone who has made an outstanding scholastic record? Then, once again, we can say that Edith is a genius.

But we must look beyond intellectual achievement. In providing Edith with Total Educational Submersion, Stern did not stop at cultural success. In keeping with his own philosophy, he insisted that his daughter be imbued with high moral, spiritual and humane values, that she learn how to uphold the democratic traits of decency, honesty, integrity and brotherhood. As a result, Edith is now a sensitive individual, filled with compassion for all, eager to give help where it is needed, to share her abilities with those who can gain from them. It is a joy to talk with her.

Of course, parents and teachers will need the skill of an Aaron Stern to motivate their children or students. Without motivation all else will fail. You can't force knowledge into a child the way you force corn into a goose to fatten it for Christmas. It just doesn't work that way.

When asked about motivation by a college professor at one of his lecturers, this was Stern's answer.

"There is nothing mystic about it. Motivate and challenge the child constantly whether at play, rest or recreation. And above all, don't lecture. Learning must be a dual process of discovery, a kind of eternal dialogue."

I strongly recommend *The Joy of Learning* to all who are interested in the improvement of American education, to all who want to see their own children develop to their fullest potential. We can help our children improve their minds, eagerly to search for the unknown and to achieve beyond their expectation. No one has yet tested the limits of the human mind. Stern describes the way it may be accomplished. He remains a modest scholar, an unassuming, dedicated man, a devoted father, with a burning desire to share his exciting experiences in the field of education with all of us.

In talking with college students, Stern said: "I love you young people, the best generation America has ever had. You are our tower of hope."

The Joy of Learning will give hope and courage to men and women everywhere, to all who believe in the democratic process, to all who feel that education can become a way of life, and at the same time, enjoyable. This method will be beneficial to all children.

Who knows how many more Ediths can be developed as a result of Aaron Stern's experience? If even but one, the Stern Method is worth trying. For, as the sages of old tell us: "If you save but one soul, you save the world."

Acknowledgments

I am deeply obliged to my family for the moral encouragement while I was working on this book and to Dr. John M. Flynn for his penetrating foreword.

Many thanks to my beloved daughter Edith, my dear friends, Ms. Lilian Fine, Dr. Leon Kilbert for their literary advice, and last, but not least, to Mrs. Shirley Babione for her expert proofreading.

Above all, I will remain indebted to my late friend, colleague and mentor, Dr. Benjamin Fine, whose eloquent introduction and editorial assistance was invaluable.

To the faculty and students, whose enthusiasm and support sustained me spirtually, I owe my deepest gratitude.

Many thanks to Magazine Managment Co., Inc., Marvel Comics Group, for permission to reprint "Aaron Stern's Impossible Escape" from 1957 issue of Male Magazine.

CHAPTER 1

The Impossible Escape

I lay there in the hole. It was a dank, frozen hole, clawed out of the black, unyielding earth by my desperate hands, and it stunk of my filth. I twisted on the mess of rags that crawled with lice and I looked up at the thatched fir boughs that served as a roof. I was dying of starvation.

The desire to live is an amazing thing. So many times I had been close to death; so many times I had wished that death would claim me; and so many times I had died in my own mind.

But now I didn't want to die. I would fight until the end. I rolled over and pushed myself up on one elbow. I felt the strain in the quickened beat of my heart. I also felt the pounding throb. The infection had made a hideous blue and bulging thing of my leg and the fever burned.

In my delirium I had thought of seizing my knife and ripping the sickened leg to the bone. And I had seen myself elated because of this violent victory over torment.

That was it: victory; to win over something. For years there had been nothing but defeat. There had been nothing except running away, always being hunted, trusting no one, suspecting everyone, being surrounded by the enemy.

More than ever then, as I crawled for the snowed-in opening to the hole, was I aware of the enemies that stalked the forest. There were the wild dogs who would rip you to pieces in a matter of seconds. There were the fiery-eyed wolves who preyed at night. There were the cunning, cruel men of the Gestapo, the local spies who would sell a man's life for a pound of sugar, and the outlaws who would cut a throat for a pair of shoes.

1

I thought of all these as I pulled into the snow. I steadied myself with my staff and tightened the tattered overcoat around me as the wind bit into my flesh. I took the first step and the pain of the infected leg shot through my whole body. Slowly I pushed ahead, my cloth-wrapped feet leaving a wide crease across the white surface. I heard neither the whine of the wind nor the far-off cry of the hungry wolves.

I was possessed with but one thought -- to get out of the forest. For two, long, frightful years it had been my sanctuary -- and it had also been my prison. Now I could stand it no longer. If I stayed another day I would either die or go mad. Even a Nazi bullet would be better.

It was in January of 1943 that I had entered the forest about 100 miles northeast of Warsaw. Like other thousands I was fleeing the Germans. You fled or faced a slave-labor camp or a crematory.

My only possessions had been the clothes on my back. I had no food, no weapons. It was bitter cold and the snow was two to three feet deep. Despite gnawing hunger, my first job had been to make a shelter. So with my hands and a piece of wood I started to dig. By nightfall I had a hole the length of my body and eight inches deep. I had made a crude blanket of strips of fir and when I tumbled into the hole exhausted, I pulled it over me.

I slept only a few hours. When I awoke it was dark and snow was falling. Trembling with the cold, I listened to the wild howls of the animals. Perhaps I would have been wiser to stay in Warsaw, getting a handful of food a day and waiting for the time when I would be herded onto a truck and taken to the ovens.

How many of my family and friends had I seen taken away to die? Days later, through the underground, we would hear what happened to them. Some would be lined up in the public square and shot, but before this they would be subjected to every form of torture and ridicule. Old people would be stripped of their clothes and herded through the streets naked. Those who didn't move fast enough would be clubbed, their arms and legs broken. The girls were publicly exposed to debasement. They prayed for the moment when a bullet would put a merciful end to their shame.

When I remembered all that, I was glad I was in the forest. The thoughts fired me with the overpowering resolution to survive.

2

The dawn of my second day was a raw, gray awakening. I crawled from the hole and began a search for wood. I had a box of matches and heat now was more important than food. I soon had a small fire going. I spent the rest of the day digging the hole deeper and gathering wood for the fire. I meant to adjust myself to the forest and its way of life -- and I would survive.

I learned to identify certain noises. I soon discovered that there were many other people in the forest and I learned how to douse the fire and crawl into the hole without leaving a trace when they approached.

Each day I learned more of my surroundings. About a mile from the hole I found a road used by the Germans to send fresh troops to the front. From a tree I watched troops come and go. When they passed I would leave my perch and search the road for discarded bread and scraps of meat and even chocolate.

The greatest treasures I salvaged from the road were a pair of shoes and a knife eight inches long. With the knife I could do many things. I carved a crude cup from a piece of wood in which to melt snow over the fire and for the first time had something warm to drink.

During the long spells of hunger I was driven to frequent acts of desperation. One night, while a heavy snow fell, I crept past the Nazi sentries into a small village a few miles from the fringe of the forest. I made my way to the barnyard of what once had been a prosperous farm, and caught a plump chicken. Yet, with a fine dinner in prospect, weariness overcame me. I couldn't go any further. I had to sleep. I found the barn and climbed up into the hayloft, the chicken tucked under my coat. I stretched out and was asleep.

I was awakened by barking. When it stopped, I crawled to the barn door and peered out. It was still dark and the snow was still falling. Dashing around the side of the barn, I fled across a field. Finally I found the road and soon I was back in the welcome arms of the forest.

Shortly after this incident I found the frozen carcass of a horse on what appeared to be a seldom-used trail less than a half-mile from the hole. As I hacked away at the joints with my knife, I noticed that the animal had been recently shod. Who owned it, and why was it dead in the forest?

3

In the spring, I got the answer. Deep in the forest, farther than I had ever gone, thrived a large band of outlaws. While there were many guerillas in the forest, too, they were dedicated to harrassing the Nazis and they worked at nothing else. The bandits were another matter. They preyed on everyone, even doing business with the enemy through intermediaries. To be captured by them meant certain death. If you carried anything of value you would be stripped, then turned over to the Germans for a price.

I learned the hard way how cunning they were. It was a warm day in May. I had earlier enjoyed the luxury of washing out the pieces of rags that I used for clothing, sunning myself while they dried. Then I had gone berry hunting.

Suddenly I was surrounded by six men. They had come upon me without making a sound. I jumped like a frightened animal since I had not seen a human being for five months. They were cut throats if I had ever seen one.

"Hello, good friend," one of them said. "We are your neighbors; we also live in the woods. Why do you not join us? We have fine huts and there are good beds and always plenty of food."

Before I realized what I was doing, I had picked up my cup of berries and was walking along the trail with them.

Suddenly I realized how foolish I was. As we pushed deeper into the woods, step by step I lagged behind until all but one of them were walking in front of me. The one who stayed by my side was the one who had invited me to come along.

Without warning, at a turn on the trail, I made my getaway. For a moment he had me by the neck and then I struck. As he stumbled and fell, I darted into the underbrush. With every wile of the hunted coming to me like a second nature. I sped across the ground with scarcely a sound, leaping across rocks and fallen trees as though it was something I had done all my life. The cries of alarm grew fainter. My escape had been good. And then I realized that the horse I had found could only have been theirs.

From then on I doubled all caution. It was just as well. Late one summer evening, as I finished my dinner of boiled grass and berries, I heard an unfamiliar sound. It was heavy tramping--eight or ten men-- less than 100 yards from the hole.

4

The sound told me just one thing; a Nazi patrol was not far off. I knew, as did the other inhabitants of the fores, that the Germans were afraid of the woods and the men in there, and stayed clear. So this meant that the patrol was lost.

Soon the sounds stopped. The patrol had decided to camp for the night. What they would do when daylight returned was anyone's guess. The best thing for me, I figured, was to stay in a tree for the night, a feat at which I had become an expert, losing neither my balance nor a minute's sleep.

I had a favorite spruce not far from the hole and as I made for it I stumbled and fell in the dark. I had no sooner hit the ground than the calm of the forest was blasted with machine guns. For nearly five minuts bullets screamed over my prone body, missing me by inches.

It was hours before I moved again. Then, hoping it was safe, I crawled inch by inch deeper into the woods. When I was out of earshot of the Germans, I climbed a tree and went to sleep.

The summer and its small compensations of berries and grass soon gave way to the harsh blasts of another winter. When the first snow came I was a little better prepared than I had been a year earlier. I had found a coat discarded by a German soldier with which I covered the bottom of the hole. The hole too, was deeper — about four feet — and provided more shelter.

I has also learned the value of a long staff. It was a fine weapon both for hunting and staving off attacks by animals. But better than this was my knife. I had become a master at hurling it, which saved my life more than once. The first time was during a raging storm near the end of December. As I huddled in the hole wondering when I would get a chance to forage for food, I heard the cries of a female wolf just outside. Like everything else in the forest, she was starved and desperate.

Slowly pushing back the thatch that covered the hole, I looked out -- and there she was, about 15 feet away, eyes ablaze. When she saw me the howls of hunger became a hissing snarl. Her fangs were wet and bare.

I faced her, pulled the knife from my belt and sent it flashing to plunge deep into her chest just as she was about to spring. About an hour later I was eating roasted wolf meat. Five days later there was nothing left but the pelt.

5

One morning, while I was searching for fire wood -- I had long since learned how to start a fire by striking two rocks together -- I heard a low growl behind me. I turned just in time to see a giant bulldog coming for me. I ducked to one side as it leaped. While it flayed the air with its claws I sent my staff crashing across its back. It fell to the ground a writhing mass of fury. The animal's spine was crushed but it was still full of fight. Backing off a few feet, I threw my knife. It pierced the belly. A widening crimson spread on the snow. The meat of the bulldog was the toughest I had ever eaten -- but it was meat.

I survived the second winter in the forest without as much as a cold. But I was glad when the grass and the berries sprang up again. For one thing, signs on the trails and the roads to the villages indicated that the local farmers were moving more freely. Was it because the Germans were suffering setbacks at the front? Or was it because people had resigned themselves to the conquest? I had no way of knowing, but I soon found out.

One day, posing as a beggar, I approached a farmer driving a small horse-drawn wagon through the woods. I asked him if he had any food he could spare. He startled me with his friendliness. Sure, he said, he had some freshly-baked bread. Would I like some? He handed me a small loaf. While I wolfed it down he offered me a ride. I accepted. As we rode along he suggested that I return to the village with him. He could get me some clean clothes and if I liked, he told me, I could stay and work on his farm. I listened carefully to everything he said, and the more I heard the promises of good food and an easy job, the more suspicious I became.

Just as we were approaching the village I was sure I heard the sound of hoofbeats. His face indicated that he heard them, too, but he obviously was not concerned. This meant only one thing to me. Get out.

Striking him across the face, I jumped from the wagon. As I leaped he brought his horse whip crashing down across my shoulders. I made the edge of the woods just as a group of German soldiers rode into view.

I was not always to be so lucky.

One day in July, while watching the road from a treetop, a branch broke under me and I fell to the ground. I cut my right hand. I prevented any possible infection with applications of saliva and urine.

6

But while the wounds healed I was unable to use the hand and this brought on a deep feeling of depression. The depression became so bad, I decided to go to the village to ask refuge from the local priest.

It was late afternoon when I started out and it was nearly night-fall as I entered the village. I tried to give the impression I was a beggar, which wasn't too difficult. As I approached the church, I was stopped by a patrol. Since I had no identification papers, I was hustled off to the local SS headquarters for questioning. When I saw the bright lights and the cruel faces all around me any feeling of resignation left me. The urge to fight came back.

I was ordered to a large room on the second floor where other prisoners were lined up with their pants down around their ankles. An SS officer went down the line. If the prisoner was found to be circumcised he was marched downstairs. No further questions were asked.

I was desperate. I told the guard I had to go to the bathroom. He motioned to a door at the end of the hall and gave me a push. To my amazement I found there was no one else in the toilet -- and that there was an open window. In panic I squeezed through the window, dropped to the ground two flights below, then ran into the darkness. There wasn't even a shot fired.

Three hours later I was back in the foul security of the hole. Most of the men who had been in the large room with me were by now dead.

This experience was enough to hold me in check until the cold weather came. And then I felt the urge to move. I was just regaining the use of my hand when I decided to make another break out of the woods.

Again I made my way to the village, again I posed as a beggar, and again I wound up in the hands of the SS. In a matter of hours I was herded onto a cattle train. Destination: a crematorium.

While the train was traveling at its highest speed I made my leap for life, hurtling over the side, and rolling down the embankment. When I regained consciousness I was a mass of bloody bruises. I carry the marks until this day.

Hiding by day, crawling by night, I made my way back to the forest. I could go no place else. My leg was bad. Then the first blizzard of the winter came. I lay in the hole without food and raved to myself as the fever mounted. To prevent myself from going mad I recited poetry while I writhed in agony.

The mental depression now was worse. I relived all the horrors of the Warsaw ghetto. I remembered the night that my wife, Bella, and I had decided that we had to escape. We had crawled into the truck and had been carried outside the gates. I remembered jumping from the truck with Bella and hastily kissing her as she fled in one direction and I in another. What was she doing now? Was she still alive. Was all this hunger and deprivation, all this misery worth it?

I had traveled the 100 miles to the woods posing as a beggar. Could I now escape from the woods by the same route? I got to my feet and stumbled from the hole through the ever mounting snow, my leg thumping in pain. I was saying farewell to the forest after nearly two years. It had been a good friend -- and a bitter enemy.

Now it was 1944. The Germans were on the run -- but I didn't know it. The allies were closing in and pushing back the oppressor.

I pushed on, stumbling, falling through the storm, blinded by the wind and snow, crazed by torment that raged in my leg. And then I found myself standing at the door of a farmhouse. The farmer, moved by my pleas and misery, said, "Come in, come in, out of the cold." My next feeling was that of hot soup coursing down my throat. . . and then of being hidden in a hole under the barn.

For the next few weeks the farmer and his wife helped me and with the hot water and towels they gave me, I bathed my leg and foot. The swelling went down -- and I was able to use it again.

What followed I find hard to describe. It was so unreal. The dawn of freedom had come -- the Nazis and everything they had represented had been defeated. The nightmare of horror was over.

When we fled from the ghetto, my wife and I had agreed to meet in Lodz if we survived the war. After spending weeks making my way across Poland by foot, I was sickened by the death, disease and ruin that greeted me there. Where would I look for her? Then as I stumbled through the rubble of the ghetto, the incredible happened. I found Bella. She had survived by a sheer miracle. Now, having remembered our agreement, she was there, living in a hovel of debris, waiting for me. I can't describe what it meant to see and hold her again.

Finally we made our way to a displaced persons camp in the American zone of Germany.

CHAPTER 2

Birth of the Total Educational
Submersion Method

Bad Reichenhall, located at the feet of the majestic, snow covered Alps in southern Bavaria, commands a magnificent view. Surrounded by mountian streams, beautiful lakes and parks, the town abounds in luxurious villas of Europe's affluent visitors. Its colorfully attired inhabitants traditionally greet each other. "Gruss Gott." Hitler, intoxicated with the unparalleled beauty of the region, plotted his insidious strategy for world domination from his picturesque retreat at Berchtesgaden located ten miles to the south.

In 1946, the American occupation authorities, in cooperation with the United Nations Relief and Rehabilitation Administration (UNRRA), prepared abandoned army garrison buildings at Bad Reichenhall as a site for a large displaced persons' camp intended to be a haven for Jews escaping from the Soviet occupied areas of Europe, where having survived the Nazis, they were now being threatened by a growing anti-Semitism partly nourished by the puppet regimes. Even if the anti-Semitism subsided, there was justifiable fear that these Jews would be permanently isolated from world Jewry by the Iron Curtain. With the tacit approval of Eisenhower, many were aided in their escape by agents of the underground Jewish Army of Palestine, motivated not only by humanitarian reasons but also politically since to establish itself as an independent Jewish state, needed immediately a large influx of immigrants to increase its population, in the face of bitter Arab opposition.

Former concentration camp inmates, weak and resigned, risked their lives to cross the borders of the Iron Curtain countries under fire. Other Jews, many old, sick, or wounded were smuggled in darkness through the rugged Carpathian mountains.

The daring and heroic exodus soon swelled to hundreds of thousands of people, including those, who, like myself, had hidden in forests, those who had obtained non-Jewish documents, as well as those who had survived the concentration camps. The townspeople stared as trucks unloaded the strange conglomeration of people, some of whom arrived without shoes or shirts. Others wore uniforms which had enabled them to camouflage their identities so that they could safely reach the border. Women carried hungry and diseased babies in their arms. Often it was difficult to distinguish the sexes, particularly since many of the women wore rags and had not been able to grow their hair back since their liberation from the concentration camps.

A skeleton of UNRRA administrators had set up emergency services to handle the influx. Food was hastily served to these people, many of whom had not eaten in days. The food was dispensed in a central kitchen, and sometimes people had to wait hours in the cold weather to obtain warm rations. As the first wave of refugees was absorbed, the facilities, which had previously housed approximately 1500 soldiers, now had to house more than 6000 persons. Three or four families shared each room. One toilet facility on a floor had to serve the sanitary needs of fifty to sixty families.

In spite of the dedicated labor of social workers and the generous assistance of the U.S. occupation forces, the task of managing the camp was gigantic. People, who had been denied dignity for years, now wandered about, aimlessly and dazed. Unsupervised children roamed the streets. Tension grew among the camp inhabitants as a passion to get out of Germany became almost uncontrollable. Frustrations grew into despair since the western countries were not eager to admit these refugees and the British administration in Palestine refused to let them go there, sealing off the access with a sea blockade.

As the people realized that what they had planned to be a brief stay in Germany might be indefinitely prolonged, measures had to be taken to prevent total demoralization. A committee of the camp inhabitants was elected which assumed responsibility for law and order under the supervision of UNRRA. Representatives of the American Jewish Joint Distribution Committee, HIAS, the Jewish Agency for Palestine, and other agencies offered their limited resources.

One day as I stood at the food line watching a few youngsters teasing a shabbily dressed old man, I decided that I would try to organize a small school. The children, running wild, were probably the most tragic casualties of the war. They possessed the majesty of a wild jungle, not as beasts, but as primitives, unconfined by the inhibitions of convention, waiting to have their attention aroused, their innate curiosity stimulated. They were excellent raw material for education, and with a school I was sure I could take them off the street and give them real interests and purpose in life.

Soon afterwards, I appeared at a committee meeting and explained my ideas for the school. "All that I ask of you is a spacious, well ventilated room and a supplementary food ration for the children."

"What are your credentials?" I told them I had gone to a university for a couple of years. Then they asked, "How can you conduct classes without textbooks and a curriculum?"

"I shall manage. Anyway, these children have nothing to lose." The committee gave its reluctant consent, and the first of several refugee schools was founded at Bad Reichenhall. Soon I began recruiting my student body. I explained to the parents that I wanted the children for the entire day and that they would be fed at school. As I expected, the parents had no objections since the children had nothing to do in the crowded quarters anyway.

Before long I had thirty youngsters. There were clowns and thieves, exhibitionists and introverts. These were children tormented by tragic memories, often desperately searching for love and affection, and seemingly hungry for guidance and motivation. There was eleven-year-old Sacha who had scouted for the guerrillas in the Ukraine, ten-year-old David who had never known his parents and had been found begging in the streets of Prague, six-year-old beautiful blue-eyed Marysia who had lost a leg when she stepped on a grenade, and the shy, melancholic six-year-old Bela from Hungary. These were children in their formative years, yet adult in their ability to survive. I was awed by them, probably the most unique and heterogeneous group ever assembled in one classroom. They were not even united by a common language.

I realized that these children needed motivation and purpose, and identification with one another. Having taken stock of the political realities, I decided to teach them Hebrew in order to help them develop a sense of pride in being Jewish. Further, I wanted them to develop an attachment and longing for their historical homeland, Palestine. My objectives were much more than the three R's.

11

Before the first class, I hung posters on the walls depicting Palestine and acts of Nazi atrocities. A makeshift blackboard was erected and small benches filled the room. I also obtained a phonograph and a pile of records. When the children filed in for the first time some stared with amazement at the phonograph. I did not demand conformity nor regimentation, but allowed the children to move about curiously.

Soon they began to form groups according to the language they spoke; Polish, Russian, Czech, Hungarian, Yiddish, Croatian, Ukranian and Rumanian. Only a few were bilingual. Usually the second language was Yiddish.

I sat at my table and observed the children's reactions. Soon some of them shyly approached me and began to talk about the posters. As they did, I would gently hug or kiss them, perhaps showing some of them the first affection which they had ever received. At noon as soon as food was brought into the room, they devoured it almost instantly. After lunch, I played Hebrew records. Those records which seemed to make the greatest impression on them I played over and over again. There was some rhythmic clapping and for the first time I noticed a smile here and there. "Haveinu Shalom Aleichem" made the greatest impact so I made a mental note to employ it effectively at a later time. It was dark before I dismissed the class. Many of the children ran over to touch me or to shake my hands as they were noisily leaving the room.

The next day when I entered the class, I was pleased to find that many of the children were there before me. "Shalom iladim," I said as I entered.
"Shalom Aaron," they replied, nearly in unison.

"From now on, " I said in Yiddish since more of them understood Yiddish than any other language. "We shall speak only Hebrew." Then I repeated the statement in five other languages. They nodded.

That afternoon we went on a field trip. The whole group counted the steps in Hebrew from one to ten as we walked along, simultaneously learning Hebrew and discovering numbers. We rested for a while in a meadow at the foot of the mountain. I reached for a flower and said in Hebrew, "beautiful flower." The children all repeated it. Then we sang "Shalom Aleichem."Afterwards we played Simon Says in Hebrew. "Hands up, hands to the face," I commanded in Hebrew as I moved my hands accordingly. "Hands touching the knees," and then the ears, nose, forehead and eyes. Tired and happy, we returned to the tune of "Shalom

Aleichem" alternated with counting the steps in Hebrew. By the end of the second day, the children had learned about 150 Hebrew words, some had learned more.

At the food line that evening, I met a committee member who had been a high school teacher. He asked me, "What kind of a wild experiment are you carrying on? Instead of teaching, you take them on trips. Discipline is what they need most." My battle with the educational world had begun.

The school continued to be mobile; the field trips presented ideal opportunities for the children to learn Hebrew. We visited the camp dispensary, the kitchen, the police station, the repair shop, and construction sites. Within two weeks I realized I had met my first objective -- the children actually spoke Hebrew. This fact was brought home to me by a refugee from Poland. "I am losing my ability to talk with my daughter," she complained. "She wants me to speak Hebrew, too."

"Then learn it, damnit," I angrily replied. "Surely you will not return to Poland to be slaughtered by anti-Semites. Your future is in Palestine."

The school continued to operate and the children to progress. There were no underachievers or troublemakers. All that these children needed was affection and motivation for learning, namely learning that immediately appealed to them and intellectual stimulation to fill the blankness of their minds. I did my best to give it to them. The school ran without pageantry, coercion or decorum. Dirty words were often uttered in several languages. These were uninhibited children free to express themselves, free to react in anger, and free to argue with me even to the point of insulting me. For example, a girl once said (in perfect Hebrew), "I wish you would drop dead, Aaron, on this very spot."

"But why, Miriam?"

"I had no lunch today."

"I am sorry I missed you. I shall make it up." I kissed her tenderly on the cheek and her face lit up. There was no envy or ill feeling expressed by the other children, for I had no favorites. Not all of the children needed this form of affection, yet, they all knew I loved them and they responded freely.

13

My school was different from conventional ones in other ways. There were no tests, marks, guidance counselors, child psychologists, truant officers, nor PTA's -- all those superfluous forms, individuals and institutions which take the fun out of learning. I received no salary nor did I seek one, because no money was available. I owed my services to the children, to their parents, and to my God. These were my children.

The children frequently disciplined each other when minor offenses occurred. For example, Boris broke a window in a farm house during a field trip. Hastily, an assembly was called together at the scene of the crime. "Why did you do it?" the other children demanded.

"I was angry. The Germans have killed so many Jews."

"You were wrong to do it," lectured Chana. "We don't know if this farmer had anything to do with the crimes. When we arrive in Eretz, Israel there will be Arab residents. Would you blame them all for the Jews who have been killed there?"

"I'm sorry," Boris said. "I won't do it again."

One day a girl asked me in class why her father climbed on her mother during the night while uttering horrible sounds. This was a legitimate question, and I answered it as such. We discussed clearly the process of reproduction and the sexual anatomy of men and women. While our discussion was in progress, Chava, aged seven, suddenly undressed herself and showed the class her body. I reacted impulsively and cried out, "Don't do it! Put your panties back on at once!" But the reaction of the other children was calm and mature. There was no giggling and no vulgar comments. Our lesson on reproduction was concluded by a visit to the camp hospital where the children studied medical drawings and then looked through the windows at the maternity ward.

The next day a girl of eleven candidly described how she had been sexually molested by an intoxicated border guard. The class listened attentively. I hoped that the experience would not affect her psychologically in the future. All that she had ever known was tragedy and this had been just one more painful episode.

Our school functioned seven days a week, eight to ten hours a day, and everyone had fun. The children gladly attended Sabbath service and afterwards we took walks, sang songs, and dreamt and talked about the future. As their verbal skill and comprehension increased, I began to tell

14

them of the drama and beauty of the Jewish history. The Bible with its poetic language inspired them deeply, particularly the battles in defense of freedom. The slavery in Egypt provided a meaningful parallel with the Nazi persecution. "I know who the contemporary Moses is," Chava cried. "It is Ben Gurion." The prophets with their eloquent and courageous messages told the children of social justice and moral values. The posters on the wall assumed more meaning as the historical sites were identified. The records, enriched by a shipment from Palestine, served various purposes. They enhanced the appreciation of music, but even more they brought Israel to the children. Some of the records were sad, while others conveyed the vigor of the reborn nation. Still others brought to the camp the militant spirit of the liberation army. The records helped the young students to identify with the struggling young nation -- their nation.

Our school still lacked the resources of other schools and so we continued to make the best of what was available. The field trips provided excellent sources of information. For example, we visited the railroad station and the electric generating plant where the children obtained first hand information about physics. Trips to the countryside provided a fine textbook for the study of ecology. They learned of the geography and topography of Palestine from a poster map. We followed current events, discussing them daily. Personal hygiene and sanitation was a critical problem for the camp inhabitants and so we spent a lot of time discussing it. The Americans in the town helped the children to acquire some English and most of the children learned German.

Although I worked with the total group on field trips and discussions, I never lectured to the students. Rather I offered individual attention to every student in the form of dialogue which could reach him on his own level. Thus, the age differences among the children did not create any particular problems. The rapport between myself and the children as well as among the children was excellent. The older children assisted the younger ones, often carrying them on their shoulders during the frequent field trips. The class formed its identity as a group.

Although the lack of adequate learning materials by the standards of most schools might be perceived as a handicap, I do not think that it was. Similarly, I do not think that the crowded poverty stricken conditions of camp living were a handicap. Occasionally, some of the families secured better housing outside of the camp and the children left my class. After they left, they gradually lost interest in school and studying. I concluded, therefore, that Spartan conditions make for growth and development and that comfort and affluence retard the zeal for learning. These conclusions were my guiding light in the work with my own children several years later.

I had avoided teaching the children in the school how to read and write, yet they learned other subjects well without the mastery of reading. I had put off this task because there was a lack of books and because teaching the intricacies of the Hebrew alphabet frightened me. However, eventually I had to face the chore. One day I came to school early and wrote the Hebrew alphabet on the board. When the children arrived, they found pencils and tablets on the tables. I told them that we were going to learn how to read and write. Then I slowly and clearly read. "Aleph, Beth. Daleth." The children soon joined me in unison and we adapted a melody to it which they enjoyed.

For the next few days, the children wrote the alphabet on the tablets. Before long all the children could identify the letters of the alphabet. Then I wrote simple words while I pronounced them: "Shabath, Shalom, Israel, Galil." I called volunteers to the board -- all were thrilled to go -- and had each one write a word that he then memorized. Within four weeks every child could write the alphabet.

My next target was numbers and arithmetic. This was a much easier task than the alphabet since the children already knew the digits from seeing them on the buildings. I divided the class into two groups; the children up to eight learned how to count and add and the older children learned simple multiplication. They practiced two and three digit multiplications while on the field trips and I was surprised at how good they were at it without pencils and paper. Fractions were also learned on our field trips where, with a pocket knife, we would carve out squares and divide them. Thus, like the ancient mathematicians, I taught geometry in the sand.

I was delighted by the success of the school. In a matter of three months, the children had not only learned Hebrew but they had adopted it as their mother tongue. They had been transformed from wild animals, beset by fears, to emotionally mature children. They were well advanced in the social and the natural sciences. They could read and write, and had learned arithmetic. Further, in light of my original objectives, they were proud of their heritage and they were dedicated to the Zionist aspirations for the relocation of the Jewish people to their homeland. All this was accomplished without threats, bribes or punishment so common in the public schools.

16

Intoxicated with my success, I obtained some tests from a German public school principal by which to assess the level at which my children were performing. The tests had been published by the German Ministry of Education and I spent three nights translating the science and mathematics questions into Hebrew. The history and language questions dealt with Germany and so they were irrelevant for these children. Therefore, I designed my own questions for these areas of their learning. Then I tested them. The outcome was fantastic; the children in my school matched and at times excelled slightly their German counterparts who had attended school for three to six years. Thus, my total educational submersion method had been born.

One day I visited an ailing friend near Frankfurt, and I was detained for another day by a cold. This was the first time I had been absent from the school. While I was away a touring American congressional delegation, or perhaps it was the Anglo-American mixed commission, visited the camp to study the refugee problem. They conducted a hearing at which dozens of displaced persons appeared to state their preferences for immigration. Most of them wanted to go to Palestine. A delegation of youngsters asked to be heard. The chairman was surprised, but he granted them permission to speak. Then, as it was later reported to me, about fifteen youngsters ranging from eight to fifteen, entered the hall singing the Zionist anthem, "Hatikvah," in Hebrew. One by one they took the stand and identified themselves by biblical names, which they had chosen for dramatic effect.

For example, one youngster took the stand and was asked, "What is your name?"

"Joseph."

"Age?"

"Nine," he replied in Hebrew.

"Where were you born?"

"In Haifa."

"Where would you like to go?"

"Home to Erezt Israel."

Similar testimonies were given by each child. They left in formation singing "Chava Nagila." As they had planned, their performance visibly touched the delegation.

When I returned to the camp, I was greeted by a committee member who exclaimed, "Aaron, that was a fine and effective Zionist presentation. Congratulations."

"What are you talking about," I asked since I had not yet heard about it.

"You actually had nothing to do with your children's presentation?"

"What presentation? Of course, I did not."

Although I have lost contact with these students of mine, I am confident that, notwithstanding their tragic background, they are capable of great devotion and heroism in defense of their Promised Land.

CHAPTER 3

Darkness at Noon

Bad Reichenhall was behind me now. It was late afternoon as the declining sun cast its long shadow upon the walls of my furnished room in the Bronx. I was lying on my bed remembering the nightmares of my past -- the Nazi atrocities, the endless flight, the jump from a moving train, the last meeting with my parents before their extermination, the cruel beating at the hands of a bloodthirsty SS trooper, who threw me on the concrete and stomped on my face.

That was the past. Now I had to face the present. I had just been discharged from a hospital with a large hole where there once had been a lower jawbone. Several operations had been unsuccessful and the cancer resulting from beatings in the camp kept recurring. Two transplants caused osteomyelitis. There was virtually no hope for me as I was told by my attending physicians.

My wife, Bella, was the mainstay of my existence during these ordeals. Little had she known when she met me as a nursing student in pre-war Warsaw that she was destined to lead such a life of struggle with me. After surviving the war, she had worked as a head nurse in the displaced persons' camp hospital. There she had to cope with the endless physical and mental wounds which were destined never to heal.

On our arrival to our newly adopted homeland in 1949, Bella's high hopes for peace and tranquility had been shattered by my deadly disease -- which soon encompassed a major portion of the medical dictionary. Yet in defiance of the gloomy diagnosis, she would assure doctors. "I know Aaron is too stubborn to die." Undeterred by the long, almost endless chain of surgeries, she would faithfully stand at my bedside until past midnight, feeding me through a straw and cheering me. Then reluctantly in the wee hours of the morning, she would make her lonely subway trip to our home in a Bronx slum so she could get a few hours of rest before going to work early the next morning.

Once Bella told a neighbor how en route from the hospital a youngster had snatched her pocketbook containing $50 -- the only money that she had. The next day, another handbag was presented to her by the poor but generous neighbors with a $50 bill and a neatly inscribed note: "We hope he will soon get well."

Unfortunately, the wish did not come true. More and more bone grafts, which slowly dismembered my body, were transplanted into my cancerous jaw -- while osteomyelitis caused them all to be rejected. But nothing could diminish Bella's courage. She often remarked in her heavily accented English, "I fail to understand why women are regarded the weaker sex. It would appear to me we have more endurance and stamina than men."

Finally, disgusted by the endless surgeries, I asked for a discharge from Bellevue Hospital. The doctors demanded of Bella, "Where will he go with a bent wire replacing his jawbone, accompanied by chronic draining?"

"I shall nurse him back to life," she replied. "How? I don't know yet. We have faith in God."

So I returned home with a twisted face. Unwilling to see friends, I spent my time avidly reading German books on anatomy and surgery. The physicians had said that any additional bone transplant would be a failure and might stimulate metastasis of the tumor. My only alternative was to live -- to live on borrowed time with an empty hole in my mouth.

Again, Bella helped to sustain me. After spending a day at work, she would come home, wash me, and while hiding her tears, lecture on the miracles of the body and the phenomena of tumor regression. She worked at keeping my spirit alive: "Surely you did not survive all this tragedy to succumb to a disease in this great country."

"You know my dear," I responded, "I have a feeling that somehow a miracle will occur and I shall conquer this deadly disease."

"I know you will." She embraced me tenderly, burying her tearful face on my chest.

20

Thus, there I was on that late afternoon, lying in bed thinking. Did it pay to survive the horrors of Nazism in order to die in the midst of freedom and prosperity? What could I do? Although I had been faced with adversities in the past somehow I had always survived. Yet how can one overcome a terminal disease?

Deep in my heart I had the faint hope that once more I would survive. I was sure it was God's will -- but how? Suddenly a thought occured to me. Why not seek the advice and assistance of the wisest living creature -- Albert Einstein? I always had a great admiration for this man, who in my judgment represented a rare blend of altruism and intellect -- one who walked in the steps of Gandhi. Einstein, of course, was not a logical choice to help a man dying of cancer for he was not a physician, but this was no time for logic. I was desperately trying to save my life. I rationalized my decision by reasoning that doctors did not try hard enough to save lives unless they were well paid and I had not been able to pay them as a free patient. Thus, perhaps I could be saved if I could obtain financial assistance. Perhaps Einstein could advise me.

Bella rejected the idea as simply unrealistic, but I was determined to see Einstein. I dressed and decided to go to Princeton. As I was leaving the house, I met a friend who asked where I was going as it was unusual for me to leave the house alone. I replied that I was going to Princeton. Jokingly, he suggested that I say hello to Einstein. Little did he know that I intended to do so.

I reached Princeton by bus and went to the Institute of Advanced Studies where they gave me the professor's address. As I approached his home, I realized the difficulty of my mission. This was a period during which Einstein had become withdrawn; just a few days before he had refused to see a reporter. As a man who cherished the sanctity of life and the dignity of man, he suffered from guilt over the atomic bomb, as I found out later. Having been instrumental in its development as a drastic step to rescue the world from the Nazi menace, he was tortured by the thought that it could destroy hundreds of thousands of lives. Further, many unscrupulous people sought to reach him for their own selfish purposes. And above all, his shyness and modesty called for total seclusion. Thus I realized that it would be unlikely that I would get to see him.

Hesitantly, I knocked on the door of his modest home. Soon a middle-aged housekeeper appeared and in her heavy German accent advised me that the professor could not be disturbed. I summoned my

21

courage and loudly stated my business in German. My strategy was simple, but daring. I was determined to state my objective so that the great man could hear the depth of my drama and invite me in and this is what happened. As I was talking with the housekeeper, the attic door opened and Albert Einstein emerged. His large, penetrating eyes were warmly focused on me. His long gray hair, like a halo, surrounded a benign, patriarchal face, full of warmth and compassion. I knew I was in the presence of a saint. Awed, I could hardly speak.

He descended the creaking stairs slowly.

"Come over here," he said, inviting me to his austere study.

I mumbled a few words which were probably incoherent. Then I heard him say, "I am so glad you came to see me." This was no sarcasm -- it was sincere. "Why didn't you come to see me earlier? Perhaps I could have been more helpful then, but after all I am no physician. I must rely on my friends' judgment. But I shall do all I can to restore your health."

I stayed for dinner with Albert Einstein. He said he would get in touch with his physician friend and do all in his power to help me. As he shook my hand at the door, he said firmly and warmly, "You must come to see me again."

As I rode the crowded bus back to New York a powerful ray of hope shone in my heart. I knew he was the only one who could help me. Yet it sounded so incredible. Why, I wondered, would this great scientist, so aloof even to members of his own family, so inaccesible to the mightiest, devote his time to a person like myself? To what could I attribute his warmth and compassion? I saw him as a true saint who showed contempt for might and wealth, but who was touched to the point of tears by s suffering human being.

The next morning a call came to my home. My landlady was bewildered when a doctor asked to speak with Mr. Stern on behalf of Professor Einstein. Soon, my visits to Albert Einstein became frequent. These were the most memorable events in my life. I recorded many of our conversations -- hoping to publish them, but later they were stolen from me.

We discussed the question of war and peace, the atomic bomb, his part in it and what he felt the outlook for world survival would be if a Third World War would be fought.

"Tell me, Dr. Einstein," I asked, "you are the father of the atomic bomb. You know what it can do to our very existence. How do you think the Third World War will be fought -- what weapons will be used, who will win?"

The great professor paused a moment in thought, then said: "You know, Aaron, I am really sorry that I ever sent that letter to President Roosevelt, telling him of the powers that a bomb of this nature could possess. The next major war, if it comes, will be devastating. It is too horrible to contemplate. I really don't know what weapons will be used nor how this new war will be fought."

We were both silent, contemplating what might lie in store for us. Then Dr. Einstein, in solemn tones, said:

"No, I can't tell you how the Third World War will be fought. But I can tell you how the Fourth one will be."

"How?" I asked, taken aback.

"With sticks and stones," came the gripping answer.

He said nothing for awhile, then began again:

"I am sorry for any part that I played in bringing the world into this dangerous situation. Oh, what horrors we commit in the name of science."

"But," I said, "you are a world-famous scientist, a physicist, a man respected and admired everywhere. Doesn't that give you any satisfaction?"

"Sometimes," he answered, "I think I'd rather be a plumber."

"Are you serious?" I questioned in disbelief.

"Indeed I am," the world-famous scientist retorted. "And if I were to advise young people starting out in life, I would urge them to become plumbers, to learn to be carpenters, to be bricklayers -- to do something useful, something constructive, and not to become scientists and place the world in a position where it can commit cosmic suicide."

But this mood soon left him. I referred jokingly to his unkempt appearance, to his mismatced socks, his baggy pants, his turtleneck sweatshirt, his ruffled, uncombed hair.

"Doesn't it bother you when people say that you are untidy and that your appearance isn't in keeping with your high station in life?" I asked.

Dr. Einstein chuckled in that whimsical way of his. "Oh, not at all," he replied. "You know, Aaron, it would be a sorry day if the bag that holds the meat is more important than the meat itself."

On another occasion we talked about the growing crisis in education, the lack of communication between the young and old generation, the need for greater respect on the part of all people, young and old, towards each other.

"What is the answer to all our problems, Dr. Einstein?" I wanted to know. "What do you suggest we do?"

"I don't know the answers. I guess we are all little children in a big ocean, and our rowboat has lost its oars."

This reminded him of a story which he related to me: "One evening, while taking the sleeper from New York to Chicago," Dr. Einstein said, "I began to get hungry. It was 6 o'clock and dinner was being served. So, I got up from my berth in the bedroom, and began to walk toward the dining car. I walked and walked for what seemed endless cars, but actually, it was only my hunger that urged me to go forward. Finally, I reached the car where food was being served.

"The train steward welcomed me and placed me at one of the small tables overlooking the window... it was getting dark so not much could be seen except a blur of light as we passed through a small town or village. Finally, the waiter came to my table and handed me the menu. I peered at it, but being unable to read without my glasses, I reached into my inside coat pocket for my reading glasses. With dismay, I discovered that I had left them in my bedroom, some 10 or 12 cars away.

"Accordingly, with a sheepish smile, I handed the menu to the waiter, and said: 'I can't read this. Would you read the menu for me, please, so that I can order my dinner?' "

The waiter, a genial, happy fellow, took the menu card, peered intently, turned it sideways, then said apologetically "I'm sorry, sir, but I'm afraid I'm just as ignorant as you are. I can't read, either."

To which Dr. Einstein added this postscript: "I guess we are all ignorant. There is so much to learn, so much to discover, so much to unearth, so many formulas to decipher, and so little time in which to do it. In one sense, all of us can't read, we all have lost or misplaced our glasses, and we have no one to read for us."

"Could a plumber help us find the way?" I asked in jest.

"No, but neither can a scientist, if he isn't wearing the right kind of lenses."

Dr. Einstein was passionate in his belief that we should maintain our democratic ideals, that we should always be on guard against traitors or misguided leaders who would lead us to destruction. He had gone through the Nazi persecution, as had I, so we both knew, at first hand, the unspeakable destruction of the human soul and spirit that dictators or demagogues could foster. Every man, he felt, should be his own master, should think for himself, should be free and honest.

"You know, Aaron," he said, somewhat affectionately, as was his wont when we spent a Saturday afternoon together, sipping tea, or while I listened to his improvisations on his beloved violin. It seemed to comfort him, to take him away from the everyday world of tragic disasters and unending conflicts.

"You know, I am a poor carpenter. If I wanted to bang a nail in straight, I would call the local handyman and assign him to the job. Oh, I would have to pay him the prevailing rate, which with overtime might be 10c a nail. Well, I would get my mirrors on straight, or the doors in proper place, and the nails would go down firm and straight.

"But, if I wanted to think straight, I would have to think for myself. I couldn't call upon the local mayor, or my senator, or governor, and no, not even the President of the United States himself. If I give up the right to think for myself, I give up my right to be a free man in a free country. And that right neither I nor you, Aaron, nor anyone else, must ever relinquish. It must always be our most precious possession, the banner that will keep us free, that will enable us to live without fear, with our heads held high."

I knew what he meant. I, too, had been through an era when it was dangerous to think for oneself.

Finally the long hoped for miracle did occur -- thanks to Albert

25

Einstein. I was admitted to the Mayo Clinic. Again Bella gave me strength. Over my protests, she accompanied me to Minnesota where she rented a small room with the assistance of a relative and the generosity of the clinic. During the tests and surgery which followed, Bella stayed by my bedside, sleeping in a chair. Once she asked the doctor, "Could I offer him my hip? After all there is so little left of him after all these surgeries."

"Are you serious? What a magnificent example of loyalty. No, Mrs. Stern. From the limited experience that we have, only a graft of a close relative such as a father has any chance of success -- yours would be rejected. We shall take his rib and transplant it into the jawbone and I assure you it will be successful."

"Why were the former surgeries unsuccessful?" Bella asked.

"Please don't quote me, but your husband was neglected. His first surgery consisted of the removal of the diseased jaw, removal of the rib, and the grafting of it all in one surgery. This was too much. Osteomyelitis set in rejecting the graft. Now we will first remove the wire substitute for the jaw bone and let his jaw heal. Then we will proceed to extract his rib and graft it. We hope we can save his life."

"You will have saved two lives," Bella replied.

Soon the surgeries were completed and hope replaced despair. Bella became a vital part of the therapy -- so much so that the clinic relocated her nearby. She would raid the library for me, and I read voraciously all that I could obtain. God only knows how she survived the eight months, as her only income was a small subsidy from the clinic.

"Bella, we should put you on our payroll," my surgeon, Dr. Figi, suggested half in jest. "Nothing could have been done without you. Where do you find your courage?"

"I do quite well," she replied. "I get my strength from Aaron's recovery."

And thanks to Albert Einstein and the generosity and competence of the Mayo Clinic, I did recover. In the spring of 1951, I emerged with a successfully transplanted jaw bone. Cured and happy with a new lease on life, I went back to New York accompanied by my loyal wife. I did not know it then, but my experiences were destined to have a great influence on the rearing and education of my yet unborn daughter.

CHAPTER 4

Intellectual Growth Starts at Birth

Unfortunately, my good health did not last. While the cancer was gone, my body, weakened by years of abuse, succumbed to new ailments. First I developed thyroid trouble, then heart disease. Together the doctors described it as an elaborate syndrome. I was repeatedly hospitalized with only occasional short periods at home. Again, Bella kept my spirit alive. Her frequent visits to the hospitals became her only recreation and the people she met there provided her only social life.

In August, 1952, during this period of ill health, our daughter Edith, was born. I was home between hospitalizations when the time came. Bella arose during the night and without waking me went to the hospital. The next morning I was called to the public phone in the roominghouse where an intern informed me, "Mr. Stern, your wife has given birth to a healthy girl."

Surprised, I replied, "How can that be? My wife must still be sleeping in the room."

I hurried to the hospital. "Why didn't you wake me up?" I inquired of Bella as she held the crying infant at her side.

"Well, I was afraid that awakening you might cause a relapse of your condition." Bella followed the same pattern almost eight years later when our son, David, was born.

As I looked at my healthy, six-pound daughter, I could not help but recall how a year earlier, Bella had been warned by a hospital physician not to have children by "the man who nearly epitomizes the whole

27

textbook of pathology, for it won't be normal. The war experiences have left a deep scar on him which will never heal."

Thus in defiance of the doctor's advice, Edith was born and I was determined that his prognosis would be wrong. However, I did not plan that Edith should be only a normal child; rather I publicly stated that I would make her a superior human being, able to make a lasting contribution to the world. When I invited friends to see her I told them bluntly that she was destined to become a "genius." By that I meant I would dedicate all my talents and energy to training her from babyhood to become a finely-balanced and superior human being, with an intelligence developed to its most remarkable potential, keenly aroused to the greatest values in life, a mind richly stored, capable of the clearest, the most independent and most humanly important thought.

Bella was opposed to my plans. She insisted that all she wanted was a normal child, not a genius or an outstanding intellect. However, I stuck to my plans, thus beginning years of conflicts with my wife who, until this time, had been my salvation. Time and time again, my dreams of making Edith into a genius and Bella's desire for a normal child were to clash. Later, I became so engrossed in "molding" Edith that her mother had to give up some of her responsibilities toward the child.

For example, after her mother discontinued breast feeding her at five months, I insisted that I should feed the baby, for as I told Bella, "This period is conducive to learning."

"Please don't deny me this pleasure," she pleaded.

"Someday, you will realize the significance of my methods." Reluctantly, Bella gave in.

Our home at that time was not the highly equipped learning environment many educators would say was necessary for the development of a superior mind. We were quite poor and we lived in a one room attic at Sea Gate, a once fashionable oasis of Coney Island. We shared the bathroom, which had extremely poor sanitary conditions, with six other families. One of the occupants was an eighty-five-year-old man who would frequently fall asleep for hours while using the bathroom. Heating in the winter was inadequate and hot water was scarce. The furniture -- which comprised all of our worldly possessions -- consisted of two beds, and old table, and three chairs, which were of too recent vintage to be considered antique, yet too old to be functional. But there was a bookcase bulging with books, and two special items which were destined to influence the baby. These were an old German encyclopedia and an old, but well functioning radio. I did not regard poverty and deprivation a handicap in the attainment of my goal.

Too proud to consider assistance from any source, we were the only family in the building not living on welfare. Not having a crib for Edith, we improvised one from a closet drawer taken from the basement.

The day after Edith came home, I re-entered the hospital where I stayed for three weeks. Upon returning home I started the developing process. "Bella from now on," I said in Polish, "the radio should be tuned to WQXR at all times. It is the only station broadcasting classical music continously. Let the volume be merely audible when the baby is asleep and louder when she is awake, but by all means let the child be always exposed to fine music."

"What will the neighbors say?"

"Well, old as they are, they sleep too soundly to be awakened easily. On the other hand, music during the day is perfectly proper."

"How will Edith react to music?" Bella wanted to know.

"Her reaction will be desirable or rather there will be no reaction at all since this will be the only environment she will know. Music will shut out everything but the most harmonious sound. This shall be the first step in her education."

Bella was less than convinced. "No one has ever treated a baby like this. God knows what will happen to her."

"Well, Bella. Apart from the fact that I am fully convinced of the successful outcome of this experiment, Edith would otherwise hear the squeaks of passing cars, slamming doors, our quarrels as well as those of our neighbors, and the constant flushing of the toilet. Intellectual growth should begin at birth and end only at death. This is the best way I or anyone can reach the baby at her age." Reluctantly, Bella gave in to me.

The radio was turned on, never to be silenced again except for repairs. The soft, melodious flow of Chopin on the piano filled the room. Edith at first moved her body nervously, but soon fell asleep calmly without a cry. She awoke later, was fed at her mother's breast, then calmly and contently, she rested for an hour or so, while the music played softly. Soon, even changing her diapers was not an ordeal, for she cried much less. Later as she was giving Edith her bath, Bella remarked, "It seems to me that she splashes her feet in the water to the tune of *Prince Igor.*" Indeed, music became Edith's constant companion.

When Edith was eight weeks old, I reported in my diary in German, "It seems to me that the best way to pacify Edith when she cries is to increase the volume of the music. In contrast, however, she becomes restless and unhappy when popular or jazz music is substituted for the classical music. An adverse reaction will even occur when the baby sleeps, for she will instantly awake crying."

She became so familiar with classical music, and loved it so much that a beautiful smile would cross her face at a favored passage of *Swan Lake* or *Carmen.*

When Edith was taken for a stroll in her Victorian carriage near our house, the radio was placed in the middle of the lawn, with a long extension cord. It would then be turned to the highest volume while my wife wheeled her around the house. When she was occasionally taken on more distant trips she was always restless, for she could not hear the music. Later the problem was resolved by a friend who gave her a beautiful portable radio.

My eccentric conduct in the house at Highland Avenue, Brooklyn, was frowned upon by the neighbors but tolerated because "He is a sick refugee who survived the hell of the Nazis." However, on the Day of Atonement, the most solemn holiday in the Jewish calendar, my neighbor, an old man, could not restrain his indignation any longer, He knocked on my door and complained in Yiddish, "We tolerate your outrageous conduct, this constant crazy music for a long time. But on this holy day of Yom Kippur, how dare you turn on the radio."

"Well, my dear man. Perhaps this is the way in which our child seeks communion with God."

"Who can understand these crazy refugees." He slammed the door and never exchanged another word with me.

Aside from the great attachment to music which Edith developed, there was nothing particularly remarkable about her early childhood. Like other young infants, she slept a lot, occasionally was cranky, and loved her food. At times she suffered from diaper rash and diarrhea, but generally enjoyed good health and gained weight normally. Her motor ability and general physical development seemed to be very good. But unlike many other babies, she did not enjoy a separate nursery room or expert medical care. When she was ten weeks old, we were able to replace the closet drawer with an old dilapidated crib given to us by a friend. The crib stood in the center of our dingy, poorly furnished room. Bella was able to provide the medical care thanks to her nursing background; Edith did not have to see a physician until she was eighteen months old.

By the time she was ten weeks old, her crib was filled with meaningful educational toys and illustrated books. Her dolls had social significance as they were of many races obtained from the gift shop of the United Nations. I considered it to be very important to have both black and white dolls, because I was determined that my child would not be prejudiced toward anyone. There was also a great variety of animal pictures from the Bronx Zoo and flashcards of the numbers from one to ten. These were never removed from her crib.

Another important factor in her early education was the conversation between Bella and myself. I decided that we would speak only in English, and in a very calm and slow manner, facing her whenever possible. She soon began to focus her eyes attentively on each speaker.

Also, I began to talk to Edith at an early age. There was no baby talk such as, "Milky drinky," or "Bu-bu, let's go bye-bye." Rather, both Bella and I addressed ourselves to her as an adult in an articulate and mature manner. "Please be quiet. Open your mouth, Edith, and let me wipe you. Where is your mother? Do you like the music? Please try to sleep some more. Do you want milk?" are examples of what she heard at approximately four months. I had named every doll and expected her to identify it. Similarly, she identified her animals a month later. At that time, the baby amazed me, as my diary states, by "recognizing approximately 400 words which she identified by gesture."

Partly because of our extreme poverty, Edith had the almost constant presence of her parents. This atmosphere, we were told, could be very detrimental to a child's development. However, because of the deplorable housing and my determination to mold her, Edith was destined to be always at the center of activities. Thus, she shared in the sorrows and the occasional joys of the family. To compensate for our material shortcomings, Edith enjoyed great affection, which she fully reciprocated. Both her mother and I held her in our arms for a good part of the day, always talking to her intelligently. In order to attract her attention, I would lower the volume of the radio and say to her slowly and clearly, "I love you so much my Edith. You are such a pretty girl. Would you like to go out?" By 6½ months, a nod of her head would suggest understanding.

Undoubtedly, one of the most effective methods of working with her was my daily routine of reading aloud. This I did not only to master English, but also in hopes I could communicate its meaning early to her. Edith was not receptive to the reading like any other infant of her age. However, this did not deter me. For weeks I read stories to her without noticing any degree of comprehension while being ridiculed by my friends and neighbors and being scolded by my wife. You may talk to her until your face will trun blue. She simply is too young to comprehend it and there might be some ill effects too," I was warned by a friend who had the good fortune to study under Freud.

Gradually, however, Edith became accustomed to the routine and seemed to like it. She would point to the radio which meant that I should reduce the volume of the music in order to read. The daily reading sessions lasted from an hour to an hour and a half. I would select a simple passage of a story designated for six to eight year-old children and slowly read: "The hungry child asked his mother for food." An illustration below the story made it more comprehensible. I would repeat the sentence three or four times and point out the appropriate part of the illustration. "You see, Edith, this is the boy and here is his mother." Edith, of course, was not able to make but a few sounds in response. I went on reading.

Later, during the afternoon hours, I would read aloud from *Life* magazine for about thirty minutes. The selections were simple and always accompanied by pictures. On alternate days, I read illustrated, softbound storybooks which I had bought for ten or fifteen cents.

Another effective part of this early training was Edith's trips with me to a neighborhood movie theatre where she watched the cartoons. Occasionally, we also watched appropriate features such as a Walt Disney film. The trips to the theater began when she was seven months old. Afterwards, at home, I would slowly describe in great detail to Bella what had happened. These descriptions delighted the baby as her facial expressions showed; sometimes a sad event would make her cry. "And the poor little cat is always afraid of the vicious dog." I could see that Edith recalled the episode which she had seen earlier on the screen. "So the poor lost sheep is looking for her mommy." The seven-month-old infant's sad brown eyes turned to her mother.

The spring of 1953 ushered in warm weather after a dreary winter and Edith was finally relieved of a persistent cold. I was able to take her out more frequently for longer strolls. As Edith reached her eighth month, I intensified my efforts. There were more monologues, more illustrated books, and a greater stress on self-reliance in feeding and toilet training. The child's alertness and sensitivity seemed to increase substantially. She responded to stimulation much better than I had hoped. My diary of April, 1953, records, "It is my profound impression that Edith, lacking the verbal skill to express herself, nevertheless understands me clearly." It was by then evident to me that my efforts were beginning to be crowned with success.

However, none of our observers, including my wife, shared my optimism. "In my judgment, her responses are no different from my daughter's," our friend commented, whose daughter was two weeks older than Edith. In fact, her remark was partly true, for her daughter showed a far greater promise than Edith as I assessed her. But eighteen years later, having relied on public school education her daughter was seeking admission to college, while Edith had been teaching college for three years.

I was so pleased with Edith's development that in an exhilarated mood a week later I recorded in my diary, "Like the spring sunshine which melts the dreary, all encompassing icy landscape, so does Edith's intellect emerge in its splendor." Henceforth, her mind blossomed as daily discoveries challenged her developing imagination.

Edith not only continued to develop intellectually, but also physically. She began to walk at ten months and two weeks. I recorded the event in my diary on June 28, 1953. "Edith remains standing, holding to the crib for periods of seven to ten minutes without any visible difficulty. Apparently she enjoys it for she smiles broadly. Today I moved the crib close to the wall and placed the baby near it, whereupon she gripped the crib and uttered hardly audible sounds. Immediately, I walked over to the opposite wall and stretched out my arms. In one hand, I held a newly purchased illustrated book with a bright picture of a lamb on the jacket. By this time, her mother ran over and sat on the floor holding her. 'Come over darling, 'I motioned with my hands. 'Here is a new book for you.' At first Edith hesitated, but soon walked the distance of about eight feet straight into my outstretched arms. "Good baby," I exclaimed. "Good baby," joined in my wife happily. Having received her reward, the new book, Edith walked right back to her overjoyed mother, who showered her with kisses, and bestowed upon the child a warm embrace. After that occasion, Edith walked unassisted around the room.

At about eleven months, she began to build full sentences. At that age, my notes report. "Today, Edith was in an exceptionally receptive mood. She ate a good breakfast while listening to *Verdi*. As her mother changed her diapers I suggested, 'Be patient, your mother will make you comfortable and dry.'

'Yes, Daddy.'

"Soon, we will go for a stroll."

"Good, Daddy." While Bella changed the diapers, Edith did not cry at all.

At ten o'clock, when we returned from the stroll, I explained the family structure of the six dolls to her. She promptly recognized the father, mother, and children. 'What does Daddy do all day long?'

" 'He works,' she replied.

" 'Where does he work?'

" 'On a farm,' she answered.

" 'What are the names of the children?'

" 'Joseph, Dan, Mary, and Luisa,' she replied and proudly pointed to the respective dolls.

" 'What animal do you like the most?'

" 'Rudolf, the lion.'

" 'Why?'

" 'He is strong.'

" 'Don't you like Diana, the small cat?'

" 'Yes, I do.'

" 'How old are you Edith?' At this question, she pulled the flash card bearing the number ten and lifted one finger. I was so pleased with her performance that I swept her off the floor, pressed her to my chest, and tenderly kissed her on the cheek. This, too, served an educational purpose, for Edith counted the kisses, 'One, two, three, four, five.' "

She developed her manual dexterity and motor ability earlier than other children, but it lagged behind her mental growth, probably because of the demands placed upon her by my intensive work. Thus, she had the intellectual capacity to write at the age of one, but could not hold a pencil sufficently well. Also she knew at one year how to control the volume of music, but lacked the manual dexterity to do so. She was toilet trained by then, wearing diapers only at night. She tried to undress herself at the same age when it was warm, but became angry when she failed to do so. Her self-reliance was so remarkable that she could play for hours without distracting anyone. However, this seldom happened as her mother or I were always at her side.

CHAPTER 5

Old Posters and Abacus

A few years ago, after I had delivered a lecture on the methods which I used in working with Edith, a renowned educator asked, "Would you recommend subject teaching in a broadly integrated area on an elementary school level? If you favor the area method, how do you think it can be best implemented?"

"Well, gentlemen, a worn out travel poster can serve this purpose in an excellent manner." A ripple of laughter greeted my reply, but I was very serious. As I had discovered in my school in the displaced persons camp years earlier, travel posters can have great educational value.

When Edith was about a year old, I talked a travel agent out of a stock of old posters with which I covered the walls and ceiling of our room. My objective was to ensure Edith would see beautiful and inspiring sights. The posters portrayed the fjords in Norway, a medieval castle on the summit of a green foothill in Bavaria, a majestic snowcapped mountain in Switzerland, Egyptian pyramids baking in the merciless sun of Africa, the Statue of Liberty with its outstretched arm, a picture of a smiling Austrian peasant in a folk dress, an airplane zooming proudly above the Manhattan skyline, and a famous Talmudic scholar submerged in study by candlelight.

She also had to see the other side of the coin, so there was a moving picture of a child with sad, large, black eyes in the midst of a war devastated city, a Korean boy in torn clothing, and Jewish refugees disembarking in Haifa.

Edith would intensely look at these pictures. Sadness would replace joy as she moved her eyes from the carefree sight of the Riviera to a war-devastated cathedral standing amid rubble. Similarly, her mood would change with the radio, switching from invigorating opera to the somber music of Rachmaninoff.

The pyramid poster was in the middle of the wall at Edith's eye level and she would stare at it for long periods. Apparently, something in the picture aroused her curiosity. Consequently, I chose this poster as an educational target. Later, each poster unfolded its wealth of information to her in geography, history, and natural sciences.

It all began innocently when Edith was fourteen months old. As I recorded it, I asked, "Edith, darling, what kind of animal is this?"

"A camel."

"Show me a picture of the camel in your cards."

"Here it is, Daddy."

"Very good."

"Which is bigger, a camel or a dog?" The search for a picture of a dog frustrated her slightly. It was misplaced under her pillow.

"Do not rush, darling. You will find it!"

"Here it is!"

In the pictures, the camel and the dog appeared to be the same size. "Both are big," she cried.

I reached for her illustrated book. On the jacket was a picture of a man leading a dog.

"No, Daddy. Camel bigger."

"Very good!" I pointed to the camel driver, "Who is this?"

"A man."

"Fine. What is that?"

"A house."

"Where are the windows?"

"No windows."

"And what is this?" A moment of silence followed. "What do you play with on the beach?"

"Sand, sand, sand!"

"Very good!" I continued. "Edith, this is a pyramid."

Happily she repeated, "Pyram."

During the following several days, I told her simple stories pertaining to deserts. One of them I recorded. "There is only sand in the desert. No water, no trees. The sun is hot. People travel through the desert on camels." She became so engulfed in and identified so much with the story that she asked for milk even though she had finished a bottle minutes before. "Camels drink a lot of water before their trip across the desert and keep it in their bellies for a long, long time." Edith pointed to her belly, "People going through the desert keep water in bottles," whereupon she pointed to her bottle.

"Nice story! More, more!"

That afternoon the radio did not play clearly which made Edith nervous. "Music no good!" she insisted. Consequently, I decided to explore in greater detail the picture of the Talmudic scholar. I did this with great care, since the picture resembled my deceased grandfather. Furthermore, I was determined to instill in the child a love for books.

"What is this picture about?"

"Man reading a book."

"Good. Edith, do you like books?"

"Yes."

"Books tell you beautiful stories. They have nice pictures. Some day, I will teach you how to read."

"Yes, Daddy -- yes, Daddy!"

"Do you like the man?"

"Yes."

"Is the man old or young?"

"He is old. What story is he reading?"

"Well, darling, the old man reads about the Jewish people of long ago. He loves to read. He reads during the day and at night. The more he reads, the smarter he becomes."

"I love books too."

"I know, darling, soon you will read for yourself."

"When? Teach me now!"

"Does the old man in the picture read his book during the day or at night?"

"I don't know."

"Well, you see a candle burning, so it must be night."

"What is a candle? Why doesn't he put the light on?"

"Long, long ago, there were no electric lights such as this." I put the light on. "People had to use candles to light the darkness." I turned off the light and in the dark, since it was twilight, I lit a candle.

"Nice, nice!" She clapped her little hands joyfully. "Daddy, I love books." She lifted the stack of illustrated children's books and kissed them tenderly.

"Yes, Edith, sweetheart, books will always be your best friends." She nodded her head.

"Give me music, Daddy." I went to a neighbor and borrowed a radio from him. Soon, the melancholy sounds of Beethoven's "Moonlight Sonata" filled the room. This was Edith's favorite and before long she fell asleep.

The forsaken camel and his drives across the hungry desert became alive in our house. The next week, I told Edith stories from the Old Testament. I explained, "The Jews were forced to work very hard in Egypt. They had to build pyramids." I pronounced the word "pyramids" slowly and carefully.

Impatiently, she interrupted. "Daddy, this is pyramid!"

I was pleased with her ability to relate. This time, I ended my story quickly since Edith became indignant at the cruel treatment of the Jews. "Bad Egyptians, bad people!" she exclaimed.

During the next two days, Edith was preoccupied with the Bavarian castle and the snow covered Jungfrau in Switzerland. She was excited over the fact that on the mountaintop there is eternal snow, while in the valley children play in warm weather. "You see, the higher up you go, the cooler it gets."

"Why?"

I evaded a direct reply since I felt that she would not understand. "Someday, I'll take you to the mountains and you will see for yourself." The Bavarian castle helped to mold her appreciation of beauty and of nature. "Pretty. Nice. Beautiful."

Although the sight of the pyramids had made her sad, I returned to it, for it presented a hidden educational opportunity. The blocks which were clearly identifiable could be used to stimulate her desire to count. By now, she knew all about the object, the surroundings, the nature of the desert, the geographic location which I pointed out to her on a globe, and its historical background. Edith was sitting on the floor and playing with her blocks.

"Come over here, Edith."

As usual, she responded cheerfully and crawled to where I sat. I expressed my pleasure by kissing her. Then I lifted her, which was difficult for me, turned to the poster and began to count the blocks by pointing to each one with a pencil. "One, two, three, four, five, six, seven."

She became so excited she used the third person. "Edith do it! One, two, three four!"

"Good."

"More, more."

"We will do it later." Before the week was over, she was counting up to twenty.

I removed the poster of the pyramids. It had served its purpose and I felt its presence was not desirable because of its effect on her. In its place, I put a poster of Haifa Harbor against the background of the majestic Carmel Mountain, a symbol of Spring and hope for the vigorous state of Israel.

Edith's educational progress was also aided by events which followed the first step upwards in our "socio-economic mobility." In late 1953, we moved from our one room attic apartment in Sea Gate to a three-room apartment in a rapidly dilapidating five story building on Surf Avenue in Brooklyn, overlooking the Atlantic Ocean. In the rear of our building was the Half Moon Hotel, which, in its early days, won infamy as the headquarters of Murder Incorporated.

We arrived at our new residence in a friend's old station wagon containing our few personal belongings and a load of books. Judging by the expressions of the neighbors, we were less than welcome. "Another shipment of shnorers (beggars as translated into English)," snickered an elderly lady to her companions.

"Indeed, it is time to move away before the building will totally rot away," replied the man.

Soon, the two old beds, the crib, the kitchen furniture, and the books which constituted our belongings were moved into the apartment. Bella, who had hoped to have a coat of paint to brighten the defaced walls, had to settle for the usual background of travel posters. Scornfully, she remarked, "Since we lack furniture which typifies living quarters, our residence may as well acquire the appearance of an office."

The silence with which our neighbors greeted us for some time after we moved in was finally broken by a widow occupying a nearby apartment. She knocked on our door one morning. "May I come in?"

"Of course," replied Bella, somewhat surprised. "What can I do for you?"

"My name is Mania and I live on the sixth floor across from your kitchen window. I am about to refurnish my apartment. Would you care to take my piano since the movers asked me $50 to remove it?"

Before the poor woman could complete her sentence, I cut in happily, fearful that my wife might reject the offer. "We shall be delighted! When can we have it?"

"At once."

That day, our meager possessions were enriched by a grand piano. But even more important, with the piano, there were 24 volumes of the Encyclopaedia Britannica, aged by years but tempting with their hidden treasures of wisdom. Indeed, from the outset, I was determined that the encyclopedia would become an effective educational tool. However, the task was formidable, for my own efforts for self-improvement and the study of English using the Britannica met with great difficulties. I found the language so complex as to make my research of a given subject futile. I was continually looking up words in the dictionary, which was time consuming and tedious. By the time I had digested most of the words, I was too worn out to pursue my subject.

Edith, always alert, watched me intensely reading the "big book."

"Daddy, give me the book."

"What can you do with it, if you don't know how to read it?" I asked.

"Let me have it, please. I will take care of it."

"All right," I said, and Edith, a year and a half old, sat herself on the floor and began slowly to leaf through the pages.

"Daddy, what is an encyclopedia? What makes it different from other books?"

"Well, Edith, an encyclopedia deals with all the events and things known to man."

"Women too?"

"Yes, dear."

"How can one person know so much?"

42

"There are hundreds or perhaps thousands of learned people who are responsible for each volume of this great masterpiece."

"You mean a masterpiece as in music or art?"

"Yes."

"Dad, teach me how to read so that I can study the encyclopedia!"

"Soon, dear."

"When I learn to read, I shall read the encyclopedia from the beginning to the end." Edith's prediction was absolutely right, for in less than three years she had read it all from A to Z.

She became so deeply attached to the encyclopedia that at least one volume could always be found in her crib, which I replaced each day with another. Unable to read, she concentrated on the illustrations which I explained to her to the best of my ability.

After Edith was in college, a wire service reporter once inquired, "Mr. Stern, do you approve of using computers in the teaching of mathematics?"

"I would prefer a simple abacus," I replied.

"You cannot be serious about that."

"Indeed I am." I made this statement at the risk of being ridiculed by the educators and electronics manufacturers who invest millions of dollars in computer teaching devices, yet I had very effectively used an abacus to teach Edith arithmetic. During one of my trips to the old book stores on the Lower East Side in search of inexpensive classics which Edith enjoyed enormously (she was permitted to browse through the books at the age of a year and a half), I had discovered an abacus. This was the first one I had seen in America. Since it appeared to me to be a rare item, I bought it for the $1.80 with which I had intended to buy four books. I saw in it an excellent tool with which to teach arithmetic to my eighteen-month-old scholar. While she was playing with it on the subway she seemed fascinated by the three different colors of the beads of her new toy and played with it for several days while I thought how to use the device effectively.

"How do you like your toy?" I finally asked.

"Fine. What is an abacus, Daddy?"

"How do you know the name of it?"

"Member the man in the store? You asked him for an abacus."

"Right, Edith, I asked for an abacus. What can you do with it?"

"Play?"

"You can also count. One, two, three, four." I moved the beads slowly from one side to the other.

"Show me, Daddy."

I raised her little finger and moved the beads, "One, two, three, four. Can you do it yourself?"

"Yes, Daddy."

Within five days, Edith was able to count all the beads -- a sum of one hundred. Soon, with the abacus she could do addition and subtraction of two digit numbers.

"Edith, count eighty-five beads and move them to the other side of the abacus."

"Yes, Daddy." Slowly, but accurately she did it.

"Move back seventeen beads. Count the ones that are left." In six minutes and fifty seconds she gave me the correct number. She added thirty beads to twenty-seven with similar speed and accuracy. At the same time, she wrote the numbers, clumsily, however, since she lacked motor ability. Within the following month, Edith read numbers up to one hundred and mastered the multiplication tables through five.

She began to read at the age of twenty-two months. It is quite possible that she was reading earlier, for, from her early infancy, she had been surrounded by illustrated books. Her ability to identify letters was evident when she was twelve to thirteen months.

When she was a year old I played with her on the beach, using blocks bearing letters. "Give me the 'A' block," I would ask her. She could correctly pick out the vowels, but she had difficulty with consonants. The selection of "W" and "Q" were especially difficult for her partly

44

because of my own difficulty in pronouncing these sounds properly, since none of the languages I spoke prior to coming to the United States had them in their phonetic structure.

At home, Edith leafed through her books and judging by the expression on her face, appeared to understand the contents at the age of one and perhaps earlier. Her attachment to the books, which numbered about fifteen, was so deep that when one became misplaced, she would cry until she could find it.

When she was eighteen months old I introduced flashcards to her. My technique was similar to that used in progressive kindergartens in teaching five and six-year-old children.

In August, 1954, I noted in my diary. "Today, because the weather is unfavorable, Edith remains indoors for the second day. She appears to be extremely receptive to instruction. Her knowledge of the alphabet is total, including all consonants. It is my belief that she will be reading within three days on a second-grade level."

The introduction of flashcards had produced good results. I had selected five cards which contained the words "cat," "dog," "man," "boy," "girl." After the fourth demonstration. Edith had made one mistake, ironically, on the word, "girl." The same afternoon, I introduced five additional flashcards with the words, "bird," "house," "horse," "mother," and "father." I was overwhelmed with the remarkable success we had as she read the words without difficulty. Before bedtime, I selected seven of the words in her book and she read them without the accompanying pictures.

Approximately a month later, Edith was reading forty words. I composed short sentences utilizing the words with which she was familiar and typed them in capitals. To add cohesiveness, I included several adjectives such as words for colors, "nice," "strong," etc., all of which she easily mastered.

Now, I sought ways in which to help improve her reading. One of these was through advertising. Signs became my most effective tool in her reading lessons. Every day, I would put her in the stroller and we would go for a long walk. Soon we became as much a part of the neighborhood scene in Brooklyn as the fruit truck. Since we took our strolls about the same time every day, about two-thirty, we would find a dozen or so children waiting to join us. They would gather at the entrance to our building and would call out impatiently, "Edith. When are you coming down?"

I would hold her to the window, and she would call back, "When the music finishes." Then when the music was over and WQXR resumed its half-hour news bulletins, Edith would be ready. "Daddy, let's go."

The congregation of children became noisier by this time and we would hear the janitor objecting. "Get out, you kids, get out. He will be down soon."

Edith, who usually ran naked in the house, would get dressed. In the elevator, I gently lifted her up to press the button. "Which is the right one?" I asked her, but she had already pressed the lower one before she was told. "Good girl."

Two neighbors already in the elevator eyed us contemptuously. "He will drive that little girl crazy," one whispered to the other, "constantly teaching, constantly bothering her. Always loud music, always commotion. What a crazy family! They should have stayed in Europe."

When the doors opened and we stepped out into the street, the children cheered our arrival. "Edith," they asked, "where are we going today?" They would follow us on our walks, listening and looking as Edith read the signs along the streets. They, too, began to learn and read them out loud.

The route I had selected for this day was Mermaid Avenue. The traffic stopped on Surf Avenue as the strange caravan of children crossed the street, with Edith and her dad at the head of the procession.

When we reached Mermaid Avenue, our exercises began. "MERMAID AVENUE," we would recite in unison as curious strollers, not familiar with the neighborhood, stared at us in bewilderment.

Again I pointed to the street sign and repeated, "MERMAID AVENUE."

"Daddy, Daddy, wait!" Edith closed her eyes tightly, covering them with her little hands, then reopened them again with the thrill of discovering something exciting. Pointing her finger to the sign, she recited, "MERMAID."

After a short pause, the caravan resumed its trip toward Sea Gate. A sign occupied the whole side wall. "SALE," I read loudly, pointing to the store window. "SALE," Edith repeated, joined by the others.

46

An   open sign was displayed prominently in the T.V. store. "OPEN," we all read loudly. There Edith happily discovered the familiar names of television sets displayed in the window and proudly read, "MOTOROLA" and "ZENITH." We waited while the other repeated after her, "MOTOROLA." Soon we moved away for reading brand names was not a part of my objective. As an educational opportunist, I wanted her to read signs which connoted a specific meaning in order to enrich her vocabulary while she learned the basics of reading. I had no objections, however, if she decided to learn the other signs.

Next on the street was a barber shop. Edith seized the initiative, "BARBER."

"Good. What does a barber do?"

"Cuts hair."

"Good, my darling." Praise was an important part of my method.

The children's chorus repeated, "BARBER."

At our main target of the day, the candy store with the newspaper stand displayed in front. Edith cried out, "LIFE," as she pointed to the magazine. "TIME. Daddy, you have this magazine at home."

"Yes, darling."

"Daddy, what is that?"

"That is a Jewish paper written in another language."

"Teach me. Daddy, teach me please."

"I will sometime in the future."

"Now. . . now!" she demanded with the impatience for learning which has become her life style.

The agitated storekeeper ran out of the store. "Move along. Beat it! I've got to make a living. This is no school."

The procession resumed its trip. "Well," I thought, "someday I will sneak out of the house with Edith unnoticed. Then we will be able to

47

devote more time there." Soon we reached the supermarket where we usually stopped.

Delighted Edith recited from a distance, "MILK, BUTTER, SALAMI" as the chorus joined her in unison.

From the distance appeared our neighborhood patrolman. "Mr. Kelly. . . Mr. Kelly. . ." Edith called.

He stopped and said, "What are you doing, man. You are creating traffic congestion. Ain't they got a school? The merchants have been complaining."

"Well, officer, that is the best way I can teach my child."

"Let her go to school."

"She is too young."

"Wait until she grows up."

"Then it will be too late."

"Too late for what?"

"For learning."

"What crazy talk," he said. "How about the rest of the kids; they surely aren't too young."
"No, they simply follow us."

"Yes, we like it," the children chorused.

"Come on, move along."

So our mobile school moved along to another and then another store, to the bakery with its tempting scents, to the real estate office with its window displaying many colored pictures, and to the laundry pouring out hot steam. Then firmly but politely, I told the other children, "Walk along the boardwalk home. We are just a block away."

"We'll see you tomorrow," they called as they went. "Good-bye, Edith. Good-bye, Aaron." Edith threw kisses at them.

48

Accustomed to the routine, she said, "Now do we go inside the store?"

"Yes, my darling," I replied as we entered the large supermarket, leaving the stroller on the sidewalk. I carried Edith as we moved along the aisles.

"Daddy . . . here. . . here. . ." I reached for the can and read part of the label. Then I asked her to read it, "FISH" she excitedly read, then "BUTTER, TEA."

"What do you do with tea?"

"You drink it."

Then we read "SUGAR." "What does Mommy do with sugar?" I asked.

"Puts it in tea. . . makes it sweet."

"Where is the tea?"

"Right here, Daddy," she said pointing to the other aisle and grabbing a small package of tea.

One spring day as we were walking along loudly reading the signs, accompanied by many children, a passing car stopped at the traffic light. Then it abruptly pulled to the sidewalk and a well dressed man got out. At first I thought he was a plainclothes policeman coming to disperse the crowd, but then he asked how old Edith was. I told him two years. "But why do you ask?"

"How can a two-year-old child read?"

"You see she does."

"How do you train her?"

"As you can see, this is my method. This is my school."

"But the other children must be much older."

"Indeed they are. They are six and seven."

"I'm six," said little Jackie.

Then I asked him who he was and what he wanted. "I'm a T.V. producer," he announced. "Would you let your little girl appear on my program?"

"What would she do there?"

"Just read." He wrote down my name and telephone number, then offered Edith a dollar saying, "I hope to hear from you soon." Little hands stretched from all directions for more dollars, but I refused to let Edith accept the money.

The children quickly spread the word around the neighborhood. "Edith will be on T.V."

"I knew Aaron's eccentricities would land him there some day," Mrs. Jacobs told my wife. Everyone was excited, that is everyone except the Stern family.

Soon I received a call from the producer. "Why haven't I heard from you? Don't turn down a chance of making a few hundred bucks. I'm sure you could use them on clothing and education."

"Would you let me make a statement on the air in which I would explain my method of teaching?"

"I cannot. It would not be consistent with the format of the show. Anyway, aren't you teaching the way the schools do?"

"Just the opposite."

"So your statement would offend a major segment of our viewers, perhaps the sponsors."

"Most likely."

"Please be realistic for the sake of your child. Don't deny her three hundred dollars."

"I'm sorry, but I can't accept." Thus Edith, who made frequent television appearances later, could have made her debut at two.

Progressing rapidly, she was soon reading advertising messages such as

"The Best Buy," "Good For Your Health," and "Will Protect Your Health," referring to products some of which were worthless and others which were downright dangerous to one's health, such as cigarettes. I did not want such advertisements to have a harmful influence on her, so we switched the reading lessons from signs to books and magazines. She would continually beg, forever it seemed, "Take me to the store to read the boxes and cans."

"No, Darling, that is for little babies. Big girls read books to learn."

"Yes, Daddy, I love to read stories," she replied.

Sometimes when we strolled discussing the books which she had read, we saw the gang of children pursuing the ritual which we had started, walking from store to store while reading the signs. "Daddy, it is so babyish. Why don't they read books?"

"They don't know how to read."

"They are big, they go to school and should be smart. Poor children." Then she said, "I love you. You teach me everything."

"You have a lot to learn."

"I will, I will, Daddy."

Thus, by the age of two, Edith was an avid reader, with a reading ability far superior to many children three times her age. Yet, there were many skeptics who didn't believe that a two-year-old child could read. My friend, Bob, was one of these. At the time there was a television program which conducted a contest of talking dogs. Bob, a great animal lover, was doubtful.

"Well, I don't know," I told him. "Perhaps there is one."

"Aaron, you must be naive."

"Bob, would you believe that a child less than two years old can read?"

"Of course not."

"I know of one."

"I'll ask my psychology professor about it." Then after a moment's reflection, he said, "Aaron, I'll bet you twenty dollars without consulting my psychology professor."

"Fine."

"Who is it?"

"My daughter, Edith."

"Aaron, you must be kidding me. Does she actually read?"

"You shall see."

That evening, Bob along with his instructor came to the apartment. Sitting on my bed since there were not enough chairs to accommodate us all, we watched as Edith, unconcerned, played with her dolls. The radio played Mozart. The instructor asked, "Do you suggest that this child is capable of reading?"

"Judge for yourself." I reached for ten neatly typed short sentences which included about seventy words. "Which one should we select?"

"Take any at random."

I took one and handed it to Edith. "Please read it, Honey."

"Yes, Daddy." Then she read, "A girl has a dog. Her father works hard."

"How old is she?"

"Twenty-three months."

"Incredible. What is your method?"

"I simply teach her."

"What method of teaching do you use?" Bob asked incredulously. "What is your secret learning weapon?"

I tried to explain that while I liked the Montessori method, with its emphasis on visual contact; and approved the best parts of the progressive method, with the John Dewey emphasis on child-community orientation. I was wedded to none of these.

"I use the individualized instruction method," I explained. "I do not believe that you can place a label on any teaching device. Use whatever is best for the occasion. Each child is different, you know."

"Now, take Edith. She responds beautifully to stimulation, to the joy of learning, to a one-to-one relationship. Edith received my full attention and at every stage of development she responded to the learning stimulus that I offered her. At no time did I force her, but she was pleased to learn, she was motivated to read, she enjoyed and absorbed knowledge as a rose bud opens in the June sun, as violets blossom after an April shower."

The professor and Bob seemed overwhelmed. "I just wouldn't have believed that a twenty-three -month-old child not only could read fluently, but from all appearances could also comprehend what she was reading. Imagine what she'll be when she's twenty-three years old!"

"She'll be a genius," I said, matter of factly. "About that I have no doubt."

The next day, Bob insisted that I accept the twenty dollars. "I can't do it, Bob." Finally, he persuaded me. This was the only bet I ever made. With the money, I purchased a new radio which served us well for many years.

CHAPTER 6

Edith Blossoms

After Edith began to read, new horizons opened up for her. One of the many books which she read at the age of two was the children's version of the Old Testament, which she tremendously enjoyed. The acts of heroism and devotion fired her imagination; she loved the humility of young David and she applauded the determination of Moses. But she also was critical of the misdeeds.

"Daddy, why is Solomon so rich?" she asked. "Why must he have so many wives?" After reading about Joshua fighting to conquer the promised land, she said, "Surely, there were some innocent people. Why did they have to die? Why didn't the Jewish people obey the law of God?" I explained to her that people have always sinned and that we should hope there will be a just world someday. "When?" she asked.

Her reading was not limited to books. At the age of two, she read in the paper that a twenty-store building was being erected near our home. During a stroll, Edith stood for a moment staring at the building, which was actually only eighteen stories high. When we returned home, she obtained the number of the newspaper, then called the editor and reported the mistake. The next day the paper printed a correction.

When she was two years and three months old, a routine physical examination revealed a heart murmur. A few months later, she contracted a streptococcic infection and was hospitalized for observation. She seemed calm and unbothered by the hospitalization. She continued to read her books and we brought her a radio from home so that she could continue to have music. Some parents of the other children in the ward complained that the music annoyed their children, and the hospital considerately put Edith in a small, separate room.

54

She was always self-sufficient. "Go home and sleep," she would tell me.

"I'd love to stay overnight with you."

"Go home and rest, Daddy. I'll be fine. Come tomorrow and bring me a lot of books."

The next morning, I brought them to her and asked the nurse how she was.

"What a remarkable child you have. Not a sound came from her during the night. She even went to the bathroom by herself. What puzzles me is why does she have the radio on all the time? She even listens to the news, as though she understands it. During the night an orderly tried to turn the radio off twice and both times Edith woke up and stopped him. Yes, I believe that she is a remarkable child."

Edith was discharged from that hospital and soon entered another one. During this period of hospitalization, she behaved quite maturely, as well.

My work with her now had an added dimension. She gained insights into anatomy and physiology. I discussed with her the purpose of electrocardiograms, x-rays, stethoscopes and the other medical instruments. She was happy and content, grasping for the new and unknown.

She understood that her mother could not visit her frequently because of her job. She would tell the nurse. "My Mommy cannot come to see me. She is working."

Unable to arrive at a definite diagnosis, the doctors assumed that she had suffered from rheumatic fever at some time. As a precaution, they prescribed penicillin daily for the rest of her life. I took a dim view of the prospects of a lifetime medication and the penicillin was later terminated in Florida in spite of the doctor's disapproval. She has enjoyed perfect health since then. Several years after the diagnosis of rheumatic fever, the Miami National Children's Cardiac Hospital diagnosed the murmur as an innocent one.

In spite of her ill health, Edith was quite active and adept at riding her tricycle. The best place was the Coney Island boardwalk, where she rode each day. Once on the boardwalk, Edith demanded a quarter from me.

Since a quarter was a lot of money for a two-year-old, I refused to give it to her. Soon she disappeared into the crowd. At first, I wasn't concerned, but as time passed and she didn't return, I became alarmed. Finally I notified the boardwalk police, who had already found her on the Brighton Beach boardwalk about two miles away. The police told me that she had asked them for money, claiming that I refused her books and food.

As Edith developed a mature mind, she began to interact with adults. One she met at this time was Albert Einstein. It was in early 1955 when I was hard at work on a book which detailed the Nazi persecution of the Jews. In addition to numerous interviews with refugees and survivors of the concentration camps, I secured comments about the era from prominent people who had either studied or who had first hand experience with it. I was particularly proud to record Einstein's observations. After Einstein had helped me to obtain the surgery, I frequently visited him and he assisted me in my work. The last time I went I took Edith along to meet the great man whose picture, along with those of Tolstoy and Gandhi, hung on her wall.

As the Greyhound bus left the Holland tunnel, Edith leafed through a biography of Einstein. Now I began to worry about bringing her along without first obtaining Einstein's permission. It was rude of me and I did not know how I should explain her presence.

When we arrived at the Institute for Advanced Studies, Edith ran directly to him. "My name is Edith. I've heard so much about you, Professor. Your picture is right above my bed." Einstein seemed slightly bewildered.

"What did you hear about me?" he asked.

"Mainly about your work on atomic energy. I love you for helping my Dad to get well."

"How did I help your father?" he asked. Edith told him what he had done. "Remarkable. How old is she?"

"Two and a half, Dr. Einstein," I replied.

"Yes. You told me earlier. But it is simply incredible." The day belonged entirely to Edith and Einstein; I never got the opportunity to ask the questions for which I had made the trip.

"Edith, what will you do when you grow up?" the professor asked.

"I will study hard to help others." Then a book on his shelf caught her eye. "May I look at this book?"

"Of course."

But the book was disappointing for it was in German. "Daddy," she said nearly crying, "I can't read it."

"Does Edith actually read?" He passed a newspaper to her and asked, "How about that?"

She began to read an article headlined, "Report from Washington."

"Do you know, Edith, my mother told me that I was seven years of age when I began to read."

"How pitiful," Edith responded. "You missed all the fun. Didn't your Daddy teach you earlier as my father does?"

"Apparently I was not ready for it."

He became so engrossed with Edith that my presence became superfluous. Edith was at her best asking questions while Einstein answered and wrote on the board. "Do you mind if I call you Grandfather? My grandparents were killed by the Nazis."

Einstein was visibly touched. "Yes. Please do."

Within an hour or so, as we were ready to leave, he said, "Aaron your daughter is destined to make a valuable contribution to science. Cultivate her talents. Let me see her again." Edith was exhilarated for a long time after the visit, but unfortunately, she never was to see him again, for he died on April 18, only a few weeks later. We mourned him deeply; a black ribbon edged his picture above Edith's bed.

Shortly after the visit to Einstein, I was referred to a social worker to help me become adjusted after my illnesses. Although the visits to the social worker and later to the New York Vocational Rehabilitation Department were somewhat of a farce, they did indirectly help me to obtain a college education.

The social worker, a woman in her forties, lectured me on the traumatic effects of my war experiences and told me that I could expect to encounter difficulty in adjusting to American society. She politely warned me, "Do not seek material wealth in a strange country with your limited skills and language barrier." Then she added, "It may sound discouraging, but above all one must be realistic. This office has the task of finding jobs for many refugees, but frankly we have little success because of the damage done to them during the war." As I left, she put her hand on my shoulder and declared, "Someday you will report to me about securing a job in a shop."

Shortly after that interview, I was requested to report to the Vocational Rehabilitation Department of the State of New York. While I waited several weeks for the appointment, I spent the time improving my linguistic skill. Soon, a letter from the Vocational Rehabilitation office arrived. I put on my only suit, given to me on my arrival in the country by the New York Association for New Americans, and reported for the interview.

At the office, I was greeted by a young and enthusiastic social worker who suggested that we speak in German since my English was still atrocious. I gladly consented, but apparently he did not realize that he spoke Yiddish rather than German. Soon he guided me through countless interviews and batteries of tests, all paid for, of course, by the taxpayers.

After several weeks, I was summoned to the manager, who questioned me about my plans for the future. I told him I intended to pursue my education. I must have shocked him, for he left the room and soon returned again with two other men, one of whom was introduced as a psychologist. They told me the tests had revealed that I had "a surprisingly low intelligence for your ethnic group, but you have shown some skill in manual dexterity." After careful consideration, they recommended that I learn to become a welder. The state was willing to pay for the vocational training, but under no conditions would they recommend that I go to college. I left the office disgusted and never returned again in spite of the many letters which followed.

It is noteworthy that during the succeeding years I met literally hundreds of outstanding academicians, mainly members of minority groups, whose studies nearly came to a tragic halt because of a similarly "scientific prognosis."

Two months after this sad experience, I went to the Dean of Brooklyn College, and asked to be admitted. At first he tried to talk me out of

58

seeking a college education, but once he became convinced of my determination, he supported my application. As he later wrote, "He first presented himself at Brooklyn College with a request which he felt was a desperate attempt to salvage for himself and his family some measure of respect after the harrowing indignities of Nazi cruelty. The request was that he be allowed to matriculate for a degree. After examining his qualifications, it was found that Mr. Stern was not only eligible for admission but on the basis of examinations, he was allowed a block of credit toward his degree." Although I had attended a university in Poland before the war, my records were unobtainable and no direct credit was given for that work.

The dean became my counselor and assisted me in many ways, including securing for me a scholarship from a Masonic lodge. Thus, I became a college student shortly before Edith's third birthday. Thirteen months later I received my bachelor's degree. During the time I was enrolled at Brooklyn College, I spent many months confined to a hospital. Having little money, I did not buy a single textbook, using instead books from the library. It is noteworthy that "the efficient and competent vocational rehabilitation office" continued to send me letters for more than a decade assuring me of its "readiness to assist me in training to become a welder." What could be a better motivation for one to pursue a college education?

My work with Edith continued during this period and I believe that my college attendance was probably beneficial to her education as well as mine. While I had always tried to be a model of a parent who sought knowledge and who placed a high value on learning, I was especially able to do this as a college student. Additionally, I was able directly to involve Edith in my learning experiences, occasionally taking her to class and discussing my courses with her.

I continued to work on my book, actively involving Edith in it. Since the book dealt with the Nazi cruelties, I was frequently criticized for exposing a young child to such emotional trauma. One of my friends asked, "Why should a child born in a free and prosperous country be subjected to the gruesome accounts of Nazi horrors?" Of course the same people had no objections to entertaining their children with television programs in which violence was rampant and where the criminal often emerged a hero. Bella, also, was critical of Edith's involvement in the book. Referring to the research, she once told a friend, "This was a big part of Aaron's life — too big."

On the other hand, I saw Edith's participation as a valuable learning experience. I believe that the annihilation of six million Jews taught her about the irrationality of hate and prejudice. There was no way that I could shield her from the violence and reality of life, so I preferred to employ it as a learning experience. Edith's grandparents, as well as many of her other relatives, were killed during the war and she had to know this. Further, I believe that she had to know the circumstances of their deaths. For example, my mother, whose appearance did not reveal her Jewish origin, chose to die in a concentration camp with my injured father, rather than seek refuge in a guerilla unit. Although tragic, this was a very heroic act and an excellent example of love and devotion.

In contrast, television has glorified crime. While our perpetual poverty did not permit us the luxury of a television set, Edith was often invited to the neighbor's home to watch it. I permitted her to see only children's programs such as Mickey Mouse and Howdy Doody, but sometimes without my knowledge she would see other shows. Once, at the age of three, she saw a western at the neighbors. Later, she asked, "Daddy, how did they ever build up the West if all they did was kill each other?"

On another occasion, however, television proved to be very harmful. One day after Edith had seen a crime episode at a neighbor's house, we went to a nearby drug store. While I browsed through the book section, Edith noticed a policeman having a cup of coffee at the lunch counter. Quietly, she approached him from behind, pulled the gun from his holster, and stuck it in his ribs. The people nearby became deadly silent as I ran over to her and carefully took away the weapon. The embarrassed policeman hastily left the store. Later when I told my neighbor about the incident, she said that Edith had seen a similar event on television that morning. Experiences such as this show how great a threat irresponsible television can be to children.

She was a great help with my manuscript she familiarized herself with the thousands of photographs which I had collected. Some of these were gruesome documentations of atrocities; others were pictures of pre-war synagogues, schools, children, adults, artifacts, and religious objects. Edith also sat with me while I conducted interviews with individuals who had participated in the Warsaw ghetto uprising, who had survived the Babi-Yar slaughter, and who had been guerillas committing sabotage against the German war effort.

During one interview, three-year-old Edith intensely questioned an elderly rabbi from Warsaw about the Ghetto uprising. "Why didn't the

Polish people, themselves victimis of the Nazis, join the Jews in the rebellion?" she asked.

"They simply did not care for the survival of Jews."

"Yes, but in the face of a common enemy? After all, they could predict their own doom which followed later during the Warsaw massacre."

"I don't know," replied the rabbi, who was becoming upset. "How old is she anyway?"

Once I learned that a woman in Chicago had a rare picture of the slaughter of a Jewish congregation during the High Holidays in a small Polish town. I called her and asked for the picture, but was refused. Then I went to Chicago, but she would not permit me to have a reproduction made. Finally, I called home and had Edith talk to her. "Wouldn't you help my Daddy with this important picture, so that the whole world could learn about the Nazi crimes, and thus perhaps prevent such an occurrence in the future?" The owner was deeply moved, and I obtained the priceless document.

Edith enjoyed the trips to the Judaic Division of the public library on 42nd Street in New York. She would carefully search the pictures in the various documents for ones which I did not have. Once she noticed a picture of a marching column of elderly Jews. "Daddy, here is a picture from Budapest."

"How do you know that it is from Budapest?" I asked.

"Simple. Here is the Danube dividing Buda from Pest". She was correct.

When I had several pictures pertaining to the same event, I could rely on Edith to select the one which I should use. "Daddy, take this one. You can see better the impressive face of the man lost in worship." Her choice was the final one.

As I had done with my research on the Nazi crimes, I made every effort to develop her character and to teach her to love other people. I stressed that violence was to be avoided at all costs and that she should be tolerant of everyone. Once, she came home from the boardwalk with her clothing ripped and her nose bleeding. I asked her what had

61

happened, but she refused to tell me. Leaving her in her mother's care, I went outside to try to find out. As I approached the boardwalk, which was about 100 feet away, I saw a group of youngsters chasing a black girl. I learned that Edith had been hurt when she had come to the defense of the girl. This, I believe was a justifiable departure from the dictum of no violence.

A key aspect of the methods which I used with Edith was that I took advantage of learning opportunities as they occured. Very routine events often provided the basis for considerable education. One morning I pointed to an old jalopy which splashed her dress as it drove by us while we were on our morning walk. "Edith," I asked, "How does a car run?"

"I don't know Daddy." This was all I needed. I had two dollars in my pocket which was all the cash I would have for a couple of days but I decided to spend it on what others might have regarded as a wasteful activity. Flagging a passing taxi, I took Edith for one of her first automobile rides since we had no car. As the taxi circled Coney Island, I explained to her all I knew about the dynamics of automobiles. By the time we arrived home, Edith knew more about a car than many adults.

At home I took the encyclopedia and read all that I could about mechanics. Then I began to challenge and probe Edith until she knew how internal combustion engine powered a car. At the end she concluded, "So these endless explosions move a car. How simple," For the time being I was satisfied, but this was only the beginning.

Later we went back outside, and I asked Edith what the plates on the back of the cars were for. She did not know and asked me to explain. I was happy that she took the bait. "Read the number on the plate." I pointed to a parked car and she read the number, 5866. "What is the meaning of it?" I asked.

She did not know and insisted that I explain it to her. I did not explain it, but rather we went back in the house. There I asked her to take her abacus and enter the figure of 5,866, then to subtract it from a million. "Fine. Good girl," I said and then I directed the conversation toward the importance of car identification and the number of cars in New York. "Do you know how many people live in the state of New York?"

"I don't know, Daddy,"

"Seventeen million. Write it down." I gave her my pad and pencil and she wrote down the number.

Edith took the initiative this time. "How many cars are in the state?"

"Fifteen million," I replied. Of course, I had just looked it up.

"Almost every person has a car, yet you, Momma and I have none."

Slightly ashamed, I answered, "Yes that is true." Then I hugged and kissed her. My objective was to plunge into the study of the geography and the political structure of New York, but Edith had raised an issue which had to be dealt with first. I believe it is very important to answer children's questions when they ask them for it is then that they are interested.

"You know, Sweetheart, I have been sick for a long time."

"Ever since I can remember, Daddy."

"How far back can your memory go?"

"A long, long time. I remember when the ambulance took you to the hospital." That had been two years earlier when she was about one and a half.

"I suffered from a bad tumor. What is a tumor, my child?"

"You explained it to me last week. It's when the cells in our body multiply wildly. Sometimes they kill the person. You asked me to multiply big numbers while talking to me about it."

"You are right, Edith. Well, I suffered from this dreadful disease for a long, long time. I could not work. That is why we have so little money. "But we have a lot of fun."

"Don't worry, Daddy. When I grow bigger. I'll work in the big library among all those beautiful books. I shall buy you a big shiny car like Simon's." Simon had the finest car in the neighborhood, a new Cadillac.

"Good, Sweetheart. I love you." Then I took the encyclopedia and showed her a color picture of a cell. "That is what happens when they multiply." Now I could continue with my objective. "Edith, it is time to go to the library."

"Hurrah." She began to clap her hands.

At the library, the clerk teased her as usual. "There will be no more books for you. You're reading them all."

"Then I will read them again," she said instantly.

At the reading table, I showed her a map.

"What is a map? Why is it green? Tell me, Daddy."

We sat down and with a pencil I outlined the boundaries of the state of New York. "Try to draw it." I gave her my pad and pencil. The outlines were clumsy. After four or five attempts, she did relatively well and we turned our attention back to the map.

"Edith, this map is of our country."

"Yes, I know. The United States."

"Right. It consists of forty-eight states, one of which is New York. How many people live in the United States?"

"I don't know."

"There are one hundred seventy-five million. Write it down." She did. "How many people live in the state of New York?"

"I forgot."

"Oh, Edith. One should never forget important things."

"I'm sorry." She was too preoccupied with the map as her beautiful eyes searched and probed. "It is seventeen million, Daddy."

"How many states do we have in this country?" I asked.

"Forty-eight," she replied. "Dad," she suddenly cried, "it's New York — our city."

I then explained that New York City was the largest city in the state of New York.

When we got ready to leave, Edith wanted to take the map with her. I explained that some books and materials could not be checked out of the library, but that they had to remain for everybody to use. She decided to take four books which dealt with the geography of New York. As a bonus, the librarian gave her three old issues of National Geographic, one of which was devoted to New York.

At dinner that evening, I asked, "Edith, what did we learn today?" She recited all the events. As she explained how the automobile ran, she made a mistake. "No, Edith," I interrupted. "That is not exactly how a car starts."

"You're right, Daddy." She corrected the error, and I realized that she was exhausted. The learning experiences of the day had covered what might have been a semester of school work for some children.

After dinner, Edith went to the sofa with the four books and the magazines, where she read while listening to the Swan Lake ballet on the radio. Within an hour she was in bed. It had been a productive day and a typical one.

Reading had become an important part of Edith's life. By now she was finishing two or three books a day, utilizing every spare moment for it. For example, we insisted that she stop at eight-thirty and we turned the lights out as soon as she was in bed. We found out later that she often spread the blanket over her head after we left the room, and read far into the night by the aid of a flashlight.

We made daily trips to the library where I permitted Edith to check out as many books as she could safely carry, usually from four to six. During one of our visits, Edith darted away from me as we were walking out the exit, and I did not realize that she was gone until after I was outside. A few moments later she ran through another door carrying several more books. Running across the street to where I was waiting, she tripped, fell, and dropped the books, tying up traffic for a few minutes. As I attempted to comfort her and to attend to her bruises, she sobbed, tears streaming down her cheek, "My knees will heal quickly, but not the books." The books had landed in a puddle of water.

One of the subjects in which Edith became deeply interested was horses. She seemed to have an insatiable love for them, reading avidly every book about them that she could get. As I was busily shopping in a supermarket, I was horrified to see Edith tearfully kick down a neat pyramid of canned horse meat. The store manager scolded her as other shoppers gathered to see what had happened. Heartbrokenly Edith complained,"Daddy, how cruel can people be, slaughtering horses to feed dogs?" I tried to explain the situation to the manager, but he demanded angrily how I could expect anyone to believe that such a little girl could read the can labels. There was no point in arguing with him.

Love, whether for horses or for family or for mankind, was an important aspect of Edith's life. We were affectionate with her and she was with us. I wanted her not only to develop her intellectual faculties but also to have love and compassion for her fellow man.

One evening as we sat on the Coney Island boardwalk, I said softly, "Edith, I love you so very much."

"I love you too, Daddy."

"What is love, Edith?"

"It is hard to explain."

"Whom else do you love, Sweetheart?"

"I love Mommy, I love books, the boardwalk, music."

"Do you love other children?"

"Yes. But I feel sorry for them."

"Why?"

"Well, they know nothing. They run around wildly all day. Daddy, what is love, really?"

I began to talk about the many forms of love, about the attachment, the willingness to sacrifice, the inner warmth that one feels towards others. Edith, as always, was alert, readily following my explanation. "You mean love is like Romeo and Juliet, Ruth and Naomi?" she asked.

"Yes, you are quite right."

Then she added, "If I had a doggie, I would love him too."

I felt guilty, for I knew that she wanted a dog, but I could not afford to have one. "Someday, I'll buy you one."

"Good," she replied and then returned to the topic of love. "Moses must have loved his people dearly."

"Why do you say that?"

"Well, in spite of their disobedience and sins, he led them through the wilderness to the Promised Land. You know, Daddy, I love the ocean, the boardwalk, the sunset. I would not want to live anywhere else." Her mind was always active and wondering. "God must love the Jewish people, too."

"Why do you think so? After all, so many Jews have been killed throughout history including your grandparents."

"That's true, but still we always seem to be able to survive. You know, Daddy, there are as many kinds of love as there are kinds of beauty."

"What is beauty, Edith?"

"The sunset, a horse, Greek heroes, flowers. I think love and beauty go together in a rather strange way."

That night in bed, I marveled at the depth of her thoughts about such abstract things as love and beauty. Also, I felt an awesome responsibility to guide her properly.

At about this time, I decided that she was mature enough to learn the biological facts of life. Although Bella objected, I decided to undress in front of Edith, so that she could learn about male anatomy. She was inquisitive, as she was about everything, and posed questions which many parents avoid. I answered her questions as calmly and as accurately as I could. We discussed the process of, reproduction candidly and Edith learned about menstruation, intercourse and pregnancy. At times her enlightenment got her into trouble with her playmates. Once she suffered a black eye for insisting that babies were not delivered by storks.

Many people have asked me if Edith played with other children. Yes, she did but she had little in common with most of them. I wanted her to enjoy life fully and I believe play is an important part of growing up. In many ways, much of what Edith did was play to her; she learned as she played and she played as she learned. However, playing with other children was not often satisfying to her. From time to time I would ask her if she wanted to play with another child, and she would usually answer no, explaining that the other child was too babyish. Once I asked her why she didn't play house and she replied that it was too silly.

Often, though, she would join a group of youngsters who were playing ball, hopscotch, hide-and-seek or some other active game. It was a satisfying kind of change for her. When I observed her from a distance, I could see no particular distinction between her and the other children. She would smile and laugh with them and she would play hard and run fast. During the game she would be totally involved, but as soon as the game was over she would shy away from the others. In spite of the similarity of their ages, she was intellectually worlds apart from them.

While Edith had difficulty relating to children, she continued to surprise and impress adults. Shortly after her fourth birthday, I graduated from Brooklyn College. After the graduation ceremonies, the dean invited me to bring Bella and Edith to visit with him. As soon as we entered his office, Edith began to browse through his personal library. He seemed slightly surprised to see a young child show such an interest in books, and he suggested that she take the book off the shelf that appealed most to her. Without hesitating, she reached for a volume of the Encylopaedia Britannica. He took the book from her, selected an article dealing with Israel, and teasingly asked her if she could read it. She began to read the article fluently. The dean was amazed and exlaimed, "but she's a genius." Then he asked her to tell him all that she knew about Israel.

Edith began, "Israel is both the youngest as well as one of the oldest states in the world," and then continued to elaborate. Obviously impressed, he gently kissed her on the forehead.

As we were leaving, he picked Edith up and said. "You must be proud of your father. He completed a four-year college program in one year and a month."

"I shall do better than that," she replied with conviction.

CHAPTER 7

The Endless Quest for Knowledge

Edith's educational progress continued and intensified as she grew older. One of her finest qualities has always been her insatiable quest for the truth, her avid pursuit of knowledge. Although she seemed to learn almost effortlessly, her intellectual potential appeared to remain virtually untapped. If, as Socrates argued in Plato's Republic, a philosopher is one "who has a taste for every sort of knowledge and who is curious to learn and is never satisfied," then Edith was truly a philosopher.

As a child, she was my closest companion and disciple; and she has always been my source of inspiration. In molding her, I always have been very concerned not only with her intellectual growth, but also with her spiritual and physical well-being. I have stressed the significance of humility and compassion. I have steered her toward non-conformity, independence of thought, and courage of conviction, teaching that the truth was important, whether or not it was popular.

I held a teaching position after my graduation, and Edith began attending my lectures when she was four years old. I believe that she was greatly influenced by the comment which I made to my students at the end of each term: "If the only thing which I have impressed you with is the fact that nothing is white or black and that you should never cease to challenge truisms no matter how tempting they may be, then I shall have succeeded in my endeavor." Edith took this statement to heart.

She repeatedly demonstrated that she was willing to challenge others in the search for truth. At the age of four, the Sinai campaign in the Fall of 1956 greatly interested her so that she kept close touch with the news from the Middle East. She hoped that Israel would not give up the land which it had conquered until a lasting peace had been established. In discussing Israel's future, which was dear to my heart also, I tried to be as objective as possible to prevent her from being prejudiced against the Arabs. I was determined she should always search for the truth, not letting her emotions rule her. I told her we could not overlook the fact that a million innocent Arab refugees had been uprooted because of the conflict. She replied, "the Arab states have so much territory they could easily absorb the refugees and that Israel had offered compensation if peace could be established."

In addition to my position, I was attending the graduate school of government at Columbia University where I took a course which dealt with the Middle East, covering its history, politics, and current events. Since the students were primarily Arabs and Jews, confrontations in class were common. Edith was anxious to visit Columbia and also to find out more about the Middle East, so I took her to class with me one day, where we sat inconspicuously in the back of the room. Because I had insisted she promised not to ask "even one single question" but her animated behavior during the lecture indicated that she was greatly interested. She later told me she found the period of questions at the end particularly painful because the Arab students were making inflammatory statements toward Israel.

After the lecture, I took her to the library. As we left, several Arab students were conducting "a documentary exhibition of Jewish atrocities in Sinai." Edith approached one of the Arabs and asked, "Where is this picture from?"

"Don't you know, little girl? These are Nazi-type Jewish murderers killing Arab women." Similar replies were given as she asked about each picture.

Finally Edith burst out, "What a lie! These pictures were taken during the Warsaw ghetto uprising; the attackers are Nazis! Aren't you ashamed to resort to such a lie?" The Arabs stood speechless while Edith continued. "I recognize these pictures since my Daddy collects them for his book." She was upset for the rest of the day.

Later, on the train out of the city, she criticized me for not taking a stand against the Arab allegations during the lecture. I explained to her that I wanted to conduct myself with dignity, unlike the other students. What I did not explain was that I had feared that if I had said anything she would also have participated in the class.

Our next stop was the school that I administered. She went to my office while I substituted for a sick teacher. The class was unruly and I was exhausted. Further, I had a headache and fever. As a result I was very permissive, and the class became loud and noisy. Edith was trying to read, but the noise disturbed her. Suddenly she opened the door, entered the class and scolded the children who were about five years older. "How ridiculous and childish you act by wasting my father's time. Education is the highest good of every human being. What a shame! What a shame that you don't appreciate it! If you don't desire to learn, why do you come here?" Abruptly she walked out, slamming the door. The reaction was short of a miracle; I had no need to raise my voice again. On the way home, Edith remarked, "You know Daddy, you should teach mature students like me so you would not have to cope with discipline problems."

At home again, she called up my schoolmate who had promised to buy her a "visible man," a plastic model with removable parts.

"I'm sorry," said Joe. "I couldn't get to Manhattan."

"You're kidding me. They can be purchased in any store." Joe wouldn't visit again without the visible man. I mildly scolded her for calling him, but she shrugged it off with, "He promised. One should live up to his promises."

A few days before Israel had invaded Egypt, the abortive Hungarian revolt had begun. Soon the Russians moved their troops and tanks into Hungary, while the other nations of the world cheered the bravery of the rebels but refused to take any steps to assist them. Edith was very interested in the progress of the revolt and was greatly concerned when it became apparent that the resistance would be crushed. For example, one morning in November, she woke up about seven and began to read Andersen's Fairy Tales. Since she had missed the seven o'clock news on the radio, she called me over and asked about the revolt. I had been shaving during the news, so I told her about the previous night's report. She abruptly informed me that she had already heard it. Then I suggested that I could go down and buy a paper.

"The paper goes to press at seven o'clock in the evening. It can't report anything new."

Slightly irritated, I said, "You can wait another fifteen mintues for the next broadcast." This seemed to satisfy her and she apologized for her impatience.

As the time for the news approached, she put away her book and waited, anxious and concerned. The announcer said, "The Russian tanks were seen en masse on the streets of Budapest crushing the last vestige of resistance." I left the apartment quickly and went to get a newspaper so that I would have time to organize my thoughts before the child began to question.

When I returned, she asked, "Dad, why doesn't the U.N. intervene? Doesn't the United States have troops in Europe?"

I couldn't explain the failure of the other nations to react, and so I suggested that we discuss it later. But Edith wanted to know at once. I successfully avoided answering, and soon Verdi began to play on the radio and Edith returned to her reading.

At eight o'clock she got out of bed and read *The Times* for about twenty minutes. She was interested in a chess problem and made notes on her pad. At about nine, she asked her mother for eggs; no one ever offered her breakfast since she was free to ask for food when she was hungry. After she ate, she worked with her abacus. To take advantage of her interest, I dictated a column of four or five digit numbers for her to add.

"You are too slow, Dad." In about four minutes, I checked the sum and it was correct.

"You will never need an adding machine," I told her.

"Additions," she said "are baby stuff."

Later, while we walked along the Coney Island boardwalk, Edith engaged me in a discussion covering many aspects of international affairs, including the Hungarian problem. "Why don't the other satellites simultaneously stage a revolt? Russia certainly couldn't crush them all. Why does NATO keep quiet?"

We talked for about an hour, then went to the library, where she checked out four books about horses. When we got home, she began to read the books during lunch and by three-thirty had finished them. Since there was nothing else to do, we decided to walk back to the boardwalk. Over there, I attempted to explain to her the gravitational influence of the moon on the seas. Since I didn't know much about it myself, she was not satisfied with the explanation. "Why don't you get a book on it, Dad? Write a note to yourself so you will not forget." I did and two days later she had the book.

Edith chose not to eat supper that night, spending the rest of the evening reading the *Times* and discussing with me the prospects for peace in the Middle East. 'How can Israel be condemned for changing arid deserts into blooming gardens." I had no answer.

At bedtime, as usual, "Could I read some more?"

"No," I said firmly. "The light will be turned off." Bedtime was one of the few rules that Edith knew at the age of four.

Already at that age, she had a remarkable memory. To test it, I once suggested that she observe the plates of passing cars while we were standing on the street corner. I wrote down the numbers of about twenty cars on my pad. Then we walked on and about an hour later I asked, "What do you remember about the cars?" To my surprise, she told me the license number of every one in the order in which they passed us. Then she reversed the order. Further, she described the color of each vehicle, but I had no way of verifying that since I had barely time to write down the license numbers. She was rewarded for her performance with an ice-cream cone.

Before too long, Edith received the visible man from Joe. It showed the anatomy of a male in detachable plastic parts. Within two or three days she learned every organ and its function. During my next visit to the outpatient clinic for an examination, I told the physician about Edith's knowledge of anatomy. Having taught it at a medical school when he was younger, the doctor could not believe that a four-year-old child knew as much about the human body as I claimed. Finally I invited him to visit us to see for himself. The next Sunday he showed up at our apartment. I introduced him to Edith as my doctor.

"Where is his stethoscope?" she asked.

"What do you want it for?" the doctor responded.

"For once, I'd like to hear the abnormal beat of my Daddy's heart for myself."

"How would you know the difference?"

"I'll compare it with Mom's heartbeat," she replied. "After all, her heart is normal."

The doctor quizzed Edith for some time. As he was leaving, he softly said to me, "You have a tremendous responsibility with that girl. I would be happy if my son who is eleven years older than Edith knew that much about anatomy." Within a week, a present for her arrived by mail from the doctor – an anatomy textbook.

At the age of four, she read the Book of Prophets. She loved it for its poetic beauty and social justice. "My child, this is the essence of Judaism, your faith — justice and charity are the same word in Hebrew."

"You mean they are synonymous."

"Yes, darling. Where did you hear this word?"

"You explained it to me after I heard it on the WQXR broadcast."

Edith recited the Twenty-third Psalm with great conviction, which impressed me deeply." " 'I will fear no evil for Thou art with me.' Isn't that beautiful!"

"It is, my child. I love it too."

"Why were the prophets so despised by the mighty?"

"Because they had the courage to oppose the unjust," I answered. "You must always help the needy and be just to others."

"I will, Daddy, all my life. Please read me Isaiah." She closed her eyes.

"Read it yourself. You do it so much better than I."

"But the words are difficult," she protested.

"You have learned it by heart," I reminded her.

"You are right, Daddy."

"Someday you will learn about the contemporary prophets."

"What is contemporary?" I explained the meaning of the word to her. "Please tell me who they are. I want to know all about them."

Soon, she learned about Gandhi, Tolstoy, and Ben Gurion, reading their biographies with great interest. "Daddy, I wish I could be big enough to help Schweitzer in his hospital in Africa."

"I hope that when you grow up, you will study medicine and heal the sick."

"Yes, Daddy. If I only could make you well."

"You will, my sweetheart."

When she was a little older, I took Edith to a Temple for the first time. She was disillusioned. "How can they please God with prayer and songs? Why do we need such a beautiful structure? Wouldn't it be better to build hospitals in Africa? Why don't these people help the sick and poor? God would like it more. Why should people eat a lot before the Day of Atonement so that they are not hungry the next day - whom are they fooling? They cannot deceive God."

"Well," I responded, "Most of the adult people are not as smart as you are. Maybe they think they are deceiving God."

"Why did the Christians persecute the Jews? They, too, believe in the Old Testament."

"I don't know. It is a cruel world."

"We must make it better."

"I hope you will," I said sincerely.

"I will. I will, Daddy." Then she started questioning again. "Why do Christians fight among themselves? We Jews never would."

"We did it in the past, too."

"Why did Christian Germany fight Christian France?"

"The Nazis did not believe in God."

"How about the First World War?" Edith continued to probe. "Hitler was not in power then." She scored an important point. In World War I, priests in both France and Germany blessed troops in the name of the same God before they were sent to the front to kill each other.

On the way home she asked, "Why do the whites chase Negroes from their church?" Again she had asked about the injustices of organized

75

religion; I could offer no rational explanation.

"When you grow up, dear, I expect you to be good, helpful and kind," I told her. "This way you will serve God."

"You mean when you help man, you serve God?"

"That is exactly so, my child."

"Daddy, I wouldn't want to go to the temple, to stand up when I am told, to sit down when I am ordered, and to sing when others sing."

There were many advantages to living in New York; it is an exciting city that is always bustling with action. Although I always lacked funds, I saw to it that Edith participated in as many activities as possible. She learned early that the finest things in life are free. There were trips to the Bronx Zoo, to concerts at Lewishon Stadium, to the Museum of Natural Science and of course, to the library. She particularly loved the Museum and it was often diffcult to drag her out from it. "One more minute," she would insist as she disappeared into the crowd. Shortly she would return excited about what she had seen. "Daddy, there is so much one could learn from the past. I wish we could live nearby so I could come here everyday."

When Edith was five, we made a long planned visit to the United Nations. For weeks I had been explaining international relations to her and we had discussed the diversity of customs, traditions, and political systems which the United Nations represented. Edith, well aware of international conflicts, knew the role that the United Nations played in such situations. Once in discussing international relations, she said, "We shall either learn to live together or we shall perish." As this was my view also, I showed my approval by gently kissing her on the forehead.

As the day for the trip approached, she began to count the hours and the minutes — "seven days, fifteen hours and five minutes." On the day of the trip, we got up quite early. I doubt that Edith had slept much for her eyes were red. After breakfast, we went to the subway station on Surf Avenue, where we had to climb about two stories or so to the platform. Knowing that it was hard for me, she cautioned me to slow up. Every so often she checked my pulse using her mother's watch which Edith was allowed to bring along on trips. "It's eighty-eight," she said. "You had better stop."

"What should a normal pulse be?" I asked.

76

"I guess sixty to seventy."

"How does a heart function?"

"It pumps blood." I was satisfied; there was no need to inquire further for there was a full day ahead of us.

As soon as we were on the train and my breathing became easier, I decided to take advantage of the hour's trip. "Edith, what powers the subway?" I asked, without stopping to think that I didn't know the answer myself.

"Yes, what does? Where does it derive its energy?" She ran to the first car to look out. Again she asked, "Where does the power come from?" But I couldn't answer.

I saw no way that the power could come through the two tracks. Since I was not going to try to bluff Edith, even though she was growing restless and even angry at the delay in finding out, I decided to ask some of the commuters. Many of them probably spent ten percent of their lives on subways, but none that I asked knew how the subway was powered. "How should I know? I ain't a mechanic," one replied.

Next, I asked the subway porter. Unable to tell us how the train ran, he looked at us with disbelief as though saying, "Why should anyone care about it?"

It became necessary to divert Edith's attention. "How many people does a car hold?" I asked.

"One hundred fifty," she quickly replied.

"There are twelve cars in the train. How many people can travel on this train?"

"That's easy — eighteen hundred."

"Each of them pays fifteen cents for his fare. How much money do they all spend for the trip when the train is full?"

This time it took her a little longer. "Two hundred seventy dollars. Daddy, where does the power come from?"

"Wait until we get off and we will find out."

77

When we arrived at Time Square Station, I asked Edith to find the phone number of the Transit Authority. Then I picked her up to a pay telephone, she deposited the coin and dialed. "Mister, who could tell me how the subway is powered?"

"What?" said the voice on the other end. I could picture his surprise. "Wait a moment."

Another man came on to the line. "Strange that people should ask about it." Then he explained about the conductor rail and how the electricity was transmitted to the electric locomotive. "Who are you, anyway?" he asked.

"Edith Stern," she replied. "Thank you." She was satisfied. I was also relieved and enlightened.

Our shuttle trip to the East Side was uneventful, and soon we were strolling toward the East River. "Edith," I asked, "does 42nd Street impress you?"

"You would think that the whole population of the city was here."

"How large is the population of the city?"

"I believe I read in the *Times* that it is eight million, seven hundred thousand," she replied.

I then called her attention to a woman walking by. "What kind of a dress does that lady wear?"

"It is a sari."

"Where are saris worn?"

"In India, of course."

"What is the name of the famous Indian leader who was assassinated?"

"Gandhi. I attended your lecture at which you spoke about his non-violent resistance to the British."

"Right, Edith. When did I deliver the lecture?"

"Seven days ago."

"You are right, Sweetheart. What was playing on the radio when we returned home after the lecture." I was testing her memory again.

"Bethoven's Fifth Symphony."

"Why was your Mother worried then?"

"Because we came home so late. Where is your pad, Daddy?"

"I don't know. I must have left it in the subway."

"That's too bad. I want to draw a picture of this building."

Since I did not want to miss any opportunity for her self-expression, I went into a five-and-ten cent store and bought a pad. Soon Edith was blocking the normal flow of pedestrian traffic while sketching the *Daily News* building.

When we finally reached the United Nations, I was worn out, but not Edith. "What language is being spoken?" I asked as we sat and watched the General Assembly. "Is it Spanish or Italian?"

"Spanish." As usual, she was correct. "I'd like to learn the language."

"All you have to do is press the button and you will hear an English translation."

"That is too easy. You always tell me how important it is to learn — to learn all that we can."

I was very proud of her. "You're absolutely right, my darling."

"Somehow all these people seem to be at peace with each other. Why must we have wars? Why don't they settle all their differences right here and now?"

"They try to; perhaps someday they will, my dear."

"With the atomic bomb hanging over their head like a sword of Damocles?"

"What is a sword of Damocles?"

"Remember, you gave me the book on Greek mythology?"

"What was the name of the book?"

"Greek Mythology."

"You are right."

"Why do you tell me so often that I am right? she asked.

That got me to wondering. Perhaps I should challenge her more. After all, Edith, is only a human, with the failings, attributes, successes and hopes of all people. She is not a robot. Nor should she think that she is always right. At the same time, the fact of the matter is that usually she is right and has the ability to cut through the cloudy maze and see what is often hidden to the average individual.

But then, Edith is not average. Far from that. She is invested with a sixth sense, with the ability to grasp quickly, to understand what is being said, what is written, what is meant, long before most persons can. That is a strong asset and she doesn't have to mince words, to grovel for attention or recognition, to seek solace from superficial achievements. She recognizes values, and has high standards and ideals which, fortunately, have been strengthened within her during each passing year.

On the way home to the subway, she fell asleep resting her head on my knee. As I looked at her peaceful face, I thought of the thousands of children who aimlessly roam the streets. If those children had been properly educated, I mused to myself, they could perhaps change the destiny of mankind. How important it is to give children a good education early in life.

Years later, when the U. S. Government asked me to conduct a study of the Head Start Program, I saw at first hand how valuable schooling at an early age can be. And I saw, clearly, that thousands of children, now suffering from mental stagnation or physical handicaps, could have their education and career training raised to high levels and become magnificent assets to American society.

CHAPTER 8

A Genius on the Loose

Edith developed an excellent vocabulary quite early and as a result frequently had trouble conversing with her playmates, who often teased and ridiculed her. She would try to even the score by using words that the other kids didn't understand. For example, she would say to a girl, "Your epidermis is showing" — a phrase which later became popular among older children. Similarly, she would tell a child, "You betray narcissistic tendencies," an expression which she had borrowed from Freud. Assuming that these words were bad the children often complained to their mothers, who in turn criticized me about her abusive language.

Having accepted a position in Rock Island, Illinois, in the fall of 1957, I moved my family there. Our neighbor, a Christian, invited Edith to spend Christmas morning with his children. Being Jewish she was not sure whether she should go. Explaining that while there is a diversity of traditions and holidays among the many religions, they have a common belief in God and justice, I urged her to go. She agreed and on Christmas morning, she was with the neighbor's children excitedly viewing the presents under the tree.

The father who passed out the presents handed one to Edith. Unaccustomed to the Christmas tradition, she asked what it was. He told her to unwrap it and inside she found a pair of pajamas. Delighted, she asked who gave them to her. In the best American tradition, the father replied, "They are from Santa Claus."

"But there is no Santa Claus," she protested. "He is simply a myth."

"Of course there is," her little girl friend said, coming to her father's aid. "He comes down the chimney every Christmas to bring us toys."

"No. There is no Santa Claus," Edith persisted.

"Daddy, is it true? Explain it to Edith."

Embarrassed, the father reassured the children that there was a Santa Claus. "Edith, you must be mistaken. You simply never saw him."

"I beg to differ with you, sir, Saint Nicholas is commemorated by the Christians, but Christmas signifies the birth of Jesus Christ."

The other children were upset. "Daddy, is there really no Santa Claus?" Again he assured them there was, at which point Edith left the house crying and walked the mile home. When I asked her what had happened, she told me the story, then added, "I left because I realized that the truth can be so painful."

One of Edith's favorite television programs was The $64,000 Question. Prior to its going off the air in the summer of 1958, Edith was probably its most avid fan. At the end of each show, when the successful contestant was invited to return the following week, he was assigned a volume of the Encyclopaedia Britannica and told to study it. The following day Edith would begin to read the assigned volume from beginning to end, eagerly anticipating the next week's show. On the day of the program she would wake up early and nervously count the hours. When the show began, the rest of the family had to be quiet, while one by one she correctly answered every question. As later events revealed, Edith was perhaps the only one who had the right answers for the show was rigged.

In addition to her intellectual feats, Edith often showed a sense of fairness uncommon to children or even adults. Shortly after her sixth birthday — which she dismissed as just chronology and refused to celebrate — we rode a streetcar to a movie theater. As we squeezed onto the crowded car, I paid my fare and we found a seat in the back.

"Daddy, you should have paid half a fare for me," she reminded me.

"I had forgotten that you are now six, but let's forget it."

A few minutes passed and Edith said, "Give me a nickel."

"What do you need it for?" She wouldn't tell me, so not having a nickel, I eventually gave her a dime.

In a few minutes, she disappeared to the front of the streetcar mumbling something about wanting to see the road ahead. Later, as we were leaving the streetcar, the driver said to me, "You have a funny girl." When I asked why, he explained that she had insisted on paying. "I told her that little girls can ride the streetcars free, but she said that she was six. Then she gave me ten cents explaining that five cents was for her fare and five for a penalty since her father hadn't paid for her." Then he said, "You must give her a lot of dough."

"No, my good man, it is simple honesty which we adults lack so badly," I said, somewhat embarrassed.

"You said it, not me," agreed the driver.

On another occasion, Bella had gone out of town to visit a friend. As we were leaving the library one afternoon, Edith said, "let's call Mother." I suggested that we wait until the rates went down in the evening, but she insisted, explaining that since her mother would be visiting later we would not be able to reach her. I finally agreed and we found a public telephone. At the completion of the call, I hung up the receiver and a dime was returned. Since I had deposited the correct change, the dime must have been returned by mistake. Without giving it much thought, I put it in my pocket.

"Daddy, you should have redeposited the dime. It belongs to the telephone company."

I agreed with her, but explained that the first person to use the phone would get it rather than the telephone company. "How would you suggest that I return it," I said.

"Let me think about it."

The next day she wrote the following note to the telephone company:

"Dear Sir:

Enclosed find a dime which belongs to you. My Dad and I used the telephone yesterday and on completion of our conversation a dime came back. Make sure that you repair your installation at this address."

She neatly printed the location of the telephone booth.

"Daddy, put the dime in the envelope and mail it." I did.

By late summer of 1958, I decided to spend as much time as possible completing my book. Hence, I happily accepted a school principalship in Florida which paid poorly but which would permit me to devote a great deal of time to writing. Further, my doctor had told me that the Florida climate would be ideal for both Edith's and my health.

Soon we were living in Saint Petersburg, where Edith started first grade at the normal age of six. Although she had been ready for several years, she did not start earlier because I was not very eager to have her in school. In fact, the only reason she attended at all was because the state laws required it. As I had feared, her school experiences that fall were uneventful and boring.

During this period, my wife and I frequently argued over Edith's future. Bella's philosophy was fatalistic. "Let her pursue studies with her age group," she said. "Surely schools are competent to educate pupils. Happiness is the supreme goal of people and one cannot attain it in seclusion." Our friends and relatives strengthened her position. The situation became unbearable to Bella as I depended more and more on my daughter for companionship, intellectual stimulation, and recreation. I could not convince her that my method of total submersion was crucial to Edith's upbringing.

We continued to discuss peaceful solutions to our dilemma, but I insisted that under all circumstances, Edith would remain in my custody. I argued that her separation from me as her teacher would cause incalculable harm to her progress. Having no solution, we settled on an uneasy truce.

In spite of the conflicts, I continued my work with Edith, who by now was teaching me as well as I was teaching her. We discussed philosophy, sociology, history, and political science. On her own, she intensively studied Gestalt psychology, a subject which she was to continue in a more general way several years later in junior college.

She still attended my lectures, where she was alert, responsive and inquisitive. If she wanted to make a point or ask a question, she did not hesitate to interrupt me, which often annoyed my students. Once I was lecturing on Darwin's theory of evolution, she suddenly interrupted me to ask, "How do you reconcile Darwin's theory with the Biblical explanation of the origin of man?" She had clearly seen the conflict between the two accounts of the genesis.

Later that year we moved to North Miami Beach where I asked the school to permit Edith to skip a grade so that she would not be so bored. In consideration of the request, they gave Edith a day long battery of psychological examinations to determine her readiness to advance. At the time, Edith still wanted a dog and to punish me because she didn't have one, she cunningly answered every question with the word dog. As a result, my request was denied. However, a few months later she was permitted to skip ahead anyway. This however did not decrease her boredom.

During the summer of 1959, we had a picnic in Crandon Park on Key Biscayne. While Edith swam in the bay, Bella asked me to walk along the beach with her. "I have something to tell that may displease you," she said.

"Nothing can shock me. What is it?"

"I am going to have a baby."

I was pleased and embraced her warmly. Then I said that the world would have another superior human being. "No!" she protested. "This will be my own, totally my own child!" The inevitable argument followed. "All you are interested in is experimentation, with no regard for your child's welfare," she charged.

I angrily replied, "Is not every parent determined to provide the best educational facilities for his offspring? Did not illiterate immigrants slave in sweatshops for eighty hours a week so that their children could advance themselves? Well I do exactly the same, but more intensely, with more vigor and dedication. Doesn't Edith lead a happy and wholesome life while, in my judgment, she is destined to make a substantial contribution to the world of science? What can be more noble? The argument subsided. Perhaps the gap had grown deeper.

As I had encouraged Edith from the time I put black and white dolls in her crib as an infant, she developed a keen sense of justice and equality in the brotherhood of man. As I did, she believed every person, regardless of race or ethnic origin, should receive the same treatment and consideration as anyone else.

In 1959, the landmark Supreme Court decision of five years earlier appeared to be another dead letter of the law. The token school desegregation efforts signified window dressing at best. An editorial in a leading newspaper poignantly summed up the situation with, "At the present rate, it will take approximately two thousand years to bring about a total school integration." The black community, disillusioned with the slow progress, became bitter and frustrated, and the racial polarization increased.

In the fall of that year, I was asked to address a gathering of black educators. I accepted the invitation, realizing that the assignment required tact, courage and sincerity. Thus, when Edith asked to join me at the lecture, I was hesitant. "Are you aware, my child, that in spite of my record of liberalism, the audience might be hostile to me for no other reason but that I am a white person?"

"Do not worry, Daddy. I am fully aware of it." Reluctantly, I consented.

The following day at the library, she disappeared into one of the many rooms, soon to emerge smiling and tightly holding her worn-out notebook. She was evasive when I asked where she had been and what she had been doing.

At the lecture, the church hall was filled to capacity. Edith and I were the only white people present. I was politely but coolly introduced. I told the educators that a struggle still lay ahead, a struggle which they would have to pursue in alliance with an englightened segment of the white community. I concluded, "No one can set back the clock of history. Justice will prevail."

A barrage of angry questions followed. "How long can we wait?" "How can you explain the delay to children who will be inferior tomorrow because they are not given adequate education today?" "Why shouldn't morality transcend political expediencies?" These were grievances which had burdened me. I had no easy answers and the crowd continued to be indignant.

During the lecture and the questions, Edith had sat by me quietly. Now she jolted my arm and with a twinkle in her eye, asked that I let her speak. Fearful that the audience would misinterpret my action by having a seven-year-old child address them. I nevertheless introduced her. "Ladies and gentlemen, I should like to present my daughter who has a few words to say." At first, the reaction was unfavorable, but gradually calmness was restored as Edith resolutely climbed on a chair.

She opened her notebook and in a loud voice read, " 'How untrust-worthy, filthy, easily given to alcohol they are, indeed they must go back . . .' " she paused. Deathly silence reigned in the hall, while my heart succumbed to an uncontrollable fibrilation. Then she slowly repeated, " 'Indeed they must go back to Ireland where they came from.' Quoted from a letter to the Boston Globe, 1880." A thunder of applause filled the hall. Tears moistened my eyes as I warmly embraced her.

At home that evening, Edith said, "Remember, Dad, the stories you told me about the plight of the Irish who had to flee their homeland because of famine and the oppression which they had suffered upon their arrival in America? Well I have never forgotten the story and I found a book at the library where that letter was printed. I think the Negro problem is quite similar. The pattern of prejudice has not changed in 80 years."

"Why didn't you tell me you wanted to quote the letter before we went to the lecture?"

"Surprise is the most effective weapon," she whispered and walked away smiling.

At Thanksgiving, Edith was to play the part of an Indian in a skit. Waiting to drive her home one day, I overheard her arguing with the teacher about the "Unsophisticated language" of the script. "It would appear to me," she said, "that second graders should possess more semantic finesse." Then she criticized the script for being "historically inaccurate" pointing out, "As everyone knows, the Indians were brutally slaughtered by the white men in their desire to take possession of the natives' land." Finally she concluded, "I refuse to participate in the show because of the historical inaccuracies and its poor articulation."

Reluctantly she was persuaded to play her part. As the parents watched, the children acted out the first Thanksgiving. Finally Edith appeared on stage as an Indian bearing fruit to the Pilgrims. "This is a token of our friendship. We Indians hope to live harmoniously with you in mutual respect," she ad libbed to a surprised little pilgrim. The girl playing the part, confused by this departure from the script, forgot her lines and left the stage in tears. As the curtain went down, I was summoned to the stage.

"How could you do it?" I asked. "You scared the poor little girl and have upset the play."

"Daddy, I simply did it for historical accuracy. I wanted to set the record straight," she replied. When I reminded her that it was only a play, she countered with, "A play which should have been based on historical facts!" I could have pointed out that in terms of historical accuracy, the Indian would have been unlikely to use the words which she did, but I saw no point in arguing further.

Realizing the embarrassment she had caused, Edith apologized to the little girl. "There was no premeditation on my part. It just happened impulsively."

"I don't understand you Edith," the girl complained.

At other times, her verbal ability proved to be an asset. One day I was driving with her from Fort Lauderdale to Miami. As I was leaving Broward county, I hastily turned on a yellow light. Minutes later I was pulled to the side of the road by a police car. The patrolman insisted that I had run the light and in spite of my protests began to write out a ticket. Edith, who had been sitting quietly, turned to the officer and said, "I don't think my Dad violated the traffic law. He turned on yellow as every prudent driver would do when a car is pursuing him closely at an unreasonable speed. However, this is totally irrelevant in this case."

"Why is it irrelevant?" the officer inquired.

"Well as a Broward County officer, you must be aware that Dade County is not within your jurisdiction. We shall prove it in court."

"Good Lord," he exclaimed, "what kind of a child is she?"

"She is not a child, but an adult midget," I replied.

The officer let me off without a ticket, stating, "I am not going to face her in court."

At home, Bella asked me why I was so pale "Mommie, I rescued Daddy from a traffic ticket on technical grounds," Edith proudly told her.

A few weeks later, while traveling to the library to work on my manuscript, I was arrested on a false charge of minor traffic violation. The belligerent officer, in spite of my protests of innocence, took me to jail, refusing to let me either lock my car or take along the only copy of my manuscript. When I was released by a judge a couple of hours later, the manuscript, including my priceless interviews with Einstein, was gone. It had been my life's work for many years. Its loss was shattering blow.

Apparently Nazi sympathizers were involved in the theft, for shortly afterwards we began to receive threatening phone calls. On several occasions our home was shot at from swiftly passing cars. The loss of the book plus the threats were devastating. My health rapidly failed to the point where I could no longer discharge my responsibilities as a school administrator.

Calm and courageous in the face of the adversities, Bella, without awakening me, called a taxi during the night of February 2, 1960, when her labor pains began. This was a repeat performance of Edith's birth; again she feared that the excitement might cause me to have a heart spasm. The next morning, I learned that I was the father of a seven-pound boy. We named him David.

David came home from the hospital to a house resounding with music. Our bitter struggle over how he should be reared was resolved in a rather tragic way for soon I became too disabled to work. Consequently, Bella had to work to supplement my meager disability pension, leaving me at home to care for David. I now had another child to mold.

CHAPTER 9

Not All is Honey

In 1960 we moved to Indiana where I served as a director of education and as an assistant to the rabbi of a Reform Temple. Life had become difficult in Florida after the loss of my manuscript and the harrassment which followed. Thus we felt that we should leave, although we were not particularly pleased about moving to Indiana. The air in this town was polluted from industrial chimneys and the people were stiff, formal and withdrawn. When I defended the record of the United Nations in a lecture, I was met with indignation. When I suggested that it might be safer to have China admitted to the United Nations rather than to have her causing trouble on the outside, I was regarded as having committed treason. It was Richard Nixon, the arch-conservative, who vindicated me 12 years later.

This was a town which saw a substantial part of its population in church on Sunday for that was a sign of respectability rather than an expression of faith. The small Jewish community, mainly descendants of German emigrants, had no less than three houses of worship and on any given day you could seat all the Jewish population in any one of the sanctuaries and still have room for more. But as Christian denominations had their respective churches, so did all three Jewish denominations -- it was the respectable thing to do. When one denomination built a new synagogue, the other denominations had to do the same thing. To fortify their respectability, many of the Jews were members of two different denominational synagogues. The Board of Welfare, encompassing the whole Jewish population, had a full-time director, but there were few needy Jews. Once a suggestion was made that an old-age home be built, but the idea was dropped when not a single applicant could be found.

My introduction commenced with a round of social visits which annoyed me since I despised formality and did not care for sumptuous meals. I felt uneasy at them since I am a vegetarian.

From my arrival, I felt that the social, cultural, and physical climate would not be conducive to my non-conformist way of life. People were reserved, but polite. After we dispensed with the ritualistic round of socials, Edith, then 6½ years old, was invited to visit another girl of approximately 8. I resented the idea for the mother of the child was a wealthy woman who was critical of my views. The family resided on a beautiful estate shaded by old trees.

I felt Edith might not feel at home in such elegant surroundings. My daughter was raised permissively in austere conditions, where superficial niceties were non-existent and formality and etiquette were unknown. There were no birthdays or greeting cards. Meals were simple. One could eat whenever he desired, or not at all if he so chose. However, there were other meaningful activities. There were books, music and debates. I became angered, "This is not Edith's environment," I told my wife. "There was no choice. She had to go otherwise the lady would be offended which could cause serious repercussions," she answered.

"I don't give a damn," I said. "I am a free man. Why should I subject Edith to such an ordeal?"

Reluctantly, Edith entered the house as I drove away from the winding driveway. I felt guilty. In less than an hour as I was reading my Sunday *New York Times*, the phone rang. It was Edith. She was crying. This was unusual for Edith rarely cried.

"Daddy, please take me home."

On our way home we did not exchange a word. This had never happened before. I asked no questions. She went into her room, locked herself in and began to read a book. Neither I nor her mother dared to enter until late evening.

Next day as I was addressing a gathering of professional women, I saw the lady's icy eyes. They were filled with hate.

At the refreshment table I approached her. "What happened yesterday?"

"Don't you ever send you daughter to us."

"Why not?"

"How can a cultured worldly man like yourself have such a rude unintelligent child? Her conduct is simply demoralizing to my children."

"What happened?" I insisted.

"When the maid called the children to the dinner table," she said, 'I'm not hungry.' "

" 'But you must eat when dinner is served.' "

" 'I will not.' "

"My children had never heard such disobedience. Furthermore, when I tried to tempt her by reciting the menu, she did not even know the various kinds of food. How uninformed she is!"

"Yes," I nodded sarcastically. "Edith indeed is uninformed!"

At 6, Edith was familiar with Homer, Freud and Plato. As I came home Edith grabbed me warmly. "What kind of world do these people live in? Their toilet must be made of gold while the Encyclopedia is untouched by human hands."

"Would you rather live there in luxury?"

"No, Daddy," she embraced me as I sat on the armchair.

I felt triumphant and very sorry for the rich heiress.

As one of my duties, I conducted lectures at the temple on the foundations of Judaism to lay groups and Christian theology students. Edith was always present. Once a student asked about the similarities of Judaism and Christianity which he referred to as the Judeo-Christian tradition. After raising her hand for recognition, Edith inquired, "How do you reconcile the Spanish Inquisition and brutal persecution of Jews in Christian Europe with this statement.

About the same time, Edith read *Crime and Punishment*. "Dad, the transition from Tolstoy to Dostoevski is like going from a sunlit valley to the gloomy darkness of despair."

"I had cautioned you not to read Dostoevski for that reason."

"In spite of it, I am fascinated by his treatment of crime and atonement. How would you define justice?"

Using religion as a frame of reference, I explained that the basis of Judaism was justice for the sake of goodness and inner satisfaction.

"You still did not tell me what justice means."

"Well, perhaps the following will help. Tzedaka in Hebrew means both justice and mercy since one is inseparable from the other."

"You put it on a philosophical plateau."

"Well, not to be abstract, justice means to treat people as you would like to be treated by them. It means to purge your heart of bigotry, prejudice and greed and to maintain impartiality. Further, it means to be truthful at all times."

She pressed me for an example. "Your friendship with Elizabeth who is a Negro while the other kids resent her is an act of justice. The care you give to library books, the errands you do for the old lady, the research you do to ascertain the truth — all these are acts of justice."

"You are saying one should be just for the sake of justice, not out of fear of penalty nor for the sake of rewards," she observed.

"Right. Further, just as a good deed should result in inner satisfaction, an act of injustice will burden your conscience. Therefore, the Jew cannot accept the premise that Christ, by his death, atoned for the sins of all people. Rather everyone must be responsible for his own deeds. For example, every faithful Catholic confesses his sins and the Father confessor then metes out some sort of penalty. This relieves the believer of his guilt. On the other hand the Jews have no easy solution to moral problems; we believe that there is no mediator between God and man. A rabbi is just a teacher."

"Daddy, take me to see a confession," I explained that as a Jew I could not confess and that it would be improper for her to listen to someone else do so. She was insistent.

"But confessions are conducted in strict privacy," I told her. "How would you have access to one? In fact the priest is sworn to secrecy. I cannot take you to a confession, but I think I know a way you can visit a Catholic church. Marty, our custodian, is a Catholic. Perhaps you can persuade him to take you to church."

Marty, who had not been to church for years, was flabbergasted when Edith asked that he take her there, but after much protesting, he finally agreed to go sometime in the near future. During the days that she waited, she read the origin and history of confession. One day Marty showed up and said, "Let's go to the cathedral."

I had requested that he bring her right back to my office, but several hours passed before they returned. When they arrived, Edith, her face pale, ran into my arms. "What happened to you two," I asked. Marty explained that she had got away from him in church. When she came back she acted nevous and uneasy. Then she refused to come home saying that she had been dishonest and was ashamed.

Marty left and I offered to buy Edith an ice-cream cone. She refused it, saying she had been unjust and didn't deserve it. "In the cathedral, I left Marty and found the confessional booths. I crawled under the curtain and entered unnoticed. Then I heard a man saying, 'I have been disloyal to my wife and abusive to my children.' The priest ordered, 'Say eight Hail Marys, attend church regularly, say the Act of Contrition, make a donation in the poor box, and make peace with God, my son.' Daddy, I have been so unjust and dishonest. How can I clear my conscience?"

For punishment, I forbade her to go to the library for three days. She agreed that that was a proper punishment.

Unhappy with Indiana, we moved later that year to Far Rockaway on Long Island. Edith now had to apply for admission at an old dilapidated school where we had to convince the principal that at the age of eight, she should be put in the fourth grade. Although the Board of Education booklet suggested that school was an exciting experience to the child, she asked, "Daddy, must I go to school? It will be boring again."

As I had done many times before, I explained that the laws require children to attend school until they are sixteen.

"But I learn nothing there. Why must I go to school and waste my time? I would be much happier at home where I can listen to music, read and have discussions with you."

"Edith, you are right, but there is nothing we can do. Perhaps they will place you in a school for gifted children."

At the school, I asked the woman in the office if I could register my child.

"How old is she?"

'Eight."

"What grade did she attend in Indiana?"

"Fourth."

"You will have to see the principal. There are no eight-year-old children in the fourth grade here."

When I asked if there were any schools for gifted children in the area, she told me we would have to commute into the city. "Oh, that is awful," I said.

"Mister, we have not yet established that she requires a school for gifted children."

I pointed to Edith who sat quietly reading the *New York Times.* "Isn't that a sufficient proof of her intelligence?" "Indeed, no," she answered. Then I went to see the principal, who after much persuasion assured me they would put her in the fourth grade, commenting, "she would find enough of a challenge there." Edith resignedly entered the fourth-grade classroom as I left.

A few hours later, she was home. When I asked her how school was, she said, "Miserable, don't ask. I won't tell you." I felt guilty for having taken her there.

Visiting the school a few days later, I inquired how Edith was doing. The teacher informed me that she was not doing well and that she did not do her homework. Then she added, "You must see that she reads at home."

"Yes, I will prompt her to read at home," I said sarcastically.

In 1960 I embarked on a lecture tour of Europe. En route home in October, I suffered a prolonged heart spasm and was taken to a hospital in an ambulance.

Since children are not granted visiting privileges, Edith was not permitted to see me. After a few days, however, I insisted that she be allowed to visit. I told the hospital officials that my recovery depended upon it since otherwise I would have my wife take me home. Finally the hospital administrator agreed to make an exception if Edith would confine herself to the wing I was in and if she was accompanied by an adult. I readily accepted these restrictions for I was anxious to see her.

Several doctors and interns were in my room making the morning rounds when Bella brought Edith in for her visit. After entering the room, she immediately asked my doctor, "What are the statistical chances for my Dad's survival? Has he had a myocardial infarction?" Astonished, the doctor asked her what a myocardial infarction was. She explained the disorder in great detail.

While I was hospitalized, Edith spent many hours at my bedside telling me about the books she had read on physiology, cardiology, and pharmacology in order "to be of as much assistance to you as I can during your hospitalization." She also gained some first hand knowledge of medicine during her visits. Because the Chief of Medicine took an interest in her, he often permitted her to follow him on his daily rounds with the interns and medical students. He explained that her presence was useful since it kept the students alert and humble.

As my stay continued, Edith became increasingly knowledgeable about medicine and medical terms. Once she asked a technician to let her check my EKG. "I would like to see the prominence and frequency of the P Waves on my Dad's tracing," she told him.

"She must be kidding me, Mr. Stern," the man responded.

One day, Edith seemed depressed when she came into my room. I asked her why she was so sad. "You receive so much digitalis. At times digitalis can be harmful to people."

Since I always took Edith seriously, I asked my doctor about it. "Doc, why am I getting so much digitalis?"

"To keep you alive."

"But too much can be harmful."

"Yes, it can be fatal, but don't worry, we are watching you carefully for reactions. Anyway, I told you not to read medical books." When I insisted that I hadn't been reading medical books, he assumed that I had gotten the information from an intern. I assured him that my source of information was outside the hospital.

Edith was fascinated by pathology. Having obtained permission, Bella took her to the pathology department. "Dad, how thrilling it is that a slight variation in the color of a biopsy determines the difference between life and death, whether a growth is benign or malignant. How great the responsibility of the pathologist is. This man alone has to make the critical decisions in the struggle with disease during surgery."

One morning a middle-aged man was wheeled into my room with an acute pain in his shoulders. The agony was clearly reflected in his face. While the nurses undressed and put him into bed, they asked Edith and his wife to leave the room. When they returned, the woman was holding Edith's hand. "What a girl you have," she told me. "What a doll! How compassionate." Then she began to cry. After assuring her everything would be all right, I asked Edith what had happened while they were out of the room.

"Well Daddy, the lady briefed me on her husband's symptoms. The persistent pain in his chest has lasted a few days and she thinks it is due to a coronary. I simply assured her that there could be any number of reasons for the pain such as muscular cramps or some other lesion."

I asked her, "What do you base your diagnosis on?"

"First of all," she replied, "I state this hypothetically. As you know, I follow the doctor on his rounds. There is a patient in the last ward who suffered from a similar discomfort. After all of the tests were made, they revealed bursitis in the shoulder."

It turned out that Edith was right; my roommate did not have a coronary. Rather the pains were attributed to psychogenic factors, apparently because he had taken a severe loss on the stock market a few days before. He was discharged about four days later.

As he and his wife were leaving, she said, "Here is a present for my little doctor." Kissing Edith on the head, she handed her a copy of *Exodus*. "Please read it. My Joe sailed on the ship."

To this date she sends us clippings about Edith. "Make sure you study medicine," was written in one accompanying note. I hope that the woman was not too disappointed when she later learned that Edith had chosen to become a mathematician.

It was mid-December before I was released from the hospital and even then I was so weak that I could hardly walk. I'd had the attacks before, but they never had been so incapacitating. Thus, we were compelled to move back to Florida for the climatic advantages. Edith, who was always looking for a way to avoid having to attend school, greeted the decision to move nonchalantly. "I'll be happy wherever we live." Then upon reflection, she added, "Great! Maybe Florida laws don't compel school attendance." I assured her that she would be required to attend school.

We gave away our few meager pieces of furniture and packed the rest of our belongings. Then for two nights before we left, we stayed with my friend Leon in Little Neck. He drove us to his house where we had dinner and talked about our childhood in Europe. Another friend stopped in to say good-bye. Then to test my ability to stand for a while, I suggested we go down to the basement and play billiards.

Suddenly Edith asked me to take her to the Museum. "How can I? It is so far and after all I am sick."

"Please let me see the Museum for the last time," she begged. "I can't go alone and Mother must stay with the baby."

"Let me reason with you, my child."

"I must go!" she shouted angrily.

After telling her no again, I went down to the basement. After the game, Leon went upstairs to complete a speech draft. My other friend remained to chat for a while, then he also left. Alone in the basement, I heard someone sudenly lock the door and run. "Open the door, Edith," I shouted. There was no reply. My screams remained unanswered because upstairs the television was playing loudly. Since I was wearing only a light jacket, I was freezing in the cold basement. I became weaker and weaker. An hour passed and I was having difficulty walking to keep warm. I thought that this was the end.

Leon and Bella had thought that I had gone for a ride with the friend who had left while Edith had gone to Leon's library where she was reading Greek mythology. She later claimed that she had forgotten I was in the basement.

Finally, using my last strength, I screamed as loud as I could. Hearing this, the dogs began to bark. Michael, Leon's son, ran down and released me. "He is frozen," Michael told the others as he helped me up the stairs. As I was put to bed, a doctor was called. Shortly, Edith appeared in the door.

"Daddy, what have I done?"

I assured her that I would be fine, but Leon was unable to control his anger. "Your own daughter locked you up — the child for whom you sacrifice your life." Ashamed and frightened, Edith left the room.

"Leon don't touch her. She is a genius. Don't scare her. Don't harm her."

"A genius, my foot! So she reads the *Times*, so she plays chess. How could she do it to you, her father? Or for that matter to any human being?"

His wife appeared in the door and listened to the account of the event. In her heavy Polish accent, she exclaimed, "How crazy you are. Everything is unique with you. You deal with not one but two or three hospitals. You change three residences a year. Your child must be no less than a genius. How about David? Is he a genius too?"

"Yes, dear, he is destined to become one."

CHAPTER 10

Another Star

My work with David, as with Edith, had begun at birth. He, too, was reading before the age of two. We bought a house in North Miami Beach a short while before his second birthday. The real estate agent drove us to the location avoiding the railroad tracks which were three blocks away and which do not enhance the value of the property. Unaware of the tracks, I agreed to buy the house. While the negotiations were in progress, David heard a train passing in the distance and called it to my attention. The price of the house was lowered by $700 immediately.

In some respects, David was superior to Edith. He possessed a remarkable ability for adapting himself to his environment. At the age of three, he would play on the beach with another child, but as soon as his playmate was taken home, he might open up Robinson Crusoe and read aloud or add numbers in the sand. He would play cowboys and Indians with the neighborhood children, then scold them for "depicting Indians always as culprits as the T.V. does, which is historically incorrect."

In 1963, I made acquaintance with a securities exchange broker, David and I began daily visits to his office where I could discuss literature, theology, and current events with him. Blonde, blue-eyed, handsome David soon became the mascot of the office. Realizing that the brokerage office could provide an excellent vehicle for David's education, I encouraged him to learn about stock transactions. Tape watchers began to ask him to check the quotes of their favorite stocks. He would read the ticker tape, then courteously and accurately report the information.

Before long, he had memorized at least one hundred fifty stock symbols. He followed their trade with great excitement, making such comments as "Here we go again. IBM is losing its bottom." The stock market also helped him to learn simple fractions. By three and a half, he knew the difference between the meaning of CH 60½ and CH 601/8. Additionally, he kept his eye on the Dow Jones tape, which helped him to read more fluently. He would draw other people's attention to the tape when it had stories in which he thought they would be interested.

"Mr. Jones, Chrysler car output dropped during the last ten day period." He knew that Mr. Jones owned a substantial block of Chrysler shares.

As David became skillful in the dynamics of the stock market, he began to form opinions about certain stocks, some of which were surprisingly accurate. People would ask him, half seriously, what they should buy. "Coca Cola or S.R.T. There are rumors about a takeover of S.R.T.," he replied one time.

In 1963, when President Kennedy addressed an airport rally in Miami, I asked the children if they wanted to hear him speak. They thought it was an excellent idea. I had Edith excused from school, and on our way to the airport, we bought a bouquet of flowers. At the rally, David gave the flowers to a Secret Service man at the fence saying, "This is for the President from Edith, Daddy, and myself." Edith and David still cherish that glimpse of the charismatic President. A few days later, David was the first one to report to me the sad news, tearfully. "Daddy, President Kennedy was shot."

On weekends, as my health permitted, we visited various places in the community. David particularly enjoyed our trips to the airport where he was once allowed to enter the cockpit of a jet. On a visit to a destroyer docked in Port Everglades, he had the tour guide explain the range of a cannon. During the same visit, he told a group of sailors, "The only thing you must be missing is girls. There aren't any." The sailors applauded him warmly and one assured him that was their main complaint.

Edith during this time continued to be bored in school. She had entered junior high school that year, and now was no longer permitted to skip grades as she had done in elementary school. She told me, "Daddy, you know, I have developed a defense mechanism which enables me to disassociate myself totally from whatever happens in the classroom, yet I do nothing that would offend the teacher." I came to have the distinction of being the parent most despised by the school authorities, because, dissatisfied with the inadequacies of the school system, I continually demanded more work for Edith.

The child told me that my frequent visits to school "put terror in the heart of the teachers."

In spite of the boredom at school, Edith's junior high school days were a period of great intellectual growth. Her thirst for knowledge was insatiable, covering every branch of the arts and sciences. We would discuss and debate jurisprudence, semantics and philosophy. In jurisprudence the starting point was now the Code of Hammurabi and she demanded that I translate the Hebrew Talmud. As her mentor, I had to devote many hours to research in order to discuss these topics with her intelligently. Bella would sometimes good naturedly tease me about my efforts. "Staying up late studying again? Have you not reversed your roles? This is the price you have to pay for your genius manufacturing."

I replied, "This is my most gratifying experience."

Not everything was academic study, however. She still enjoyed music, and she took violin lessons. I'm sure the neighbors would have preferred that she had taken up knitting instead. "Don't you have any homework?" a neighbor once asked her as she practiced. Even I would sometimes plead with her to quit practicing for the day.

"What is the matter, Daddy? Can't you take it? How about me? I also like fine music but I'm forced to listen to my own cacaphony." In the end, she became an accomplished violinist.

I had taught Edith to play chess when she was three, and we often played. David would watch us. One day he said, "How about playing a game with me?"

"Who taught you the game, David?"

"No one, I just watched you."

Two years later, by the time he was six, he regularly defeated me.

While Edith did not shy from physical activities — she once said of physical education, "If I cannot exercise my brain at school, at least, I can exercise my body" — she was not particularly athletic. David, however, was quite athletic; my educational work with him did not hinder his physical development. He played ball and occasionally exchanged a black eye with a playmate. "It was self-defense," he maintained. "It is the survival of the fittest. I was attacked."

In junior high school, Edith tried to cultivate friendships with her classmates, but it was often difficult. For example, a girl might be invited home for dinner. Sooner or later, Edith would invite her into her bedroom, which was stacked to the ceiling with books. These alone were usually enough to dampen the relationship, then the girl would inspect Edith's closet. "Are these the only dresses you have?"

"How many do I need?"

"By the way, there is a sale at Lerner's."

"I really don't care about it. I can wear these for another year or two," Edith replied. She had very little in common with the other children.

Usually before a test, Edith's popularity would increase. Her classmates would call her on the telephone. However, she could not always offer assistance because she cared little what happened in class, and seldom opened a textbook. Once she said, "Dad, as I sit in the class observing the other students, I find that many of them have greater potential than I do, yet they are destined to drown in the sea of mediocrity, without incentive and guidance. For example, take Helen. She grasps concepts instantly, but she has no desire to explore further. Why should she? She had straight A's which is all that society, her parents, and the school expect of her."

At school, Edith occasionally grew irritated, and deliberately tried to embarrass the teacher. She might cite a passage from some noted author with whom the teacher was unfamiliar. Once in social science class she quoted from a book by Erich Fromm to make a point. The teacher's lack of knowledge was at once clear. At the end of the class period, Edith told her instructor how sorry she was and that she wouldn't do it again. Then for weeks she lapsed back into her nonchalant attitude, in which, like a prisoner in a penitentiary, she marked the passing days on the calendar.

Having the advantage of being Jewish, she was delighted with the privilege of being able to observe both Jewish and Christian holidays. "Thank God, the holidays are coming," she would exclaim.

Sometimes she would urge me to stop paying my school taxes on the ground that the schools are a total waste.

"I would be subject to a legal suit and I don't have the funds to go to court."

"All you have to do is to subpoena me as a witness."

"I'm afraid it isn't that simple."

"What about me? You are being taxed financially while I am being subjected to this unproductive experience daily."

I continued to make frequent trips to the school and thus maintained my reputation as a "nuisance." "We have far brighter students than Edith," the principal told me. "If there is enough challenge for them why should you complain?"

"I have no doubt that there are brighter children than my daughter, but the point is they are not sufficiently motivated. On the other hand, Edith is."

"You are pushing her too hard. We are interested in developing the totality of the student's personality."

"What a cliche."

"Good day, Mr. Stern. There is nothing we can do for Edith. Next time send her mother instead. She appears to be a more reasonable person."

At home, I had to tell Edith that I was unsuccessful again. She would not be able to take advanced work, or a language course, or a science course. Philosophically, she responded, "This too, shall pass."

Meanwhile, my visits to the school brought ridicule from her classmates. "Your father was at the school again. Perhaps if you had a boyfriend, you would be less bored, prima donna."

"You are not doing too hot in classes anyway," suggested her neighbor.

"Indeed, I don't do well," Edith replied.

The parents of other children also criticized me. "Mr. Stern, you are obsessed with education as if it were the supreme goal of a human being. My son regards the school as too tough. He has trouble finding enough time to pursue his other activities."

"What are they?"

"Football. Baseball."

"I'm sorry. Edith does not indulge in these activities."

"How about cooking, sewing, and cleaning?"

There was no need to reply. When I told Edith about the conversation, she was really upset, particularly since she regarded such activities to be prime examples of how society has tried to subjugate women.

Two years later the boy dropped out of high school and took a job pumping gas in a service station. When Edith is home on vacation, she always urges me not to stop there. "I don't want to embarrass the poor kid. He is such a bright boy. It is a shame he didn't finish school."

Edith always knew the exact location of each book in her library, which numbered in the thousands, including a new *Encyclopaedia Britannica* presented to her by the publisher, but at the end of the school year, she could never find her textbooks. "Edith, please find your books or I will have to pay a fine," I would beg.

"Believe me, Daddy, it isn't deliberate. Perhaps, I subconsciously lost them out of resentment."

"But you love books."

"Of course I do, but these symbolize the school." Eventually Bella came to her aid and found the books.

Once I was shocked to learn that the geography text which was used in Edith's junior high class contained a map showing all of Africa still as English and French colonies except for the Union of South Africa, Egypt, Ethiopia, and Liberia. The nations which had gained independence in the fifties were not shown. In response to my complaints, the principal told me funds were not available to buy newer textbooks. As I inquired further, I found that this situation prevailed throughout most of Florida.

I thought that perhaps I could help the situation by publicizing it. However, at about the same time Edith was told she must take a course in home economics before she could graduate from Junior High. While we were unhappy with the mediocrity of the schools in general, there was no area which upset us as much as home economics. Edith was not the least interested in learning to cook and sew, while I thought that it was a waste of taxpayers' money to teach domestic skills at school, especially since the academic subjects were so inadequate. I visited the home economics class, where I viewed the elaborate display of new washing machines, ovens, and other kitchen paraphernalia. I asked the teacher if all of that equipment was expensive. "Yes," she replied, "you are looking at some of the finest home economics equipment in the country. It costs many thousands of dollars," she said with pride.

I was outraged. Fighting to control my anger, as I went to the principal and told him, "We spend millions to teach girls to cook and wash clothes, things which every girl is exposed to at home from infancy, while we deceive them in a vital content area such as geography. This is cruel and tragic. What a price we will pay in the future for our neglect. It would seem to me that this is the only country in the world where academic credits are granted for such non-academic subjects. This is the only country that spends public education funds for washing machines."

Edith was now twelve years old and in the ninth grade. I was determined that I would put an end to her public school education, since I was sure that the remaining three years of high school would be totally wasted. I planned to find a way to have her admitted directly to college. I believed that such a step would add years to her life and life to her years.

I knew that it would be difficult to do and that obstacles stood in my way. I was engaged in an intense campaign to have a bill passed in the state legislature to authorize the City of Miami to pay me damages for my stolen manuscript. Furthermore, an accident had caused temporary paralysis in my right arm, while my heart episodes had become more frequent and of longer duration. It was not a good time in my life to begin a new battle.

To make the move more difficult, Bella was firmly opposed to taking Edith out of school and entering her in college. She felt that since Edith

106

nad already skipped two grades, she was far too young for college. She once said to me, "You have stolen the child from me -- I said nothing. You stole her childhood -- I voiced no protest. Should anything happen to her as a result of this experiment, I shall never forgive you."

Bella's opposition was fortified by the school authorities from the superintendent to the last teacher. Finally, Edith was frightened and frustrated by the conflict between her parents, a conflict which was of long standing and which threatened to end in a divorce. Nevertheless, I was determined to undertake what Bella thought was a "crazy scheme."

As my first step, I issued a press release stating I would not permit Edith to attend high school under any circumstances. I wrote, "I feel that the public school system is inadequate and will retard my daughter's intellectual growth and development." A conference was soon arranged with the school officials who told me that if I took her out of school, I would be prosecuted "since public education is compulsory until the age of 16 in Florida." I replied that I would prove in court that my training at home was by far superior to the public school. Whereupon the official answered "Edith will enter college before graduation from high school only over my dead body."

Undeterred, I continued to pursue my plan. First I went to the University of Miami where I was greeted at the guidance department with disbelief and ridicule when I asked that Edith be permitted to take the battery of entrance examinations. Her IQ had been tested in New York five years earlier at 201 and I knew well that her scores on the entrance examination would be quite high. This I hoped would at least disarm, if not defeat, my opponents. Unfortunately, the university did not permit her to take the tests.

The next target was Miami-Dade Junior College where I met with the head of the counseling service. To my surprise, he greeted my suggestion with a great deal of enthusiasm. I complained that school authorities are more concerned with peace and tranquility than with progress. I felt they opposed Edith's admission to college because they were afraid it would establish a precedent and encourage other gifted children to seek early admission to college. This, of course, was my hope and one of my objectives. A broad smile crossed his face and I knew that I had won an ally.

My hopes were further brightened when I showed him Edith's term paper in mathematics which was already beyond my comprehension. He admitted that he was not a mathematician, but in his opinion "the excellence of her organization and the proficiency of her language indicated work at the level of a college sophomore." As our discussion ended, we shook hands, and he assured me that he would discuss the matter with the college president. He said they would notify me soon of the decision.

I had won a battle, but being realistic, I was aware that a struggle still lay ahead. Since Miami-Dade Junior College was within the jurisdiction of the school superintendent's office, I knew the school officials would continue to oppose Edith's admission to college, if only as a matter of maintaining their prestige.

Shortly after the meeting, I went to Tallahassee, the state capital, to fight for the passage of my bill. During the several weeks I was there my daily phone calls home revealed that the college officials had not tried to get in touch with me. Bella sarcastically remarked over the phone, "If they need her, they will call her. I shall refrain from bothering the college."

Finally, I won passage of my bill. At the time I was jubilant and returned home with renewed energy. As soon as I could arrange it, I met with the college president. From the tone of his voice, I knew that he was under pressure not to admit Edith. Nevertheless, he authorized her to take the admission examination.

Edith scored in the upper 10% of the applicants seeking admission to college -- a remarkable feat for a twelve-year-old girl. A final conference was arranged with the guidance department head. As he congratulated Edith, she said, "I could have done a lot better if I had not spent the two nights before reading books." She neglected to tell him that she also had completed the test in about half of the allotted time, relinquishing her opportunity to check back over her answers -- a custom which Edith still follows in examinations.

We met again with the president, who informed us that Edith would be admitted as a full-time student in the coming summer semester. I assured him that he would never regret his decision; since Edith would definitely justify his confidence.

Edith's admission to the junior college went smoothly. Unlike many high school graduates who have difficulty adjusting to the demands of college, she entered academic life secure in her belief that she could meet the new responsibilities without difficulty. Although Bella had wanted her to take a breathing spell before starting, Edith insisted that she be enrolled for the early summer term.

To reassure Bella, I took her with me the first day when I went to pick up Edith. She nervously paced the halls outside of the classroom. "God knows whether the presence of all the students won't terrify her. Will she be able to follow the lectures?"

"Don't worry, your fears are unjustified. She could have entered college a year ago."

Soon the bell rang and Edith came out of the classroom. "How was it?" Bella asked.

"Perhaps it was less boring, but I still managed to finish a science fiction book."

Edith did quite well in college that summer scoring A's in both her courses. When the term was over, she attended a two-week session at a conservation camp near Ocala. This was the first time away from home alone and she was reluctant to go. The other campers were boys and girls aged from ten to fourteen. By prior agreement, Edith was assigned to the oldest group. She was twelve and in junior college; they were fourteen and in junior high school. In the past, she had difficulty getting along with similar children and now she had to live with them for two weeks.

I had asked the camp managers to keep her enrollment in college a secret. However, the children wanted to know about one another and Edith also, of course. They asked what grade she would be in in the fall and what school she would be attending. Eventually, having no choice, she had to disclose her secret. Then they laughed at her because they thought she was lying. She called home reluctantly to request her school transcript which I mailed. After she showed it to them, the children viewed her with suspicion and left her alone for the remainder of the session.

In September, Edith returned to college. David was now five, and Bella thought he should start school, arguing that since my health was bad, taking care of him was too difficult. She pointed out that sooner or later we would have to enroll him in school, "so we might as well give him an early start," she argued. I fought to keep him at home, but she was right. I did not have the strength to keep up with him.

Since he was too young for public school, we decided to enroll David in a new branch of the Hebrew Academy. The school principal told me to take him to a child psychologist who would determine if he was mature enough for first grade. After a twenty-minute examination, the psychologist advised me that David was not ready to confront a classroom situation. I did not agree with him. Rather, as I had done earlier when the test reports showed that Edith was not ready for advancement, I convinced the principal to enroll David in spite of the psychologist's recommendations.

David was relatively satisfied in first grade. I had taught him to speak Hebrew when he was two, which was quite helpful since the classes were conducted in both Hebrew and English. This made school more interesting to him. He was one of the top pupils in the class, although he rapidly began to forget much of what I had previously taught him. His vocabulary began to shrink and instead of the three and four digit multiplications he had been doing, he was now doing simple additions. Further, he came home tired after a forty-five minute bus ride. I was sick a lot, and thus unable either to enforce the ban on television or to work with him much.

Edith, meanwhile, was excelling at Miami-Dade Junior College. She quietly pursued her studies, earning straight A's, while still reading avidly. Having been trained years earlier to research subjects thoroughly, she had no need to take lengthy notes in class, nor was she overly concerned with tests and term papers. "An effective professor should guide and stimulate independent research. The library, rather than the classroom, should determine the student's scholastic progress," she insisted. She felt "sorry for the students who spent an entire class period laboriously and indiscriminately writing down every word the instructor said."

For the first time in her life, Edith was well accepted socially. Students would drive her home after school, many of them visited her on weekends, and the phone was seldom idle. As in the past, she continued to play chess with David.

At thirteen she was about five foot six, with dark brown hair falling to her shoulders in, as she described it, "classic beatnik style." With her dark rimmed glasses, she was reported in the press to be "scholarly attractive." She was the type of girl who could pass for thirteen or twenty. I had arranged with the junior college that her age should not be known to the other students, and, although the newspapers quickly discovered her, many of her classmates did not know how young she was. At times, this led to amusing situations.

In a creative writing class, she was given an assignment to write a poem which could be easily understood by thirteen or fourteen-year-olds. The following day, she was asked to read her poem in class. During the discussion of it, one student of about twenty said. "The poem has great merits for its esthetic beauty and its meaningful message." Then he continued, "How in the world would you expect a fourteen-year-old child to understand it?" Edith exchanged meaningful glances with the instructor secure in the belief that her secret would be well guarded.

One of her schoolmates was a middle-aged woman. One night while Edith and some other students were at the woman's house finishing a group project, the woman told her fifteen-year-old daughter to go to bed. The girl complained to Edith and asked, "Did your parents treat you so inconsiderately when you were my age?"

"My treatment was pretty much the same," Edith replied, concealing her laughter.

Sending a child Edith's age to college also presented problems, marking a new phase in my relationship with her. Previously, my work with her had been quite productive, satisfying for the most part her mental, physical, and recreational needs. In spite of the fact that her genius had placed her out of contact with her age group, she functioned cheerfully, with books and music. I did not have the heartaches of many parents whose children are rebellious. While there was not complete agreement between Edith and me on everything — I encouraged her to be an individual — there was a common scale of values and priorities.

Now, her entrance to college altered our relationship. I was faced with the problem of a college student who in many ways was not old enough to have adult responsibilities. For example, I had to tell her to brush her teeth, to polish her shoes, to take a shower, and to abstain from starches since she gained weight easily. In return, she constantly argued, "If I have formally entered adult life, I request the right to conduct myself as I see fit, whether it is brushing my hair or going to bed." I could not yet, however, abdicate my responsibilities as a parent.

Our relationship also changed in other ways, particularly because going to college resulted in a transformation in her. In public school, she had been hopelessly bored by the slow pace of instruction and she had viewed her schoolmates with some contempt. Now in college, her ability and resourcefulness were challenged and she sought and gained recognition from the other students. As part of this new liberation, she grew somewhat rebellious toward her parents and society, an attitude common for the generation of which she was now a member. At this time, in spite of her young age, she began to smoke.

In the fall of 1966, the paraochial school closed the branch which David had attended because of financial difficulties. Rather than have him spend hours in traffic going to the main building of the school in Miami Beach, we enrolled him in a public school. Now he became much more of an ordinary student. His previous desire for knowledge was tempered by school regimentation and conformity and Bella continued to press him to be a normal child saying, "One genius in the family is enough." These experiences slowed his development, but he remained a bright youngster whose imagination would spring forth at the slightest challenge.

One of the consequences of my work with Edith was her popularity with the press. Because I was interested in improving education for all children, I welcomed publicity as a means of getting my message across. However, Edith did not care for it, regarding it as an invasion of her privacy. While she was at the junior college, I gave a lecture in New York in which I mentioned her. Afterwards, a reporter, who had been in the audience asked me if he could write a magazine story on her. I agreed, hoping that the story would help education. That night I called Edith and asked her to be cooperative and polite to him. She agreed.

The next day, the reporter braved a hurricane and flew into Miami on the last plane. Edith, meanwhile, had dressed herself as a maid, and greeted him when he arrived. Disguising her normal voice — she once described it as "a neutral accent with a touch of Brooklyn in it" — with a Southern one, she informed him that "Miss Edith just left this morning for a prolonged weekend in Atlanta." The reporter left without his interview.

Edith did very well in the junior college program, completing the two year sequence in a year and a half with an A average, and thus fully vindicating me. At the graduation ceremonies, she won a standing ovation from the faculty, students, and parents. After the ceremonies I gave her a twelve dollar radio, the most expensive present she had ever received in recognition of her achievements.

After her graduation, she entered Florida Atlantic University in January of 1967. Although she could have secured admission to almost any prestigious university, I selected Florida Atlantic, a newly organized school, because it was located only about thirty miles from our home which served the dual purpose of permitting her to have a measure of independence while still having her close enough that she could visit us on weekends. I was not yet ready to send my fourteen-year-old daughter hundreds or thousands of miles away to be on her own.

She was now a junior in college and was to live in a dormitory on campus. This led to some concern by the university officials. The dean of women suggested that because of her age, Edith should have a ten o'clock curfew. This time, Bella came to Edith's defense. She told the dean. "Since Edith is mature enough to be a college junior, she should enjoy the privileges granted to other students." The dean consented and I was overjoyed that Bella had finally been converted.

In many ways, Edith was a typical college student. We would frequently visit her and often on weekends, she would come home with loads of dirty laundry, as college students everywhere are likely to do.

During that term at Florida Atlantic, she told me that she had decided to become a mathematician. As we walked along the Fort Lauderdale beach one evening engaged in one of our frequent debates, I could tell that she was preparing me for a shock. This became more apparent as she buried her head in her arms as we sat down in the sand. "Edith, what's bugging you?" I asked.

At first she insisted that nothing was, but finally she said, "Dad, I have reached a decision. One that might be contrary to your expectations." She knew well that I had wanted her to go into medicine." After months of soul searching, I have decided to become a mathematician."

Surprised, I interrupted to ask if the decision was final. She assured me it was. I then reminded her that math was not her best subject. "But why?" I asked. "Are you searching for martydom? Are you being masochistic?"

She agreed that mathematics was not her strong subject. Impatiently, I continued. "Edith, as you will agree, a physician personifies the most noble aspirations of man. What can be more fulfilling than to heal the sick? There are so many dreadful diseases to be conquered such as cancer and heart disease, both of which have claimed the best part of my life. This is the frontier that ought to challenge the best minds. Or if you don't want to be a physician, you could become an attorney. After all, compassion and commitment to the ideals of justice are your outstanding features. There is a wide spectrum of professions for which you are better qualified than mathematics. As a mathematician how will you be able to contribute to the welfare of man?"

"Dad, I have weighed the pros and cons of this step. I have considered your feelings, but I still think it is the best decision. First, I am not going to follow the road of least resistance. Second, I believe that it is time that I cut the umbilical cord from you. Third, since mathematics is not my strongest subject, I feel I must overcome and master it. It is time that I stand on my own feet and become knowledgeable in a field which is alien to you. I have to act as an independent individual. Isn't this consistent with your values and concepts? Wasn't it you who taught me to meet challenges and to seek the truth? I regard college teaching as a very noble profession. It doesn't always pay well, but I have no desire to obtain wealth anyway."

"Edith, I must confess that this is the most triumphant moment of my life."

Although David was not progressing particularly well in school that year, he closely followed current events. For years, historians will speculate whether Hubert Humphrey's staunch support of the Vietnam involvement and his abrupt switch to the doves' side later cost him the presidency in 1968. As far as David was concerned, Humphrey was discredited in the spring of 1967 before the anti-war sentiment had become so popular.

Humphrey, crossing the country in an attempt to build support for the administration's policies in the face of a widening credibility gap, was scheduled to address a rally one Sunday afternoon in Greynolds Park, a short distance from our home. When David came home that day, worn out from fishing, I asked him, "Would you like to go with me to the park to hear the Vice President? While we are there we can take a boat ride, do some botanical exploration, and then just talk." He eagerly agreed.

The park, an attraction for the local hippie community, was tightly guarded by a police detail and Secret Service men. From the makeshift platform, the local politicians delivered speeches while the audience ate free hot dogs and drank soft drinks, waiting for Humphrey's arrival. One dignitary took the microphone and pledged "vigorous support to our brave boys who sacrifice their lives in the defense of our country in Vietnam."

David was unmoved by the eloquence of the distinguished looking speaker, "Dad, I fail to understand why should our boys sacrifice their lives in the defense of our country eight thousand miles away."

"Be quiet, David. We will discuss it later."

Soon a chain of limousines approached. The ever-smiling vice president got out and, accompanied by Secret Service men and local dignitaries, climbed to the platform. According to the notes which I took, he began a vigorous attack on those "who fail to see our humanitarian task in defending the South Vietnamese against the Communist aggressors." Murmurs could be heard from some of the hippies and a few posters appeared denouncing the war. Humphrey, with the zeal of a Baptist preacher, continued. "After all, in compliance with our moral and treaty obligations, we must defend this remote outpost of democracy. We must assist a friendly, freely chosen government. . ."

David was outraged by Humphrey's speech. Finally, he could no longer restrain himself. "What an unadulterated lie. Where is democracy when the political opponents of Ky perish in jail?"

"Be quiet, David. Don't interfere with the man's freedom of speech."

"God, what a lie!" David yelled out.

The Secret Service agents, preoccupied with keeping a close watch on the hippies, were unaware of David's determination to mount the platform and give the "true" version of Vietnam. Unable to cope with him, I had to carry the child out of the park with my hand covering his mouth. "What is your boy screaming about?" a policeman asked as we were leaving.

"He wants an ice cream cone," I said.

"Here is a dime. Buy yourself some ice cream, little boy."

Overcoming my restraint, David threw the dime back to the officer and shouted, "Give it to Humphrey to fight his war."

At home, I scolded David for his conduct. "I'll control my outbursts in the future. But you know, Dad, if Humphrey should ever run for President, I think he will be defeated."

"Why do you think so?" I asked.

"He obviously lacks objectivity. Otherwise he would not have defended our involvement in Vietnam."

History proved David's prediction to be absolutely correct.

CHAPTER 11

David is Being Introduced to Charities

Tamara was a pretty blonde, and since blondes have all the fun, Tamara was always well-dressed. This provided a sharp contrast with other college girls, who neither had the funds nor inclination to look at all times sharp. On the contrary, some degree of shabbiness, before the sociologists invented the term hippy, was an accepted attire on the college campus and it may have added some degree of sexiness.

To be sure, Tamara attended all her classes regularly, has taken her lecture notes scrupulously, if not discriminately. Her marks were average. Her term papers were laborious but not imaginative. After all, a girl has no alternative but to go to college if she wants to marry a nice man. One may say that Tamara was withdrawn, having little social intercourse with peers of both sexes. In summation, there was nothing remarkable about our girl.

Nothing -- with one exception. Whenever some extra-curricular activity would be scheduled on weekends, Tamara could not attend it. The reason for Tamara's consistent non-participation was sharply brought home to me one Sunday afternoon.

One Sunday, David and I went to see a first run picture. As we surged towards the exit after the show, our attention was drawn towards a young lady in modest clothes, who loudly and in a lamenting voice solicited funds for the "poor forgotten, asthmatic children." It was unmistakably Tamara -- but a transformed one, her eyes flashing, resolutely pushing the charity box toward young couples. This gesture made it truly compelling for young men, with the silent approval of their dates, to donate money. Having recognized me, Tamara was slightly taken aback. Naive as I was, I commended her profoundly for her civic comport, after the onrush of patrons ceased.

"What," did Tamara reply in astonishment, bordering on disbelief?

"Don't pull my leg," she insisted. "Civic pride, civic duty, to the tune of 60% net profit." She looked cynical. "I offer my altruistic services on weekends for a neat profit of approximately $100 for six hours of work."

Slowly we departed from our warrior as I regretted every penny that I had ever donated to organized charity. We remained speechless until finally David broke the silence.

"Would it not be proper for a governmental agency to scientifically survey research needs and then make the proper appropriations rather than allow such shocking misuses of public funds?"

Many hospitals exist not for the benefit of the patients, but solely for the enrichment of their owners. Sad as it may seem, the private hospital is frequently run on the same basis as the private corner drugstore or the large Macy chain - to put profits into the hands of the proprietor.

While in a capitalistic society we applaud the profit motive, a line must be drawn when it comes to the exploitation of sick, needy persons who are often in desperate straits. And what is even more despicable, too often these hospitals also exploit the good nature, the good will and the good motives of thousands of kind-hearted men and women who volunteer their services without charge to the hospital owners, but without benefit to those who are the ultimate users of these services -- the patients themselves.

We had been told that a minor operation was advisable for our son. What should we do? So many operations, we learn, are unnecessary, contrived in the interests of the surgeons. Figures reveal that more than 1 million patients are placed on the operating table each year even though they do not belong there. But we are guided and directed by our doctors, so what could we do? We waited, procrastinated, wondered: is it necessary?

Finally the day arrived. I no longer could postpone the inevitable, David had to have his tonsils removed. Sternly the pediatrician urged me forthwith to make an arrangement with a hospital, and by "sheer accident" he referred me to one of which he was a co-owner, a fact which I was not aware of at this time. Since this was 1968 rather than 1922, David required an anaesthetist, surgeon and the rest of the music, and of course a lengthy two or three day hospitalization.

Having no choice in the matter, I promptly began to shop over the phone. Unfortunately, there was no reservation to be secured anywhere other than at this hospital. My negotiation there was not dissimilar from one that you might conduct buying a T.V. in a discount store. Soon the room fee declined from $40 to $30 and finally to $25 as did proportionately other expenses such as drugs, etc. The management's deportment did not inspire much respect. But after all, we bask under the sun of free enterprise.

I almost felt like Abraham offering his son for sacrifice, as we drove early in the morning to the hospital.

As I was pacing nervously, the long corridor leading to the operating room, waiting impatiently for the end of the surgery, I noticed in the corner a desk at which two ladies were working, fervently dressed in the hospital volunteer garb. As I approached these motherly looking ladies, they solicitously inquired whether I needed their help.

"No," I replied, "I wait for my son who is being operated on, this very moment."

Warmly did the lovely ladies comfort me. Soon, a conversation ensued. With great pride they explained to me the succor that they bring these poor patients by distributing meals, doing errands, delivering mail, etc. "Are you being paid for your efforts," I asked.

"God forbid. Our only reward is service to the less fortunate."

Unable to suppress my anger, I suggested, "After all, this is a private hospital run for profit just like any other enterprise. The service you render is to the management rather than to the patients, who pay a great deal of money for their stay here, irrespective of your noble intentions."

This was enough to cause ire to the gray-haired lady who angrily replied, "You foreigners simply don't understand Our American Way of Life." David, who was uncomfortable after surgery, laughed as I told him this story.

As I entered David's room on the day of his discharge, I met the

119

hospital administrator, who scolded the child for his criticism of hospital policies.

"We are here to assist you and the only reward we and the volunteers obtain is your recovery."

"Only the last 5 words of your statement are correct. I only stated the facts. These people should know that they serve a profit-making organization rather than God, "replied David calmly.

We left the hospital in great hurry. "What a tragedy it is that people are being so cruelly fooled from the cradle into their graves," commented David philosophically as we approached home.

One day David tuned in to the Annual T.V. Marathon Fund Drive to combat a deadly disease. I noticed how his mood had gradually become pensive.

"Dad, what a dismal spectacle this is. The master of ceremonies profusely perspires, as his lips, dry from screaming, dip into a cup of water. His eyes melodramatically misty, he strikes a martyred saintlike pose as he extols the virtue of charity. Starlets, ever mindful of their ratings, kick their feet in a rhythmic cadence. In the midst of all this, poor children, their bodies painfully twisted by this horrible disease, parade in a Roman circus fashion. Everyone is intoxicated with fervor, as more and more money pours in. My God how obscene, how disgustingly self-serving this is. The stars long for an opportunity to enhance their professional status, while posing as pious humanitarians. Politicians improve their image and mend fences.

Did anyone ever ask how the money is being spent? What progress towards a cure, if any at all, has been made in the course of many years of research, to the tune of hundreds of millions of dollars?"

Having realized immediately that this was a new educational opportunity, one that would also enable David to ventilate his ire, I asked my son, "Would you like to do an in-depth study on charities? An assignment of this magnitude is truly challenging."

"Gladly," replied my 12 year old son as his eyes lit up brightly.

My young scholar spent the next week in intensive research, as he diligently sought to obtain data in the library and interviewed officials of many relief agencies.

Shrouded in mystery, the vast labyrinth of charities of all sorts like a web encompasses every sphere of our society. Frequently, crooks, supposedly operating legitimate institutions, at times camouflaged as religious organizations, enjoy a tax-free status and immunity from government investigations. This, coupled with the high esteem is which Americans hold religion, makes the swindler's task easy and safe.

Because of the shrewdness of the operators and the clandestine character of some charities, no estimate could be obtained of the funds raised annually in this country. Figures ranging from $80 billion to a staggering $200 billion, or $1000 per every soul in this country, could be considered realistic.

Finally, David submitted to me a neatly handwritten 12-page report with the poignant comment, "What you learn from it will surely shock you."

The following excerpts will testify to the accuracy of his prediction:

"It is indeed tragic that tens of billions of dollars, donated by generous citizens to assist their fellow men in distress or to pursue medical research to wipe out a deadly disease, are often being "legally" expended on so-called administrative costs to the tune of 80%.

Lax laws, or the absence of any laws applying to charities in many states, attract cunning swindlers who in the spirit of "free enterprise" wrap themselves cleverly in religious or patriotic cloth and siphon off, with total impunity, 100% of the donations, amounting to tens of billions of dollars.

However for argument's sake, let us assume for a moment that no misuse of charity funds in any alarming proportions takes place. How can the hundreds of research institutions, scattered throughout the width and breadth of our country, function effectively? How can these fragmented isolated institutions, lacking expertise and adequate facilities, perform the titanic task of conquering leukemia, asthma and rheumatism? Indeed, this is virtually impossible.

It is imperative that the Federal Government set up or direct one of its existing agencies such as the National Health Institute in cooperation with top scientists to conduct a coordinated monumental struggle to wipe out diseases. Its priorities must be based on statistical data, with preference given to the one that strikes the largest number of persons, rather than based on the caprice of a media star who because of his or her popularity can mobilize enormous funds through personal appeals to combat a disease which actually strikes a negligible number of people. Such an energetic move is of vital importance to the progress of medicine. It would also save the tax payers billions of dollars fraudulently taken from them by cunning criminals under the guise of piety.

No less vital is control of the plethora of relief agencies, where misrepresentation, misuse of funds, and cruel discrimination against minorities reach epidemic proportions.

In order to assure fairness and dignity to the less fortunate, the government guided by laws must assure assistance to the neediest.

We should eliminate the mushrooming welfare agencies, which at best duplicate the activities of existing governmental organizations, and at worst, which is frequent, harbor insensitive, corrupt opportunists and arrogant social workers. These agencies attract workers who pontificate rather than assist and scold rather than aid. They arbitrarily dispense services and funds in a manner which often subjects the recipient to indignities and discrimination.

The government, notwithstanding political expediencies, will have to take a hard stand to curb this national disgrace."

So deeply impressed was I with this remarkable study that 4 years later, hoping to be called as a witness, I planned to read it to the congressional committee investigating fraud in charities. Unfortunately, I was unable to secure an invitation.

David can also be sarcastic. Last year, one of the administrators of a "Boys' Town" was interviewed on the NBC Today show.

The unexpected publication of an audit revealed that the institution housing several hundred youngsters had a few hundred million dollars stashed away, while it was aggressively soliciting more funds.

The astonished interviewer asked the priest, "What could you possibly do with more money? After all, you have so much, and your needs judging by the size of your institution are truly limited." The priest paused for a moment and replied, "Well, everybody raises funds. Look at Harvard University. They are so rich yet they seek more funds."

"Of couse they seek money and justly so. Being one of the world's finest universities, Harvard is deeply involved in all kinds of research," answered the interviewer.

At this moment David angrily turned off the television, remarking to me with cynicism, "Perhaps these pious people research the technique of exorcism. That can be expensive too. On the other hand, maybe they try to maintain the standard of living to which they have become accustomed in the face of rampant inflation." "You mean the children's standard of living," I interjected.

"No, daddy, that would be too costly and above all sinful. I mean the administrators', who have vowed chastity and poverty, standard of living."

In June 1976 the New York Times printed on its front page a story entitled "Audit of Catholic Order's Funds Shows Missions Got Under 3%." Incredible as it sounds, the story revealed that "leaders of a Roman Catholic missionary order acknowledged today that its representatives raised some $20 million in the last two years to feed and clothe the poor abroad but had sent only $500,000 overseas. . . The document showed that less than 3 cents of every dollar raised by Pallotines has reached the order's foreign missionaries. . . The order had invested millions in Florida real estate ventures and uncollected loans (given) to Maryland political figures."

One of the loans was reportedly advanced to Governor Mandel of Maryland, "who faces a federal court trial in September. . . The money was reportedly used to pay Mr. Mandel's divorce settlement."

"Dad," said David with a sardonic smile, "what a remarkable display of ecumenical spirit." (As everyone knows, Governor Mandel is Jewish.) "What is even more gratifying is that from the way the money was used the Catholic Church has apparently altered its adamant stand on divorce. Hopefully, birth control will be next. Remember, dad, the paper I did on charities 6 years ago?"

"Yes, David. I think that was an excellent expose."

"My God, how naive I was then. How much more atrocious the malady really is, cutting across all ethnic, religious and racial barriers. Its devastating effects act like cancer that eats away the very fabric of our society."

In response I turned my face and concealed a bitter grimace, for I was deeply ashamed of the older generation with its legacy of greed, filth and deceit.

CHAPTER 12

The Limelight

Edith's admission to Florida Atlantic University was well publicized. News stories proliferated as reporters gathered at the university to interview "the girl genius." Hundreds of requests for interviews poured in. The phone was constantly jammed. Mail in bag loads arrived at home and at the college. Still shunning publicity, Edith became so angry that she requested the school administration to place a guard at the dormitory to screen the visitors and weed out the newspapermen, some of whom disguised themselves to conceal their identity.

My view on this issue was different. While I wanted to assure Edith the highest degree of privacy, I was also eager to tell the world about her success, hoping to encourage children and parents to seek quality education and to disarm my critics who often viewed my methods "as the obsession of a mad scientist who eagerly sacrifices his own child to test his dangerous concepts." However, my aims were frequently misinterpreted in the press, as reports, in an effort to make the stories more provocative, depicted Edith as a "frustrated and unhappy child who had been transformed into a computer."

Foreign journalists too appeared on the scene. Their editors, rather than accepting wire service releases, wanted direct interviews. The State Department, recognizing the child's propaganda value, published a story about her in the U. S. Information Service foreign publications, including the ones behind the Iron Curtain. A high ranking State Department official telephoned one day to ask me to extend every courtesy to the foreign newsmen. He said "it is rare that foreign papers have anything nice to say about the United States. Perhaps the stories about Edith were the first favorable ones printed behind the Iron Curtain about our country since the second world war."

Edith and I were interviewed over the Voice of America during which we told our story. Although the Voice of America is frequently criticized for editing and managing the news, our experience with it was quite satisfactory. My criticism of the public school system was broadcast to the four hundred million listeners without changes. In fact, it was broadcast in its entirely four times.

Edith often tried to foil the efforts of the newsmen. Once when she was interviewed over the telephone on a nationwide broadcast, the interview lasted too long and she became restless. Finally, she asked her roommate to flush the toilet. Listeners throughout the nation must have been surprised to hear the sound of a flushing toilet terminate the interview.

Edith's photographs must have been valuable, for many photographers, unable to penetrate her classrooms or dormitory, followed her around on the campus to take candid shots. She greatly resented such tactics. Once as she ate in the university cafeteria, two men sat down opposite her. As one began to fix his camera, she suspected his intention and made a face at him. Undeterred, he went on tinkering with his camera until the outraged Edith stood up, stuck her tongue out, and angrily asked, "How much will this picture bring you?"

"Young lady, I have no intention of taking your picture in any pose whatsoever." Embarrassingly, the elderly gentleman proved to be an official of the State University system on an inspection tour.

Once when I was in New York on business, I was introduced by an acquaintance to an official of CBS as the "guy who breeds geniuses."

"What does he breed?"

"Geniuses."

"You have a good sense of humor," said the official.

My acquaintance then told him the story about Edith and showed him some newspaper clippings. Impressed, the CBS man invited me to visit him at his office the next day.

That night I was not able to sleep. This was my great opportunity to tell the whole story to the world without editorial comments. I was hopeful that I would be able to expose the inadequacies of the public school system and to present constructive alternatives.

The next day I was at CBS at the appointed time. The official explained that the network was interested in doing a show on Edith, but he had been unable to find Florida Atlantic University listed in the directory. I explained that it was a new but good school. The producer wanted some time to consult his associates, but was fairly certain CBS would do the story, which he assured me "would be told in full without taking any statement out of context."

Back home I had to face my "adversary." "Listen, Edith, this is no ordinary publicity. This broadcast will permit you to address yourself to twenty-five million people. It will give you the opportunity to make a substantial contribution to the battle for better education, to share with the public your experiences, and to make any comment you choose."

She protested that she was not much of an authority on education, but I disagreed. "You have a most unusual educational background, one which directly contradicts the public school philosophy. Let the world know about it so that others might benefit from it." Finally I won my point.

Weeks went by. I heard nothing from CBS, until I learned that the official to whom I had spoken suffered a heart attack. I feared that was the end of the interview, but one day he called, explaining that his ill health had upset the schedule, but that CBS was ready to do the show.

The long-awaited day arrived. The University spread the red carpet for the film crew headed by a veteran reporter. Edith was embarrassed as the news about the broadcast spread among the students, fearing that they would resent her. Everyone wanted to be in the show as sites were carefully selected and the dormitories readied for the indoor shots. Edith's roommates called their relatives around the country telling them they were going to be on television.

One afternoon the filming began. I should point out that since I do not have access to an accurate transcript of the tape, the dialogues reported here are based upon my own recollections. While they are perhaps, paraphrasings of the actual interview, I believe that they accurately reflect the content and the exchange of views.

First, Edith was interviewed. "What prompted you to leave junior high school?"

"I was bored. There was no challenge."

"Was it really your decision? Or was it your Dad's?"

"The decision was mutual."

"What do you consider to be the main trouble with the public school system?"

"It provides no stimulation. The teachers' motivation is poor for by and large they are incompetent. You have to be academically mediocre to get along with your classmates. One cannot progress at his own pace. The formative period of pre-school is totally neglected. In my case, there was a deep schism between my training at home and the work at school. I was resented by my schoolmates."

"You have just stated that you found the teachers poorly motivated and incompetent. To what do you attribute this?"

"With all due respect to those teachers who are bright and deeply dedicated despite the mediocre standards, the curriculum of teacher colleges is appalling. Much of the time is wasted on Mickey Mouse type courses. No mastery of the field of specialization is required. It is no secret that many students who are unable to maintain the minimum scholastic average at the schools of liberal arts and sciences transfer to education courses where they do quite well. As a matter of fact, some of my friends at this school take education courses and they will verify my assessment."

"How does it feel to be with students so much older than you?"

"No problems at all."

"How is your social life?"

"Good. I understand you intend to interview some of my friends. You will see whether or not I am well accepted."

"Bella, who had taken a dim view of my work with Edith, appeared next. I wondered what stand she would take, addressing herself to millions of mothers.

"Mrs. Stern, as a mother, you must have been worried about the ambitious program which your husband envisioned for Edith."

"Indeed, I was deeply concerned and frightened. I feared then that her emotional growth would not keep pace with her intellectual development."

"Was that fear justified?"

"Not at all. Now that she attends college, she is much happier. Emotionally Edith is well adjusted. Her social life is rich and full."

"Would you recommend such a course of action to other parents?"

"Most definitely. I would urge them to work with their children from infancy. Having done this, they will find the school pace to be totally unacceptable."

"From the news reports, I gather your views have radically changed."

"That is true. Do not forget that the whole educational world opposed Aaron's work. I had faith in the experts' judgment."

"How does Edith relate to you?"

"Unlike many mothers, I have no communication gap with her. We understand each other quite well. She is affectionate and reciprocates my love."

The next day I was interviewed. Then a number of Edith's friends had their turn. The reporter asked questions such as how they got along with Edith, if her age was a problem, and if she was snobbish. They all gave a very favorable impression of her. David also was interviewed. He frankly related how school was boring him.

As a finale, a gray-haired, distinguished-looking professor emeritus of Columbia University, who was then a professor at Florida Atlantic, went to the microphone. The reporter asked, "As a professor of education, how do you view Edith's progress?"

"I am appalled. Here is a child who became the scapegoat of her father's obsession. Emotionally immature, she cannot cope with college pressures. You can see how frustrated she is. Indeed it is a tragedy."

The professor, visibly agitated, could find little consolation in the faces of the onlookers who, to say the least, disagreed with him. There was something grotesque and tragic in his deportment. After the professor's interview, he warned Bella about "the horrible consequences which might follow, such as a nervous breakdown, maladjustment and perhaps suicide."

Having failed to persuade the mother to "take energetic steps in order to safeguard the child by immediately withdrawing her from the university," he turned to the reporter who had listened attentively to the conversation.

"I beg you in the interest of education, do not broadcast these interviews for they can destroy the nation's faith in public school education. They might cause a great deal of harm to our youth."

Having no stomach to listen to these stupidities, I left abruptly, waving goodbye to the reporter.

The following weeks were very eventful as press conferences and T.V. appearances claimed our time. So busy was I that I did not learn whether CBS had broadcast the show or refrained from doing so due to the pressure exerted by the educational establishment.

Edith, however, became concerned as time went by and CBS did not air the show. "While I have never followed newspaper stories about me, this time I am embarrassed. The university and my friends who were interviewed would like to know when the interviews will be broadcast," she complained to me.

Sometime later, after she had graduated from Florida Atlantic and begun her graduate studies at Michigan State University, Edith called home. "Dad, I just watched the show which CBS did on the Pentagon with great interest. It really took guts. Apparently the educational establishment is more powerful than the military since CBS declined to air our interview."

"Which interview?"

"Remember the one at Florida Atlantic?"

"For the moment, I had forgotten about it."

"So had I until I watched the Pentagon show," replied Edith.

Although CBS chose not to broadcast the film Edith's remarkable ability to function well at fourteen away from home finally disarmed some of my ardent critics. Hence a measure of exoneration by the public and the educational establishment could be noticed. The impact was so great that some of my critics now adopted a "me too" attitude. An official who had blocked my efforts to have Edith tested at the University of Miami said, "I always knew she was destined for greatness." The county Board of Public Instruction which had resisted my efforts to take Edith out of school suddenly decided to award her an honorary high school diploma, the first in their history. The Dade County Commission, whose assistance I had vainly sought when I was opposed by the school board, awarded a certificate of appreciation to the girl who "has become a wonder in her own time as the fruition of a scientific, educational experiment by her father, Aaron Stern."

The most amazing and gratifying result of the publicity was undoubtedly the letters which arrived from tens of thousands of people from around the world. Unfortunately, I only had the funds to answer a few of them. Edith had become so well known that some letters were addressed simply to "Genius, Florida Atlantic University." To test it, I asked a friend in New York to address a letter to "Wunderkind, Florida Atlantic University, Boca Raton, Florida." She received it promptly.

Some of the mail came from religious fanatics who described Edith's success as "a sign of the coming of the Messiah." In some letters, opportunists sought endorsements of their ideas and products while others offered lucrative financial rewards for the advertisement of their educational products. One suggested that we lend our name to a "Correspondence School for Molding Geniuses." I was proud of Edith who stated, "I will not prostitute myself into deceiving the public for any sort of material gain."

There were the inevitable letters from psychologists, psychiatrists, and educators warning me that "the course on which you embark might have disastrous repercussions on the child's development. Pushing a child beyond the chronological limits leads to maladjustment and often suicide." Since Edith was extremely happy, functioning well in an adult society, we disregarded this advice with defiant laughter.

Some letters arrived from, as Edith termed them, "members of the fat-dripping suburbia" telling how much Edith had missed the "joy of being a cheer-leader and participating in high school dances with her peers." These Edith dismissed as "trivia which glorify mediocrity."

Many letters arrived from former convicts and drug addicts who complained that their education was inadequate and, as a result, their lack of purpose and boredom led them to crime and drug addiction. One lamented."If the school failed to inspire me toward academic growth, the least they could do is to equip me with vocational skills. What choice had I after the high school drop-out other than stealing cars?"

Similarly, there were numerous letters from frustrated parents and students who angrily stated their disappointment with the school system. One Cleveland housewife's letter deeply touched us.

"Since Joe, an exceedingly bright boy of thirteen, wastes his stay in school, I decided to teach Mary how to read and write before she entered first grade. The school frowned upon such an idea. Now Mary, age nine, who attends third grade, does not know yet the rudiments of reading and writing. What are we to do with her? My husband's meager income prevents us from sending our bright youngsters to a private school. We have no funds for tutoring. Plase advise us what to do as I am despondent." Unfortunately there was no solution I could offer.

In spite of the concern of many well-wishers that "Edith, with her high intelligence, will not be able to get married, for man was meant by God to be superior," there were quite a few marriage proposals. Edith had fun displaying the pictures of her prospects to friends. I also received a few letters from women, married and single, of which the following is an unusual example. "I am 30 years of age, white, attractive, happily married. I have always wanted to raise at least one bright child who would make a lasting contribution to the sciences. Thus far my two children show no outstanding features. In spite of the newspaper reports quoting you that 'Edith's accomplishments are entirely attributable to your educational technique' I am confident that it is due to your genetic structure. I should like to have a baby with you. Would you consent? Michael, my husband, will have no objections." A Los Angeles Post Office box identified the correspondent.

My wife, slightly embarrassed, suggested, "Perhaps this is a golden opportunity for you. You have always complained about our marriage."

The most disturbing revelation was that the mail from this country was divided between those who applauded my efforts and those who opposed them while the voluminous mail which we received from India, Pakistan, Formosa, Japan, Israel, and the whole of Europe, representing a cross-section of the population including American troops overseas, lauded Edith's accomplishments and my efforts to advance her.

Especially warm were the letters from members of the U.S. Armed Forces. Some were obviously due to nostalgia. Many were deeply moving.

One corporal from Korea wrote, "Now that I am far away in this God forsaken country, I came to realize the significance of education and the extraordinary sacrifices which Koreans bear to secure one. I wish my schooling had as much meaning to me."

A lady wrote from Germany, "Hitler could not have weakened the moral fabric of Germany without destroying our intellectuals and institutions of higher learning. A good education is the only hope for the world rent by hate, disease and poverty."

An Israeli engineer wrote, "The only way that we will conquer our Arab adversaries is through education. Thus, we will enlighten them about the futility of blind hate which might devour them rather than our presence in the Middle East."

As for the chronological barriers, a German professor wrote.

"How come that our young people enter professional schools on completion of secondary education at eighteen, without the benefit of four years of college? Does it mean that an American doctor, attorney or engineer is better equipped than his European counterpart? Definitely not."

A Peace Corps volunteer teaching in Asia stated: "I wish my instructor had as much success in teaching me my mother tongue as I have in teaching English to the natives, some of whom walk miles to school barefoot."

A Formosan girl wrote in broken English, "I am only fourteen years of age and look forward to enter the university to pursue mathematics. My teachers are of the opinion that we need educated people and since I excel myself in mathematics, there is no need to waste time for me in secondary school. I cannot understand why would your school authorities, as the nespaper reports, object to your entry earlier to a university."

During one of her brief vacations when we were sorting the mail, Edith remarked: "Dad, I am frightened about the future of our country. It would seem to me that we glorify mediocrity in contrast to the awe

132

and great significance which people throughout the world attach to education. Have you analyzed the mail?"

"Yes, I have."

"Weren't you appalled by the fact that not one word of criticism came from abroad? After all, the same stories were published throughout the world. How can one criticize a parent for his diligent efforts to secure the best, most meaningful education for his children?"

Encouraged by the publicity and the letters, I decided to make an effort to convince the educational establishment of the worth of my teaching methods. I had been successful with my own children and I saw no reason why I couldn't be successful with other students. In fact, at the displaced persons' camp in Bad Reichenhall I had taken children who were running wild in the streets and successfully educated them. Surely my methods could be at least as successful with American children, even with underprivileged ones.

One of my efforts was directed at the Florida State Department of Education. In 1967 I had a speaking engagement in Tallahassee, the state capital. At the time, the state school system was at a boiling point with the teachers threatening a strike which finally became a reality in the following year. Additional funds were needed for education just to maintain the status quo, but the Republican governor lacked rapport with the Democratic legislature. This problem was further complicated by the governor's campaign promise of no additional taxes. I believed that this was an opportune time to share my educational experiences with the state authorities.

First, I sought an appointment with the governor, but as usual he was out of town. Then I met briefly with the head of the House Education Committee during a special session of the legislature dealing specifically with the school crisis. He told me, "Well, it sounds exciting. Leave me your number and I'll call you to appear before the Education Committee." The call never came.

Next I saw the state superintendent of public schools, and explained my ideas. He asked, "Where am I going to secure funds for your project?" I explained that it would require very few funds. I was only asking for a couple of rooms without elaborate facilities so that I could demonstrate that my total educational submersion would work with other children. I wanted a group of young children, preferably under-

133

privileged ones, for a period of six months. I was confident that I could raise their IQ's by at least twenty percent, and I could demonstrate teaching seven-year-old children to multiply three digit numbers in less than a week. He also thought it sounded exciting and asked me for a scientific resume of my methods. I told him that I didn't have one.

"How can a man of your scholarship neglect such an elementary step?"

"It is plain common sense," I explained. "My greatest asset in working with Edith was adhering to plain common sense without dogmatic guidelines. It is so simple that I would not even attempt to define it in any scientific terms. Indeed, it worked for Edith."

"Well, I'll schedule a discussion for you with a few of my staff members and a representative from the College of Education at the University."

"That would be fine." I returned to the waiting room. Soon, two women came to see me; one was a member of the superintendent's staff and the other was a professor of education. We went to lunch and I began to explain my work with Edith and David.

"What are you trying to prove?"

"Nothing, I simply desire to equip my children with as much knowledge as I can."

"Don't we all?"

"I doubt that."

"Mr. Stern, have you visited one of our public schools, recently?"

"Not really."

"Do you know that we do exactly the same?"

"How successful are you?" There was a long silence. "My dear ladies," I said, "our generals command a rich well-equipped army which does exactly the same as Moshe Dayan, whose Israeli armed forces are poor and ill equipped, but determined and dedicated in the pursuit of a just cause. How does the recent victory of Dayan compare with the pathetic

134

situation in which we find ourselves in Vietnam?" I'm not sure they understood the analogy.

"Would you care to visit the university and meet my colleagues?"

"No, thank you." Within an hour I was on the Greyhound bus heading for home and wondering whether the American Medical Association wouldn't reject an effective cure for cancer, if such a method had been conceived by someone outside their ranks. Then I thought of David who was hopelessly bored in public school.

Another source from which I tried to obtain support for my methods was the Department of Health, Education and Welfare office in Washington, D.C. Using my meager resources and over Belta's protests, I traveled to the capital. "They will turn a deaf ear to your proposals," she said. "Why waste precious funds at a time when we deny ourselves essentials?" I went anyway.

After checking into the YMCA, I went to the Office of Education where my efforts to see the commissioner failed at first, but eventually succeeded. Then I was directed to the acting director of the Division of Elementary and Secondary Education Research. I had a series of conferences with him and he also read the parts of my book which deal with my methods. The official was impressed. Then I asked, "Why does the public school system, which unquestionably is in a mess, refuse to implement these improvements?"

"Unfortunately we have no jurisdiction in this matter. It is up to the respective state departments of education."

"The federal government spends billions of dollars on schools. Surely it is interested in the improvement of the quality of education. You award huge sums on research. Why not on my proposals?"

I was told that the congress extends appropriations and suggested that I submit my proposals to them. When I asked if the Office of Education would support me, he said that they couldn't.

"Sir, my proposals deal with a dramatic breakthrough in education, one which will revolutionize the whole field at a nominal cost. I would like to establish pilot projects in every state, and in order to subject my technique to the most severe test, I would like to enroll three-year-old underprivileged children of minority groups. These youngsters, who are believed to be of low scholastic potential, would be housed in austere surroundings. I'm confident that they would achieve the second grade level in only a few months at a total cost of less than ten million dollars. The administration of the funds should be under strict federal controls while the scientific evaluation I should hope would be entrusted to private independent universities."

"These are grandiose plans. How realistic are you in your assessment?" inquired the official.

"Could you please arrange for me, right here, while I'm in Washington a demonstration of my technique in one of the least successful schools? It would take me no more than eight to ten hours to teach two-digit multiplication to a group of ten second-grade youngsters."

"I'm afraid I could not arrange that."

At our last meeting we were joined by a few other high-ranking officials of HEW. "Why don't you attempt to implement your proposals on a state level?" asked a young man.

"I have tried. They're not interested in changes."

"Surely they must be aware of the crisis prevailing in our school system."

"Apparently not," I replied.

Disenchanted and poorer by $300, I was sitting at a cafeteria table wondering how to explain my extravagance to Bella who had postponed the purchase of a badly needed refrigerator for the past two years due to lack of funds. I visualized her telling me, "So another fiasco, Don Quixote. When will you learn your lesson?"

One of the officials approached me.

"My dear man, I know how disheartening it must be to you. This department sees many visionaries, with worthy proposals, who, like you, meet a deaf ear because of bureaucracy and their inability to muster political support or any number of other reasons. But above all, the greatest obstacle to innovation is the fear of change. You know, people feel that if God had wanted us to fly, he would surely have given us wings."

136

CHAPTER 13

The Emancipated Edith

From time to time, various quiz shows sought Edith as a contestant. The most persistent one was *To Tell the Truth*. Unable to reach her, they called me in the summer of 1967. The producer argued that the affidavit which was broadcast before each show would be an excellent way to tell our story objectively. I thought his argument had merit, but, as usual, Edith disagreed. "I refuse to be an accomplice to misleading advertising. I've turned down lucrative offers before, and I'll turn down this one," she stated.

"But Edith," I pleaded, "please weigh carefully the merits of the affidavit. The producer will have no choice but to state the whole truth and thus vindicate me from the allegations that I stole your childhood. And think how many youngsters will be inspired by your achievements. You will advance the cause of quality education."

Edith gave in. "Set the wheels in motion," she said.

Soon the producer mailed airline tickets and made reservations at the Americana Hotel in New York. After some arguing, Edith finally consented to accept, as I recall, $500 to "defray the cost of sightseeing, concerts, and a Broadway show."

On our arrival at the hotel, a representative of the show greeted us. "I hope you will enjoy your stay in New York. We at the studio are thrilled to have you, the most celebrated youngster in America. Please drop in this afternoon at the office. The taping is scheduled for tomorrow." Soon we were on our way toward the East Side to visit the galleries. Edith discovered the book stores where she spent about twenty percent of our budget.

When we returned to the hotel, the doorman eyed Edith, inexpensively dressed and laden with books, then curtly advised, "This is not the service entrance."

"Thank you kindly for the information, my good man," replied Edith as she walked through the main door.

At the producer's office we signed an agreement, then jointly drafted an affidavit. After the producer's staff typed it, we carefully read it and found that some changes had been made. "Did you say I will hopefully obtain my bachelor's degree at eighteen? You are wrong. I should earn it when I am fifteen or earlier." The girl didn't believe it and went to check with researchers.

"I am told that no girl has ever finished college at the age of fifteen," she said.

"Fine, then I will establish a precedent," Edith replied. The next day we returned for the taping. As usual, there were two other contestants, one of whom was a daughter of Mayor Lindsay and the other the child of a writer. Edith was sarcastic. "As you can see, Dad, ours is a land of equal opportunity. It is purely coincidental that out of three million city kids, the producer could find these two only."

"Edith, do not look for utopia. These are brutal facts of life. My struggle for better, more meaningful education has as its objective the uplifting and advancement of the broad masses of people, toward a better life, the development of their skills and talents."

"Dad, I'm grateful to you for your work with me, now as I compare myself with these unfortunate ones who suffer from intellectual poverty in the midst of affluence."

"Edith, I think these girls are bright by comparison with others."

"Most unfortunately, you are right, Dad."

Prior to the show, the contestants were briefed and questioned. Edith, of course, towered above the other two children with her encyclopedic knowledge. The staff quizzed, "If a panel member asks you what your curriculum consists of, what would you say?"

"What is curriculum?" the two contestants asked, as Edith politely restrained her laughter.

PLAYING PIANO AT 3

EDITH, 2 MONTHS OLD,
TENSELY LISTENING TO CLASSICAL MUSIC

EDITH, AGE 3, EN ROUTE TO
VISIT ALBERT EINSTEIN

FROLICKING WITH A FRIEND

AT 6, ON A BOAT RIDE

EDITH 8, DAVID 1

EDITH, AGE 5, WITH FRIENDS

EDITH 9, DAVID 2

DAVID, AGE 8, CONDUCTING AN
EXPERIMENT

I TOO ENJOYED GOLDEN BEACHES

DAVID, AGE 1, LISTENING TO A STORY

DAVID AT AGE 5

EDITH 4, DAD AND MOTHER

AT THE LIBRARY

MATHEMATIC COMPLEXITIES
SIMPLIFIED

A TIME TO MARVEL

BOOKS WILL ALWAYS BE MY MOST
PRECIOUS FRIENDS

EDITH EXCHANGING JOKES WITH HER STUDENTS

EDITH, AGE 16, COUNSELING A GRADUATE STUDENT AT
MICHIGAN STATE UNIVERSITY.

READING AT THE PICTURESQUE CAMPUS
OF MICHIGAN STATE UNIVERSITY

RECREATION

EDITH AND HER FELLOW GRADUATE
STUDENTS AT MICHIGAN STATE UNIVERSITY

TEACHING HIGHER MATHEMATICS AT THE UNIVERSITY, AT 15.

DAVID, AGE 15, CAPT. NEEB, BARBARA PETERSON, AGE 14, SUBSEQUENT TO THE YOUNGSTERS' EXPERIENCE PILOTING A PLANE

"What have you learned about photosynthesis?"

"I don't know the meaning of it," replied one of the girls.

Edith later bitterly complained to me that "it is tragic that these girls will attain great success by the virtue of parental wealth and position, while so many gifted people are destined to struggle for survival."

Our first skirmish came when the makeup woman appeared. Edith refused to be made up. "I fulfilled our agreement to an iota. There is not a word about makeup or grooming of my hair."

"But it is in your interest. You will look better on the air," pleaded the woman.

"I'm quite happy the way I am."

"Would you like to change your dress? We have one available."

"Most definitely not. There is nothing wrong with my dress. I have worn it a year and I like it."

After a quick rehearsal with the substitute panel, Edith, composed and slightly indifferent, was on the air. The other contestants, in contrast, appeared to be insecure as shown in their nervous facial movements.

At the end of the show, Edith was expected to stand up. She was hesitant, but the other two girls gently prodded her. "I really didn't want to stand up," she explained later. "They don't have to know me."

When we were ready to leave, Mrs. Lindsay graciously invited us to the Gracie Mansion. Edith politely rejected the invitation. "You are the first person to decline such an invitation," the disappointed lady replied.

"I am sorry, but our schedule is so crowded," gently apologized Edith. Later I asked her why she rejected the invitation. "Dad, I don't need any more publicity. I'd rather spend an evening at Lincoln Center." A few months later, Edith turned down an invitation from President Johnson with a succinct note: "I shall not break bread with you until our troops are withdrawn from Vietnam."

The rest of our stay in New York was very pleasant. Edith was intoxicated with the diversity and cosmopolitan character of the city which she had not seen for seven years. Reluctantly, she left the Staten Island Ferry, claiming its five-cent fare was "the last vestige of fiscal sanity in the sea of inflation."

The visit to our old neighborhood was nostalgic and triumphant. "Here is the genius about whom her father bragged so much. We thought he was crazy," remarked our old neighbor.

The concert at Lincoln Center, a Broadway play, the Guggenheim Museum of Natural History overwhelmed her. Her mood was so good that without bickering, she consented to an interview by a syndicated columnist, and by a New York Post reporter. "I think I can lift the moratorium this time," she said cheerfully.

We quickly ran out of money and had to return home instead of seeing the World Exposition in Montreal as we had planned. At the airport, David, Bella, and a few friends came to greet us. "You know, Edith," her seven-year-old brother said, "I was so mad sitting at the T.V. set for I knew every answer."

I had no doubt that David could answer the questions, for while as expected he did poorly in school, he was intelligent and quite knowledgeable. One of my best educational projects with him began later that year. In December, 1967, the world's first successful heart transplant stirred the hope and imagination of people everywhere. We thought the event was significant not only because Dr. Barnard had dared to cross a new frontier in surgery in the face of strong criticism, and thus bring a new ray of hope in the struggle against this deadly disease, but also because it meant hope for the day when my own heart could be replaced by another, vibrant one.

David came to me early in the morning after the news of the transplant was first released. "Dad, I can visualize you playing ball with me and riding a bicycle."

"That is wishful thinking. How do you expect my heart to be so improved? Be realistic."

"I am realistic, Dad. Dr. Barnard in South Africa has transplanted the heart of a young person into a much older patient than you and it functions well."

140

"That might be so, David, but we cannot predict how long it will function and whether the body will reject this alien organ."

The expression on his face suggested deep disappointment as he tiptoed back to his room. I knew the child would be unable to fall asleep again. Nor did I. As I lay there, I contemplated going to South Africa as an experimental patient. There was little to lose, but much to gain. Then I thought about David. Why not seize this opportunity for educational purposes and exploit it fully? Since the boy was concerned with the prospects of a transplant for me, it might provide an excellent incentive for learning.

The next day I thought a lot about the heart transplant, but I said nothing to David. In the evening, I asked him to check my heart while I was lying down to rest. He enthusiastically took the stethoscope from my headboard and began to listen to my heartbeat. "You don't have a spasm at the present. The beat is rhythmic and full."

"Do you think I should take a Quinitine?"

"No," he replied.

"David, what a puzzle this muscle is. It is so simple, yet so complex."

"Yes, Daddy." His eyes lit up.

Gradually I guided his interest. Finally, I suggested, "Suppose I let you investigate all you can about heart transplants so that I can make my decision based on your recommendations."

"Dad, I would love it." He warmly embraced me and a kiss sealed the deal. From that day on, most of David's activities focused on news surrounding the heart transplant. Once more, I had turned my liability into an asset.

David began to read every news release with an insatiable zeal. One day he said, "It seems to me that the major problem is rejection. It is ironic that the defense forces which protect the man against hostile bacteria also attempt to destroy a transplanted lifesaving organ."

"Is that so?" I asked.

"Indeed, it is."

"Let's study it then."

"Fine, Dad."

I told him all that I knew about the immunological defense in the body, drawing on my limited background in biology, but that was not enough for David. He then consulted his sister's biology textbook, and unsatisfied with it obtained information from other sources on tissue characteristics and tissue matching methods.

"Dad, it is a shame there was not more thorough research in this area before the first heart transplant was performed."

"Well, David, apparently the medical profession did not regard this breakthrough as feasible or desirable so soon. Perhaps Dr. Barnard, impatient in his desire to save a patient's life, simply decided to proceed on his own after years of cherishing his dream."

"Dad, I love him for it. He is my hero."

Following the death of Louis Washkansky, Barnard's first transplant patient, the criticism of the operation gained momentum and then subsided. His success with Philip Blaiberg a month later brought about a proliferation of heart transplants everywhere, and within six months well over a hundred hearts had been transplanted.

One day David happily reported to me, "Daddy, it seems to me that a major milestone in heart transplants has been reached; a serum was developed in Holland which promises to combat effectively the rejection immunity of the body."

"Did you learn that at school?"

"You must be kidding me," he replied.

One morning he excitedly woke me up quite early. "Daddy, your heartbeat was much slower and fuller when I checked you with the stethoscope." He was right. My next visit to my doctor confirmed it. As we discussed my frequent heart spasms and the administration of a new drug which the doctor had previously prescribed, he explained that the purpose of it was to reduce my heart rate, an objective which the drug accomplished. I smiled. The cardiologist, accustomed to my pensive moods, was surprised.

"I know it," I said. "My son diagnosed it."

Soon I realized that I had an opportunity to broaden David's interest, this time in the social sciences. One day I came home with a box of pins and a world map which I had purchased for seventy-five cents. David immediately asked, "Daddy, what is that for?" Then after a few seconds, "Don't tell me, I know. We will follow the heart transplants as they occur and place a pin in the respective cities."

The map was placed in his room on the wall above his bed. Each time a heart transplant operation was reported, he inserted a pin.

"David, where did the latest heart transplant take place?"

"In France, Daddy."

"Was it successful?"

"Well, the patient is still alive."

"What do you know about France? Since the country is so advanced medically, we should like to know more about it," I prodded him gently.

"Oh, I have done that already." It was difficult to conceal my pride as he proceeded. "I looked up France in the encyclopedia. DeGaulle is the President." Then in rapid succession, "France had a tragic history. The Nazi occupation and the futile war in Algiers and Indochina. I think we should leave Vietnam at once. The French mistakes there should have taught us a lesson."

Now a new opportunity for branching out to a yet broader area was available. During the next few days, David learned about the Geneva Convention governing the conduct of war. We drew comparisons between the Middle East conflict and Indochina. Quite often, I acted as a devil's advocate to challenge him. The debates became heated. Finally David, who had been deeply opposed to the American involvement in Vietnam even before the incident with Humphrey a year earlier, and who abhorred violence, suggested that there are just and unjust wars.

"Well, what is your definition of a just war?"

"The struggle against Hitler. Nazi Germany was determined to annihilate the Jews and to subjugate all the conquered people to serve the German Reich in slavery. Likewise Israel had no choice but to resort to arms in defense of its people against enemies who in their own words are determined to push Israel into the sea. On the other hand, one cannot visualize North Vietnam being a threat to the U. S. no matter how much we resent their political system."

I could not resist his charm and logic. "Here is a dime. Run over to the store for an ice cream."

"I would rather do it later. NBC news will be on shortly."

Relentlessly pursuing the transplant project, he learned about twenty or so different countries. Of course, he also followed the transplants conducted in the United States. In the process, my boy learned about the diversity of opinions and about the interactions of social and religious groups as they debated the merits and demerits of the transplants. He also learned about the legal ramifications and the cost of medical services.

Undoubtedly, the greatest challenge came when a heart transplant took place in an Iron Curtain country. I decided to explore the complexity of a different socio-political system.

"Well, Dad, having read about the Soviet Union and its allies, I'm sure glad to live in the U.S.A."

"So am I," I answered. "But why do you say that?"

"For example, you are an outspoken critic of the war in Vietnam and our public school system, yet you will not be harmed for your views. In the Soviet Union, however, you would have been put in jail for criticizing the government's policies."

Little had David realized when he began the heart transplant project that he was destined to acquire a vast body of knowledge.

Edith continued to progress well at Florida Atlantic, both socially and academically. People had always been concerned about how she would relate to boys, but now the questions became more frequent, especially from reporters. They wanted to know if she dated, if she got along with boys, and if she planned to get married. These questions could be expected, particularly in a society which based the status of a woman largely on the accomplishments of her husband.

My determination to accelerate her progress was in part influenced by the fact that she was a female. Too often I have observed girls of superior intellect torn between men and the pursuit of their own professional goals. For example, there is some degree of merit in the reluctance of many medical schools to admit women students since they are too frequently lost to matrimony before graduation. A recent survey at a nursing school disclosed that a substantial percentage of female students sought admission solely for the purpose of meeting a "nice doctor."

The tacticians of Madison Avenue cleverly portray a woman as a sex kitten whose supreme bliss in life is to linger in luxury. Her half-naked body can sell anything from a toothpick to a generator. The price of this is devastating in terms of the waste of the tremendous talent of women. I would guess that if we ever fail in our contest with the Communist world, it would be due to their successful utilization of the abilities of their women. Such considerations weighed heavily in my determination to help Edith become a superior person.

She is a militant adherent of the woman's liberation movement and her accomplishments readily dispel the myth of male superiority. "Remember, Dad, the press interviews you conducted when I was little and the disbelief expressed when you maintained that a woman could surpass a man? I guess you were right. I think that your work with me was the beginning of an effective woman's liberation movement."

With regards to marriage, she has said that in its present form it has lost its relevance, ramaining static as the society became more complex. To substantiate this, Edith cites the staggering rate of divorces. "Marriage will become more meaningful when the woman is an equal partner, financially liberated, independent, and capable of assuming her own role in politics, society, and the sciences. Her choice of a mate will be determined by compatibility rather than by expedience, by genuine love, rather than a search for security. Of course, education and the liberalization of divorce laws are essential in bringing about the change."

I once asked her if she planned to get married. "Since I don't regard marriage as the ultimate goal of a woman, I would only be able to fall in love with a creative man who would challenge and stimulate me intellectually, one who as a high code of ethics and who would place spiritual values above material ones."

Edith has contempt for girls who look forward to a housewife's role. "I fail to see the glamor and challenge of scrubbing floors, washing dishes, and cooking. Perhaps girls who look forward to being housewives are unwilling or incapable of developing their intellectual faculties. With the rapid progress of technology these menial tasks will be fully automated anyway."

Once an interviewer asked her. "How about boys? Do you meet them?"

"Yes, I meet boys, Florida Atlantic is a coed school. As of the moment, however, I have no matrimonial plans. First, I want to get my Ph. D."

Another common question was, "Would you raise your children the way your father raised you?"

"Yes, I would. Most definitely. If I marry, my husband will have to consent to rearing our children as I was."

"Would you recommend his methods to others?"

"Absolutely yes, provided that the parent possesses a high degree of culture and a commitment to this goal. I can't say for sure how much others will benefit from it since I am the first product of the program. However, I do know that the intellectual horizons of a child can be greatly expanded, edging out the mediocrity and lust for comfort which are so commonplace in our society."

"Truthfully, are you happy, Edith? Are you well accepted socially? Does the age difference constitute an obstacle?"

"I have been perfectly happy for as far back as I can remember. My social life is rich and full. The age difference creates no obstacles at all. I am completely at ease with people, and judging by the way my schoolmates treat me, the feeling is fully reciprocated."

"What is your aim in life, as a woman and as an individual?"

"I am a woman in a biological sense only. I seek no privileges nor will I tolerate restrictions. I abhor distinctions bestowed through marriage, such as a First Lady. The society will have to judge me on the basis of my merits and my merits alone. In marriage, I shall seek mutual respect and affection, compatibility and challenge. This is my definition of marital happiness."

146

Once during a press interview at Florida Atlantic University the fourteen year old Edith introduced her twenty-two year old roommate, majoring in education, with the following comment: "Within a month she will graduate to teach kids of my age at a junior high school. Simultaneously, I shall teach students of her age higher mathematics at Michigan State University."

Although the affidavit on To Tell The Truth had presented our story correctly, the press continued to distort it. Of the many misconceptions printed, I most resented the ones which portrayed me as a cruel, strict father. Instead of being a rigid disciplinarian, I was extremely permissive. As a child she had on several occasions hurt me in anger and once she destroyed some of our furniture. On another occasion, she intentionally broke three windows in our house. I had them repaired without a comment.

One evening in May, 1968, while Edith was at Florida Atlantic, I received a telephone call from a radio station in San Francisco. The caller requested an interview with me, explaining that a UPI release about Edith's scholastic triumphs had appeared in the Chronicle that morning. He said the story had created a great deal of interest, resulting in many calls to the station. Reluctantly I agreed. When we were on the air, he introduced me as Edith's "Demanding Dad" from the article. As it was reported in the story, "He based his training on four things: discipline, diligence, motivation, and speed." Then he continued, "The residents of the Bay area are shocked by your cruel methods employed on a baby. Is it possible that incarceration in concentration camps has so dehumanized you?" David, who was on the extension line remarked sarcastically, "My Dad's cruelty prompted him to become a vegetarian."

Once I received a call from an Associated Press editor in New York. "Mr. Stern, to separate the facts from fiction, I would like to send one of my most gifted reporters, for an interview with Edith and your family. I know you are annoyed by the inaccuracies and exaggerations about your daughter, my man will do an in-depth penetrating story to set the record straight."

"I'll do my best to arrange it. Give me a few days to get Edith's consent."

"He'll be there in four days."

The next four days were devoted to bargaining and persuasion.

"Edith, darling, this man is a famous reporter. He won't be tempted toward melodrama. I think that a true picture of you will emerge from this interview."

"Dad, I don't care. Having read all the lies printed about me, I really don't care what the world thinks about me. The answer is no."

I called the editor back and advised him that I was unable to arrange the interview. "Mr. Stern," he replied, "my reporter is a charming fellow. He will reach her somehow."

"Fine, but do it at your own risk."

In May of 1968, the newspaperman called from the airport and asked me to meet him that morning at Florida Atlantic.

"Don't underestimate Edith," I told him. "She's tough."

At first we could not find Edith, but finally I saw her strolling with a young man. "Edith, meet my friend," I introduced the journalist.

She politely greeted him. "How do you do, sir."

"Where can we talk?"

"Right here. Let's sit on the grass," replied Edith.

The accompanying cameraman was out of sight. The reporter was charming. But nothing could persuade her. "I really don't care for publicity."

"Edith, these people spent a lot of money to send the gentleman here."

"I have made my views clear. I refuse to be cajoled or bribed." The reporter, who most likely had learned from the numerous press accounts about Edith's admiration for the *Star Trek* television series, cleverly told her, "Young lady, you are as stubborn as Spock in the last *Star Trek* episode."

That excited her. "So you are a *Star Trek* fan too."

"Yes, I am."

She smiled at him. "One who watches *Star Trek* cannot be altogether bad."

After that the reporter had no difficulty. We spent a delightful day together, ending with a dinner at one of the best restaurants in Boca Raton. There we met Edith's mathematics professor. Knowing that Edith avoided such places, he remarked, "This is the last place on earth I would expect to find you."

"It is with the compliments of the fourth branch of government, the almighty press, that I, a little pauper, can be found here."

"So you finally granted an interview."

"How can one deny a *Star Trek* fan?"

While eating in fancy restaurants was a rare event for Edith, she could frequently be found in establishments offering more modest cuisines. Once when I was visiting her, she suggested that we go out to eat. "Dad, I know a place where you can obtain all the fish you can eat for a dollar nineteen."

While as a vegetarian, I was not particularly impressed, I replied, "Fine. Let's go."

A friend of hers joined us. As I watched Edith devouring additional portions of fish, again and again, I couldn't help but wonder if her food absorption wasn't greater than her intellectual capacity. Reading my thoughts, she whispered, "Food in the university cafeteria is so lousy. We eat here every Wednesday."

"I wonder how long the poor guy will remain in business."

"Don't worry, Dad. This is his contribution to better education. Besides, he has six other days to heal his wounds, for this deal is offered only on Wednesdays."

Edith completed her Bachelor of Arts degree in August 1968. Since the graduation exercises had been held earlier, she was scheduled to attend the ceremonies the following year. However, she objected to attending exercises under any circumstances. Furthermore, she had decided to attend graduate school at Michigan State University — a distance of 1700 miles — which made it unlikely that she would return for the graduation.

Branding such ceremonies as "empty symbolism," she adamantly stated, "I will not parade down the aisle wearing grotesque attire in a circus-like parade."

"But Edith," I argued, "this is sort of a milestone signifying a major educational attainment. Your mother and I would be proud and happy if you were to attend it."

"Dad, I plan to pursue my education. You seem to overestimate my degree. I have earned it, as you know, effortlessly. It is not much of an achievement. Since when do you, a proponent of non-conformity, subscribe to this middle-class philosophy?"

Edith was of course right and there was no point in arguing with her. Graduation exercises, or formalities of any nature for that matter, meant very little to me and Edith knew it. There was no sense in pretending. I simply wanted to cooperate with the university which had been so kind to Edith. Not long before, the registrar had confided to me over lunch that while other colleges suffered from a lack of facilities, FAU's greatest problem was a lack of applicants. When I had difficulty believing it, he explained that because it was a new and not well known state university, rather distant from population centers, students were not familiar with it. Furthermore, FAU is the only university in the state system that by design has no freshman and sophomore classes. Hence, the university had only 3700 students in facilities capable of handling 10,000 to 12,000.

I had a great deal of affection for Florida Atlantic University which, in my judgment, has an excellent faculty — many of whom are my friends. The school had been very helpful to Edith, and its president had secured a generous scholarship grant for her. "Don't ask any questions about where it comes from," I was told when I inquired about the source. Since the registrar had also told me that the publicity associated with Edith's attendance at the school had been an asset to them (they had received several hundred letters from everywhere in this country and abroad as a result), I was determined to arrange publicity so that the school would further benefit from her graduation. When I failed to persuade Edith to attend the ceremonies, I made other arrangements.

Shortly thereafter, and not so coincidentally, the wire services pestered me over the telephone. "What about Edith? When will she graduate?" I explained that she had already graduated. "When will the exercises be held?" they asked. "We would like to take some pictures and arrange an interview."

A decision was soon reached. Edith would have a private graduation ceremony in the office of the president with only a few selected guests present. The news was "discreetly" released to UPI.

Edith was outraged. "I will not attend this circus! I refuse to wear the garb." Someday I will donate a scholarship to a deserving student in appreciation for the generous grant given me, rather than parade for the press. Please, Dad, I like this school and its faculty, but don't force this ceremony on me."

Finally, after much persuasion, she capitulated, "Well, Dad, it is obvious that I have no choice but to go, however, I refuse to wear the cap and gown."

At the scheduled time, David, Edith and I went in to the office of the president. Bella was unable to attend the ceremony because of illness. Selected school officials, a student photographer, and a wire service reporter were there also. Edith finally consented to put on the gown of the dean of faculty who always kept it handy in his office.

After the graduation formalities were over, she was warmly congratulated. When Edith posed reluctantly for pictures, the president asked David, "What about you? When will you go to college?"

"It would be presumptuous on my part to make a definite commitment, but I am confident that I shall surpass my sister by entering college at an earlier age," replied the seven year old boy.

The UPI reporter, disbelieving his ears, began to ask David questions. David's anwers were well chosen while he displayed remarkable articulation.

"He's a genius. Two geniuses in one family. Please repeat for me the statement you made to the president."

David obliged him by repeating the statement word for word. A day or two later the American and world press reported the graduation ceremony and quoted David's statement verbatim. Screaming headlines proclaimed a "Second Genius in the Family." Thus David stole the show. Edith was at home "recovering from the pageant." Pointing to the many newspaper accounts, she smilingly remarked, "We pride ourselves as being the country of peaceful transition. David, with my blessing, will be reigning now."

151

CHAPTER 14

Fifteen Year Old Professor

At last the hoped for and dreaded day arrived. Edith was to leave for Michigan State University to begin her graduate studies in mathematics and to assume her role as a university instructor — the youngest in history. Waiting for this day had been trying for all of us. Many thoughts crossed my mind during the long, sleepless nights.

Will she succeed? How can I permit a fifteen-year-old girl to leave her parents for such a long journey? How will she be able to conduct university classes? She is still a child. Will her youthfulness interfere with her duties? Will the older students respect her? How will she adapt herself to the cold climate? Her wardrobe is so skimpy. Won't she be cold?

In my mind rang the warning of the New York physician who had prescribed penicillin for the rest of her life. Had I been wrong in overriding him? He had said to keep her warm at all times and suggested that we relocate to a warm climate to help prevent a recurrence of rheumatic fever. Won't the transition now from a warm to a cold climate cause her troubles?

How will she be able to manage her budget? She is only taking seventy-five dollars with her.

Perhaps the prophets of doom were right. Perhaps she will fall flat on her face. This could be catastrophic to her.

Bella, who was delighted with Edith's remarkable success in college, chose to be silent, but her eyes betrayed a deep maternal fear. I knew she was having the same doubts.

"Daddy, don't be worried; you have given me self-reliance, broadened my cultural horizons, and introduced me to values which I shall always treasure. Have no fear. I'll pass this test too with flying colors. It is you I am worried about. You are so engrossed in my progress. Believe me, in spite of the distance, I shall always be at your side. Remember, you have David to work with."

"Edith, I have not said one word to suggest apprehension. I have full faith in you."

"Let's be frank. Verbal communication is superfluous for us. I can easily sense your concern."

To reassure myself, I thought of the many steps I had taken to advance her education, to prepare her for this day. Fifteen years had elapsed since I had told the nurses at the hospital that she was destined to be a genius and now she had exceeded my most ambitious expectations. Why should she fail now? But since parents are destined to worry, there was no way I could lift this burden from my heart.

"Edith, I shall always be as near as the telephone. If anything goes wrong, simply lift the receiver or come home at once. Remember, most youngsters of your age are just entering high school. They have no responsibilities."

Bella was in tears, hugging Edith and unable to speak. As the plane carrying my beloved child disappeared into the sky, I felt that a part of me had died. I couldn't help feeling that my life had suddenly become empty, for not only was Edith my daughter and dearest companion, but I also realized that I had perhaps egotistically tried to fulfill myself through her accomplishments, a sin of which most parents are guilty to some extent.

As we drove home from the airport, Bella reminded me, "We still have David. Please restrain yourself from your genius-making so that he remains with us longer."

The press was determined to cover Edith's story at Michigan State. Before her departure, reporters called her long distance to plead for interviews when she arrived in Lansing. She reluctantly agreed.

Shortly after her arrival, The Detroit Free Press ran a story which said in part:

". . . are you, as some educators claim, the 'victim' of your father's concepts of 'total educational submersion'?"

"Now you are really away from home for the first time and you've caught a cold and you worry a bit about whether you'll be able to draw a straight line on the board if you have to teach freshman algebra."

"Will you sink or swim?"

"Right now, you seem to be paddling right along."

Worried, we called her.

"How are you doing, sweetheart?"

"Just fine, Dad."

"We read the story in the Free Press with apprehension."

"The exaggeration is in the best tradition of journalism, Dad."

Edith embarked on her career as a college instructor without fear. On the day of her first class, she confidently went to her room. One glance at the students convinced them that she meant business. Her youth was neither an asset nor a liability, since her deportment was consistent with her duties.

She blended into the huge university without fanfare, enjoying the comfort of relative anonymity. All requests for interviews had to be, by her own decision, cleared with the chairman of the mathematics department, who seldom granted them. While her phone was unlisted, Edith's social life was full and rich. She attended concerts, availed herself of campus cultural activities, had many friends of both sexes and successfully pursued her work in her dual capacity of instructor and graduate student.

At Christmas vacation after her first term there, I asked her how it felt to make a debut as a college instructor at her age.

"Well Daddy, at first I was kind of scared. Then in the privacy of my room, I calmly and objectively assessed the situation. I concluded I possess the knowledge and the students are here to learn. Age differences or other considerations are totally irrelevant. I simply entered the class in a business-like manner, at ease, and began my lecture."

154

"Have you encountered any problems at all related to your age?"

"Really nothing of consequence. A few of my students petitioned me to improve their grades, but soon realized how firm I was."

One day, following my lecture at a university, I was delighted to meet a transfer student from Michigan State University.

"Have you taken math at MSU?"

"Yes, I did."

"Who was your instructor?"

The student mentioned a name which I have forgotten.

"Well I know a young lady who is teaching mathematics there. Her name is Edith Stern. No relative of mine," I quickly added.

"Oh yes she's a tough cookie. My friend took her classes. Brother, is she demanding. No wonder her name is Stern."

"Is she really as young as the press reported?"

"Most likely not. How could a sixteen-year-old child reach such a level?" he answered.

"Well I guess you are right. The press cannot be trusted."

Once when she came home to visit, I asked Edith if she would like to meet with some of her former school friends. "Frankly, no. What do I have in common with them? Also meeting them would be embarrassing since some have just graduated from high school." Nevertheless, she inquired, "How are Michael, and Mary? Did Leon secure a scholarship? Do you know where Arnold moved to?"

The only childhood friend whom she has and meets occasionally when she comes home is Mark, who is Edith's age and who attended two grades with her. As I recall he was as bright as or brighter than she when they were in the second grade together. I worked with both of them during our field trips and found Mark no less receptive than Edith; in fact, in many instances his interest in the sciences impressed me very favorably. She was close to him when they were children, but the friendship ended when we moved to Indiana. After we returned to Florida they would occasionally meet. When she graduated from Florida Atlantic he was still in the tenth grade, although as an outstanding student attending honor classes. When meeting Mark, Edith nostalgically reminisces about the bygone days, but truthfully, they have little in common. When I suggested that we invite him to her graduation at Miami-Dade Junior College, she consented, but added, "Dad, the boy is so very young."

At Michigan State, Edith had many friends and she loves them. Some of them are single, others are married; some are exotic and others are regular American kids. Her friends include a Catholic priest, a nun, and several foreign exchange students — whose language and customs fascinate her. She once shared a suite with a Chinese girl from Taiwan who now is a biology professor and who has invited Edith to Taiwan to visit her. Her other roommate was a black girl from Alabama and earlier, other white American girls. One of her friends is a young man who had to interrupt his work on his doctorate when his wife became unexpectedly pregnant; he took a job in a small college in Michigan. Edith likes them both and frequently visited them on weekends. She shared her faculty office at Michigan with seven other instructors where they had a ball playing practical jokes on each other and celebrated the completion of a term with a bottle of champagne.

In many ways Edith is a typical member of her generation. Like other people her age, she is fun loving. She would laugh her head off at movies such as Twelve Chairs, clown playing baseball during a faculty picnic, and giggle carefreely reading Mad Magazine or a Playboy book of jokes. She loves exotic foods, sternly scolds a friend for not returning her science fiction books, unashamedly sheds a tear reading Love Story, cheerfully played in the snow with her fellow graduate students, and exchanged salty jokes. On weekends, she often visited with friends on their Ohio farm and then would ride all night on a bus back to Michigan.

Edith's clothing is very simple. In regards to dress, she points out that there are two considerations, aesthetics and the utilitarian aspects. So she buys inexpensive dresses, disregarding the fashion trends, "I shall not let anyone dictate to me what to wear," she declares. "These are the advantages of being a homo sapiens."

Once I attempted to discard her worn out sandals. She fiercely yelled, "Don't do it. I'm attached to my sandals." I protested that she had worn them for the past three years and that they looked atrocious. "I don't give a damn what others think," she shouted. "I love and wear them to my classes."

In her somewhat Spartan upbringing, Edith learned self-discipline and to subordinate emotions to logic, the basic ingredient of scientific objectivity. When pursuing a worthy objective, she has a single-minded dedication. She rejects comfort, expediency, or complacency. As to the power of mind over matter, she practices it so effectively that when she broke her foot, she did not seek medical attention until the next day after prodding by friends. When I found out about it, I asked Edith how she could neglect such an injury. "Well, I had very little pain. Besides I had exams to study for." The doctor, however, did not agree with her; in his opinion, she must have had a great deal of pain.

Similarly, Edith's dentist was astonished over the way she endured the pain caused by a mouthful of cavities. Edith claimed that she had no pain or discomfort, to which the dentist replied, "Impossible."

During the summer of 1969, Edith spent her vacation at home. In order to supplement her income she accepted a position with IBM. The Miami News reported in a headline, "IBM gets smart — hires human computer Edith." The story began with "That mechanical genius of the computers, IBM, is about to come eyeball to eyeball with its human counterpart, 16-year-old Edith Stern. The result may well be a standoff. At the very least, it will set the machine pulsating."

In order to comply with the law, Edith, a minor, had to obtain working papers from the local Board of Education, in order to render services as a scientist. To me, this was a magnificent triumph over the sickening mediocrity.

Edith is a seasoned traveler. As a student. she obtained fifty percent discount on her flights on a standby basis. Once, en route home from Michigan, she was bumped off in Cleveland where she spent a day and a half in the airport reading books, totally oblivious of the passing time. Finally, I called the airport and secured a seat for her.

"It really was comfortable. The airport is well heated. I had the opportunity to read without interference. There were many students at the counter, most of them trying to get home for Christmas. I felt they should have the priority. After all I am Jewish."

"But how about your parents worrying to death?"

"What was there to worry about? You knew the plane arrived safely in Cleveland."

"Couldn't you call us?" "I was reading and simply forgot," apologetically remarked Edith.

On another occasion, although suffering from chicken pox, she decided not to postpone her trip home. In spite of the rash on her face she was able to enter the plane. Then she spent almost the whole trip in the rest room in order to protect the passengers from the disease. Some women attempting to enter the comfort room became alarmed since it was constantly occupied. Finally, they summoned a stewardess who broke in. She screamed when she saw Edith, whose face and arms were covered with a bright red rash. The stewardess led her to a seat while the whole aisle was deserted.

I was at the airport waiting for her arrival. Since I had been unable to persuade her to enter a hospital in Michigan, I had arranged a room for her in a Miami Beach hospital.

"I shall not go to a hospital. Take me home."

"But you are sick and contagious."

"Daddy, I am awful homesick. Put me in isolation at home."

Soon David caught it. They had a fine time convalescing together.

When she came home from Michigan, Edith enjoyed frolicking with her family. During our frequent trips to the beach, our favorite retreat was a lifeguard's elevated stool. We climbed into it in the evening, deeply inhaling the fresh air, while gazing into the blue Atlantic. Edith explained to David "the mysteries of nature" and he in turn lectured her on marine life, a subject on which he has become somewhat of an expert. Like many other teenagers, Edith liked to swim far from the shore. When I called her to come back she flashed me a peace sign and yelled, "I am safe. I swim well."

At home, Edith, like other sisters, teased her brother, and sometimes it climaxed in a good-natured fight. On other occasions, she challenged him to a bicycle race around the lake, often beating him. She would cleverly con him in a game of Monopoly, but she invariably lost to him in chess.

Upon her return home, she immediately would remove her many awards and diplomas from the wall — to the chagrin of her parents. She once attempted to destroy her honorary diploma from North Miami High School. "Apparently the Board of Education felt guilty for the indignities to which we were subjected when you fought for my release from junior high school. Thus, to appease us, they awarded me this honorary diploma. What a farce. What stupidity."

Edith remains an avid reader. Her first trip while on vacation was to the book store in search for "gems." Her library was catalogued and entrusted to David's loving care. During one summer, she left her stereo, records, and some books with a girl friend in Michigan. The girl was evicted and Edith's priceless possesions disappeared. She never recovered her things and was bitter about it.

During her visits, she liked to tease me. Once she said, "Dad, I will give you two days to define topology intelligently." Topology is one of her specialties.

"I cannot even comprehend what it is. The nearest I can come to it is topography." I know practically nothing about mathematics.

"Very funny," Edith responded.

"That is really the truth. Had you studied medicine, law, sociology, psychology, or almost any other field, I could at least follow your progress. But, of all the subjects you had to choose theoretical mathematics so as to deliberately keep me out."

"One must conquer the unconquerable, otherwise there would be no challenge. Remember, a teacher once told me that I would never master mathematics. This is a challenge. It was also important for me to cut the umbilical cord from you. Otherwise, perhaps I would be studying medicine today. Anyway I might try for an M.D. after I obtain my Ph.D. in math."

Edith is quite interested in world affairs and her dedication to the ideals of social justice are deeply ingrained. She was opposed to war and violence and passionately campaigned for Eugene McCarthy in the 1968 presidential primaries. In fact, she utilized her press interviews and T.V. appearances to promote him.

Once during a radio appearance Edith was asked to comment on the Middle East crisis. "As a Jew, I'm in sympathy and in full accord with the heroic stuggle of Israel to stay alive in the face of formidable adversaries dedicated to her destruction. But I'm also fully cognizant of the plight of Arab refugees who are so mercilessly being exploited by the Arab states. Thus any settlement in the Middle East will have to provide financial means to compensate these unfortunate ones."

The interviewer, who was pro-Israel, interrupted, "Isn't it true that the Arab states have persecuted the Jewish inhabitants, confiscated their wealth, and forced them to flee for their lives?"

"That might be so, but in my judgment two wrongs do not constitute a right, no more than the North Vietnamese cruelties justified My Lai."

Edith can also have a good time pursuing causes. One day she called home from Michigan, and since she sounded hoarse, I asked her if she had a cold. "No Dad," she replied. "I just returned from the state capital. We were demonstrating for the liberalization of abortion laws. It is a good cause and a lot of fun to scream and to clear one's lungs out on a chilly spring day."

"I can hear some giggling in your room. Who's there with you?"

"It is Sister Anna. She just arrived from the convent to receive her Ph.D. She will sleep over with me."

"Does she approve of your views on abortion?"

"Of course," Edith said. "She's liberal."

Religion plays an important part in her life, but it is religion based on intellectual perception, not emotional ritualism. Man can only love and serve God through his relationship to other human beings. There is no way to appease God through prayer or supplication. Religion must be militant. Social justice is what counts. God's battles are to be fought in Mississippi rather than in ornate temples and cathedrals. The rest is deception and self-perpetuation for the sake of comfort and pleasure.

Edith likes to quote the philosopher, Martin Buber:

"The annihilation of six million Jews is a great tragedy, but even greater is the fact that the whole Christian world stood by indifferent while this unparalleled act of genocide was perpetrated."

An interviewer once asked, "Edith, what are the alternatives?"

"Struggle, involvement, purpose in life, establishment of ethical values."

"Did you say restoration or establishment of moral values?"

"I was unequivocal. I said establishment of moral values. Mankind has been always decadent as far as one can trace human history. However in an age of military and scientific sophistication, it becomes a matter of life or death. We shall learn to live together or perish." Edith had made the same statement when she was five years old.

In 1970 Edith was awarded her master's degree in theoretical mathematics from MSU. That summer she worked at Eastern Airlines in the computer department to replenish her depleted funds. Once I visited her at Eastern headquarters. She met me at the security booth, obtained a pass for me, and then led me through a a labyrinth of halls into her spacious office. On her desk were a few pieces of paper and a pencil. She casually scribbled some notes and I asked her if that was all that she did. "Indeed," she replied, "There is not much challenge here. I'm simply relaxing in boredom. I really don't know why they pay me so much money."

Later, I spoke to the manager of the computer science division, who assured me that Edith provided a very complex service to the company, and as a temporarily employed scientist she was greatly underpaid. "I wish you could persuade her to accept a steady position. Her income would double and she and her family would obtain flight privileges. Then, she could take a leave of absence and continue her studies." I told him that she would never interrupt her studies. Then I asked how she related to her co-workers, all of whom were much older. "Quite well. No problems at all. They are all fond of her." Before she returned to Michigan, the division gave her a send-off party.

Edith, who has fulfilled at eighteen almost all requirements leading to a Ph.D. in theoretical mathematics, could have had her doctorate earlier if she had obtained a fellowship which would have enabled her to take more courses. This, however, she adamantly refused to do, to the chagrin of her family.

"I regard a grant as totally unethical, inasmuch as the recipient renders no service in return for the money." Then she added in a less pensive mood, "Besides, teaching gives me such great satisfaction."

There are critics still fixed in their prejudices who argue that I have victimized Edith with my educational program. While they are willing to admit that she is academically superior, they believe that since her intellect has been developed, she must be deficient in some other aspect such as personality, emotional maturity, or social relationships. They find it difficult to accept that she is a well-rounded, happy person.

It is true that Edith possesses an insatiable desire for learning which I hope will never end. Similarly, she adheres to high standards of ethics and personal integrity and has a passionate commitment to the ideals of social justice.

But it is also true that she is always cheerful. She once said, "I really have not found anyone as happy as I am. I attain effortlessly all the goals which I have set for myself."

Her emotional stability is remarkable. She easily and readily adapts to any environment whether it is the university, IBM or Eastern Airlines. To the best of my knowledge Edith has never resorted to drugs and she suffers from no frustrations. At Michigan State, she abruptly stopped smoking when told her lungs were congested.

A psychology professor once asked me about her sex life. I replied, "I really don't know about it. No parent of an unmarried daughter can ask such a question unless she chooses to discuss it. If she is promiscuous, she becomes pregnant and it becomes obvious. None of this is true in Edith's case."

I have been accused of casting her in my own mold. While we share many common values, we certainly do not have an identity of views. She has chosen a field of study which is so remote from my own that I do not understand the nature of her research.

She successfully relates to others as witnessed by meaningful social ties. Her roommates have always respected her highly, and Edith was quite successful as a teacher. She is deeply attached to her parents and her brother. When we had a financial crisis, she enlisted the aid of a co-signer and borrowed a thousand dollars for us from the university credit union.

In spite of frequent predictions to the contrary by educators, Edith, a product of the Total Educational Submersion method, is a cheerful and well-functioning, happy individual.

CHAPTER 15

Do We Really Care to Improve Education?

In pursuing my educational program, I have continually struggled with the schools, listening while teachers and principals charged that Edith and David were unintelligent and uninspired, watching as my children attended school year after year, hopelessly bored by the mediocre pace and lack of challenge. I can draw one conclusion only: our school system is flagrantly inadequate.

My work with David and Edith has been in many ways the antithesis of what they encountered in school. I worked with them on individual levels, guiding, probing, urging them on to new heights. From their early infancy, I stressed the importance and significance of education and knowledge. When they had questions, I helped them find answers; when they were interested in something, I helped them to explore it. I fear that if I had been indoctrinated in a teachers' college their accomplishments would have been quite meager. Fortunately, I was free from the inhibitions and dogmas which flourish in the schools and often retard, rather than promote, the educational process. It is against this background that I sincerely hope that my children's experiences and achievements will become a significant aspect of the educational debate in this country.

One cannot deny that our educational system at best fails to meet the challenges of our dynamic, industrial society. The failure appears to be even greater for the exciting promises of tomorrow. In our affluent society teaching, this very noble profession, is financially unrewarding and often commands very little status or respect. In many cases, teacher education attracts the least promising applicants, frequently including those who have failed to meet the higher standards of admission required by the other colleges and branches of the universities. Talented young men and women, with the exception of some very dedicated ones, prefer other professions where social prestige, remuneration, and the opportunity for advancement are much higher. In teacher colleges, the students are taught methodology often to the detriment of subject matter. Thus, we frequently end up with teachers who have very little knowledge in the content area which they are supposed to teach.

Many schools are overcrowded with 50 to 60 students per teacher. In some places, school discipline is totally lacking. Quite often teaching requires an act of personal courage in the face of physical danger. The school curriculum is frequently out of date and, as a result, out of step with the requirements of an industrial society. Athletic activites usually obtain more recognition and a larger share of the appropriation than academic ones. Parental involvement through the P.T.A. is superficial with a strong emphasis on trivia, parties, outings, and parades.

Boards of education, under whose direct jurisdiction the schools are placed, are often comprised of poorly educated, but influential people, who at times retard the school's progress rather than help it. The nearly pathological fear of federal intervention had repeatedly hampered much needed financial assistance, while many communities, in their short-sighted desire to prevent greater taxation, defeat bond issues needed to aid education.

I would seem that a prime goal of American education is to preserve the status quo, yet such preservation is the greatest deterrent to our progress. Many school administrators at all levels frown upon innovation, which they feel challenges their competence, compels them to adapt themselves to a new set of circumstances, and thus undermines their security. The bastion of this opposition is centered in the teachers' colleges whose very survival would be placed in jeopardy if the anachronistic and inefficient curriculum and methodology were discarded.

Where improvements and innovations do take place, it is often in ways which miss the main point of the problem in education. It is analogous to organized religion which in searching for magnitude and splendor, builds elaborate temples and cathedrals, losing sight of the central theme -- God, himself. Similarly, our schools have grown in size and complexity while the quality of education has declined rapidly. The ancient Talmudic sages maintained, and justly so, that, "The only thing that counts in education is the desire to learn and the dedication and competence of the teacher."

Thus, Edith and David's education at home was not with fancy gadgets and expensive instructional aids; rather their school was the world. Everyday objects and events provided the basis for exciting learning experiences, the key being a successful use of the sights and sounds which surrounded them. The schools, however, often act as though one more gadget or one more teaching aid will provide satisfactory substitutes for the desire to learn and the quality of the teacher.

What can we as parents and citizens do to improve education? As parents we can broaden our children's cultural horizons, introduce them to research, debate with them, discuss the events of the day, and in general set a worthy example. This will require that we spend time with them in intellectual activities, working to develop their brains as they develop their muscles. Remember that no more than ten to fifteen percent of the intellectual capacity of the human brain is being developed -- the rest is literally being wasted. It would be beneficial also to curb their habitual and often indiscriminate television viewing -- particularly since so much of television programing is worthless trivia, often glorifying crime. Of course, curbing television viewing may require parents to overcome their own addiction to T.V.

As citizens, we can insist that the establishment improve education. I urge everyone to insist on quality education which is responsive to the needs and intellectual growth of the child. Since the people pay for the schools, they have every right to demand that the schools do an excellent job, that the schools should be accountable just as a business should be. However, I have been waging such a fight for many years with a striking lack of success. As reported in previous chapters, I have lectured across the nation and in Europe, and made statements to the press, discussed education with local, state, and national educational administrators, and sought to secure funds to demonstrate how education can be improved, however my efforts have been militantly opposed by school authorities.

My last such effort began in the fall of 1970 when, as I was casually glancing through the pages of the *Miami Herald*, an unusual notice attracted my attention. The Florida Senate Committee on Primary and Secondary Education was scheduled to conduct a public hearing aimed at the "improvement of the quality of education." Although my numerous proposals for changes in the school curriculum and methodology which had been directed to the State Department of Education and the various boards of education had been totally ignored in the past, I felt it was my duty again to expose the inadequacies of public education and to propose changes based upon my successfully tested methods.

The climate in Florida seemed better for change than ever before. In particular, I was gratified by the changes which had occured in the political situation in the state. A young, dynamic governor had just been elected and his proposed sweeping fiscal reforms impressed me. Furthermore, an influx of youthful, energetic, and generally well-educated people was now in both houses of the state legislature and even a few such young people had secured seats in the cabinet. I hoped that these changes heralded a new era for Florida's outdated school system.

The cold, if not outright hostile, treatment given to me by the assistant school superintendent when I inquired about the details of the hearing did not dampen my enthusiasm. As one who had acquired the distinction of being a resented person by the school establishment, I was fully aware that my presence at the hearing would be less than welcome.

The day of the hearing arrived and the meeting was called to order. Soon it became apparent that the speakers at the hearing were preoccupied with concerns other than the quality of education. In spite of the obvious failures of the public school system, failures which place the very survival of society in jeopardy, not one speaker addressed himself to the issue at hand. As though totally oblivious of the crisis and the purpose of the hearing, the speakers could have been talking at a General Motors and United Auto Workers contract bargaining session or at a city commission meeting dealing with garbage disposal. One speaker, representing a teachers' union, requested collective bargaining rights. Another, on behalf of a rival union, demanded equal representation. An official spoke about pension funds.

Finally, I took the floor. "Gentlemen, I hope that you share my shock. These hearings were meant to deal with the improvement of education at a time of crisis, yet none of the speakers who have appeared here, people who have one hand in the taxpayers' pocket, have addressed themselves to the issue at hand. These are the very people whose lack of competence contributes to the failures of our school system and whose income is derived from school taxes.

"It is indeed tragic that I, of all the speakers, the only one who never sought a penny for my efforts, address myself to the issue and submit proposals for a dynamic school system based on a successfully tested educational method. As legislators, parents, and taxpayers, I hope that you will in your wisdom support and implement my proposals. I stand ready to serve you in any capacity."

When the hearings were over, one of the senators approached me. "Don't think that we turn a deaf ear to you. We visit schools and we are aware of their crisis, and above all we are determined to meet it. I for one, am interested in your proposals. Let's get together."

I was in a joyful mood as my tiny Volkswagen sped along at the maximum speed limit on the way to see the senator. Perhaps now, I felt, after years of bitter struggle, my long cherished dream will be fulfilled. Times are changing; the torch is passing from the old worn out generation to the young impatient one. Cliches are making way for new concepts and ideas.

Just a week before, I had been warmly received at Nova University, a new dynamic graduate school in Broward County. After my lecture to the Behavioral Science faculty and graduate students, my host, Dr. John Flynn, asked how many of the people present would entrust their children to me. Almost everyone raised a hand. This, I felt, was not merely courtesy, but rather an emphatic vote of confidence. Furthermore, there was no bitter opposition on the part of the professional educators as I had been accustomed to encounter at many universities. Thus, I was hopeful that Nova would be willing to cooperate with me in demonstrating my educational methods.

The meeting with the senator was very cordial and informative. He kindly assured me that my proposals were sound and advised me that there would be $1,200,000 available that year for research and development in education in Florida. He said that in his judgment, no project had more merit than the demonstration school which I had proposed. I explained to him my frustrations with the school administrators in the state, that I was convinced that the State Department of Education was determined to preserve the status quo at any price, and that it would make every effort to kill my proposal. "In their judgment," I said "there is nothing wrong with the school system." The senator, however, felt that times had changed and that the people were no longer tolerating complacency and incompetence. Encouraged, I thanked him and departed.

As I expected, Dr. Flynn, on behalf of Nova University, consented to undertake the scientific evaluation and to provide assistance in the implementation of my proposed school. Similarly, the administrator of the Nova public school complex adjacent to Nova University expressed his delight in my program and offered to house my school. Shortly afterwards, I sent a proposal to the State Department of Education.

Weeks went by and I did not receive even so much as an acknowledgment of my proposals. Finally, a UPI story headlined, "Plan to Rate Pupil Learning Called OK for 19th Century," reported on the disposition of $1,200,000. It had been designated for research and development. The money was to be used to measure how well students learn. In the article, the Chairman of the House Appropriations Committee was quoted, "They are archaic in their view. Eight percent of the things they are measuring are not how well somebody learns, but things like how many teachers per student, how many square feet, toilet facilities."

In my judgment, this perfidious act bordered on criminal conspiracy. Unable to restrain my indignation, I called the State Department of Education and after a frustrated search for the superintendent, a bureaucrat picked up the receiver, "Whatever happened to my proposals for a demonstration school?" I inquired.

"They were unanimously rejected," the official replied nonchalantly.

"On what grounds?"

"It was felt that they would destroy the moral fiber of our youth."

(Perhaps this phrase was coined earlier by the former Commissioner of Education of the State of Florida, Mr. Christian. For this is how he appraised my proposals subsequent to my lecture at the Florida State Cabinet meeting on July 17, 1973.

As one could expect Mr. Christian's claim to competence as a educator was based on his earlier career of a college athlete and later coach.

Yes, as for his preoccupation with morality, it's noteworthy that he had to part soon after with his lofty position because of a conviction charging him with acceptance of bribes and kickbacks in the performance of his duties and later served a jail sentence for income tax evasion. For the record, Mr. Christian at the time of this writing blissfully receives a pension of $25,000 per annum for his "services to the State.")

"You can't be serious?"

"Indeed I am. But more importantly, we are quite pleased with the high standards of public education in Florida and see no need to reform it."

Choked with tears, I terminated this futile conversation.

That evening, Edith called from Michigan: "Have you heard yet about your proposals, Dad?"

"They were rejected, my child."

"How will the $1,200,000 of research funds be spent?"

"According to UPI, to study how well students learn, a plan which according to the article is obsolete before it ever gets off the drawing board."

"Dad, it is common knowledge that our schools fail miserably, Why do they spend money to study it? What a waste?"

"Prepare yourself for another shock, Edith. Eight percent of these funds or about $100,000 will be designated to study such things as the ratio of students to toilets."

"Apart from the fact that such a study is totally irrelevant to the school crisis, I would compute it for a fee of $50 or less. Better yet, I would do it for nothing if someone will convince me that such information will advance the cause of education," replied Edith.

Thus once more my efforts to improve education were cynically defeated.

The main part of the proposals is included in a slightly edited form. It clearly and succinctly states the total educational submersion method, its philosophy and objectives.

OVERVIEW

"Total Educational Submersion" refers to a method of education in which the student is an integral part of the instructional program. A brief synopsis of the method is provided by the following excerpts of a letter dated January 13, 1971, written to Mr. William Cecil Golden, Associate Commissioner by Dr. John M. Flynn, Associate Professor, Nova University:

"His (Stern's) approach to education has two logical components which probably should be considered separately. One is his

169

methodology and the other is his priority or value structure about what should and should not be included in the curriculum. People who disagree with the content of this latter component should not let it interfere with objectively examining his teaching methods.

"The methodology is basically an individualized instruction approach — one which takes the child where it finds him, capitalizes on the child's interests, and uses as instructional materials both books and the environment. In many respects, his method is not new; it resembles Dewey's in some ways and certainly parallels many modern trends such as individualized instruction, relevance of learning, and to some extent, contingency management and discovery learning. On the other hand, I believe that it incorporates a flexibility which is not often present in other current approaches. For example, the method is quite opportunistic in capitalizing on the child's interest.

"Stern's methods, of course, have not been tried on a large scale. With his own children as well as his camp school students he was able to give a lot of individualized attention, which would not, of course, be easily possible in a school situation as it is presently structured. He is quite realistic about this limitation, but nevertheless believes that his methods can appreciably improve education. I tend to agree with him on this point."

The proposed project offers a contrast to both traditional educational methods and to other current innovative approaches. The ills of traditional practices have been berated frequently and only brief mention will be made of them here. As is well known, our schools – both in Florida and across the nation – are failing to meet the needs of society: in far too many schools, the curriculum is irrelevant to life, the pedagogical approaches are from another era, and the teachers themselves are poorly trained and often inept.

Educational leaders, of course, agree that change is needed in our schools; they disagree, however, on what change should be. Approaches include individualized instruction, modular learning units, behavioral objectives, increased use of technological devices, contingency management, programmed learning materials, staff differentiation, and reorganization of subject matter.

The main thrust of the new educational approaches tends to center on individualized instruction and behavioral objectives. Individualized instruction is also at the center of the project proposed in this document,

170

but behavioral objectives tend to be the antithesis of the total educational submersion approach. While behavioral objectives can be beneficial for some purposes, they are artificial and can be detrimental to the educational process. The proposed project is in no way a reaction to behavioral objectives, per se, but behavioral objectives clearly focus on a highly structured approach, as contrasted with the pragmatism and spontaneity of this project. Instead of leading children through pre-set sequences of objectives, total educational submersion will take the interests of the children and will build the instruction around those interests. Where the former approach is somewhat rigid and sterile (even though it is in the name of individualized instruction), the latter is flexible and natural. It makes the educational process relevant to both the students and the world, capitalizing on the daily interplay between the child and his environment. Much of the problem of motivation can disappear in this approach, for what the child is interested in is also what he is learning about.

Total educational submersion, as the name implies, makes education synonymous with life. It utilizes community resources, topical issues, and everyday events. Thus it is extremely relevant and meaningful to the students.

The proposed project has as its overall objectives the following:

To make school more relevant and meaningful; to develop a well informed person capable of functioning in our dynamic society; to stimulate intellectual growth, creativity, development of innate talents; to motivate to the fullest potential children to become enlightened, alert, responsible citizens dedicated to ideals of social justice; to strengthen the moral fabric; to prepare the academic minded for further studies; and to improve vocational training while restoring its dignity.

PROCEDURES

The salient points of the proposed total educational submersion project are detailed below.

General Methodology

1. Optimum Use of Existing Community Resources

Boredom and stagnation caused by the isolation of classroom experiences often deter students in their progress. Every community possesses a rich reservoir of facilities, ranging from hospitals, laboratories, courts, factories, etc. where learning becomes a living experience, stimulating the urge for discovery. Vocational facilities will overcome the stigma associated with vocational training. Accessibility to the prime sources of learning in the native setting practiced by experts in their respective fields, will enhance the quality, inspire enthusiasm toward learning and bridge the gap between school and the world at large, between theory and practice.

2. Community Involvement

Racial polarization, generation gap, indifference, and "virtue of non-volvement" (noli me tangere) pose perhaps the greatest threats to the survival of our society. The great social drama — struggle for social justice, conquest and eradication of hunger, disease and prejudice — must be a vital part of the curriculum. Students' active participation through educational processes as well as identification with community life lead to development of civic pride which is imperative to growth.

3. Teaching Technique Based on Diaglogue

Perhaps one of the greatest shortcomings of the school system has been its catastrophic reliance on the monologue-lecture. This unilateral process prevents the student from debating an issue and arriving at an intelligent conclusion. Furthermore, lack of qualified teachers and well written books diminishes the quality of learning. Students' reliance on textbooks, class-notes, and a rigid bureaucratic school routine prevents their independent, creative research.

Under the proposed project, learning will be regarded as a multilateral spontaneous process. Dialogue, debate and discussion from the earliest age will enhance judicious judgment, development of personality, poise, maturity, and linguistic facility.

Less reliance on textbooks and the absence of lecture notes will encourage independent library research.

4. Grades Abolished

A wholesome class atmosphere provides a sufficient incentive for learning — arts gratia artis. Informality and the ability of the teacher to relate constitute the greatest asset. As some students cope more successfully with tests, irrespective of their knowledge, than others, it is impossible to evaluate progress accurately with them. This makes the use of tests counterproductive.

5. Broad Use of Television

Television can be an important adjunct to school if it is properly employed. Recent surveys revealed that high school students spend four to six hours daily watching television. The more time they devote to it the less successful they are in school. For the purpose of the study, the programs watched were non-educational such as quiz shows, Westerns, comedies, soap operas, etc.

In the proposed school, instructors would use the educational tools, radio or television, i.e., documentary films, news broadcasts, and the educational channels.

6. Growth of Students at Own Pace

Rigid conformity to chronological barriers is at best capricious, arbitrary, and at times harmful. Each child should be encouraged to grow mentally at his own pace.

7. School Activities to Last Ten Hours, Six Days a Week

In order to secure a wholesome atmosphere, conductive to learning and growth, the joy of discovery would replace the boredom of a compulsory class attendance. Daily trips by buses manned by highly motivated instructors would provide a productive synthesis of recreation and in-depth learning. This coupled with a lack of home assignments would be welcomed by parents as well as students. Daily field trips are basic to the successful implementation of the method.

CURRICULUM

1. Area Studies in Place of Subject Studies

Area studies aimed at breaking down artificial barriers and duplication make the learning process more effective, meaningful and enjoyable. A capable, ingenious teacher with a wide background of reading can convey to the students with much greater effect such historical facts as Napoleon's defeat in Russia by having them read that description in a good translation of Tolstoi's *War and Peace.* The industrial revolution in England is made real and vivid in several of Dicken's novels or the condition of Italian city-states is dramatically presented in Shakespeare's *Romeo and Juliet;* students would also get the benefit of the rich and beautiful English language. With similar ingenuity the teacher can

173

provocatively lead the students from physics to chemistry, biology to anatomy, and so on.

2. Greater Student Freedom in Decision Making

Compulsion stunts a child's mental growth. Rigid curricula choke off students' spontaneous enthusiasm for learning. Compulsory studies related to the student's preferred and chosen field bring out his resentment or inability to understand and thus interferes with his intellectual progress. Students should have a greater choice in selecting their areas of study.

The maturity of students is being underestimated. A strong responsible student government at all levels of education represents a first experience in democracy. Peer approval or disapproval is an essential factor in progress and the maintenance of harmonious relationships in class; it helps the teacher to relate better to the students and enhances esprit de corps.

3. Heavy Emphasis on Current Events

In this fast moving world with events continually shaping our destiny and with rapid transportation shrinking the world dramatically, the study of current events is essential. No less than 1½ hour per day should be devoted to it in conjunction with the area study. Students should read the *New York Times* daily from the age of about 11 to grasp the full awareness of the great dramas (e.g., student dissent, international crises) paramount to the formulation of ideas, judgments and identification.

4. Heavy Emphasis on Ecology

Pollution of every conceivable kind threatens the very survival of the world's population. The study of ecology can inspire dedication to fight this threat on a personal level. Additionally, ecology provides an excellent educational tool for the study of science and humanities, in their broadest spectrum. Full awareness and active involvement in the battle must require highest priority. Daily field trips are imperative.

5. Foreign Language Study at the Age of Four

The pre-school formative period presents an ideal opportunity for study of a second language. Children born in Switzerland are bi-lingual. In many cases fluency in three languages was common among three and

174

four year old Jewish children in Poland (Polish, Hebrew, Yiddish). The population composition of South Florida makes bilingualism desirable and easily attainable (Spanish).

6. Sex Education at the Age of Four

Frank and accurate treatment of sex education is essential to normal growth and prevents frustration, fears, vulgarity, and mis-information. Parental inability to explain coupled with reluctance to face the problem pose difficulty to a youngster in the early age of discovery.

7. Home Economics Revised

Home economics as currently taught in our public schools must be drastically revised. They should be not compulsory, but elective courses, because training at home in these matters is sometimes good and sometimes non-existent. Exorbitant funds for expensive kitchen and laundry equipment would better be spent on books. Practical home economics courses, if offered, should be taught with the simplest and most basic tools, to prepare students, both boys and girls, for emergencies. Emphasis should be placed on health, first aid, nutrition and the economics of consumption.

8. Physical Education

The hero worship and exaggerated partisanship associated with inter-scholastic, competitive athletics negate educational objectives. Physical Education should stress mass participation, and calisthenics to develop the body in harmony with mental growth. The goal is "a healthy mind in a healthy body."

ENROLLMENT AND REGULATIONS

1. Student Enrollment from the Age of Three

The process of education under ideal conditions should commence at birth and cease only at death. Psychological studies strengthen my thesis that the learning capacity of pre-school children is enormous. While learning should begin as early as possible, at the age of three children display insatiable intellectual curiosity and readiness to learn, and they are old enough to be taken care of easily at school.

175

2. A Minimum of Conformity and Regulation

A productive, uninhibited, learning climate can best be secured through informality, free expression, and spontaneity. The learning process can only be joyful, meaningful and productive when associated with total freedom. Initiative should not be curbed by stagnant regimentation and conformity. Let all the flowers blossom. A teacher should be a friend and confidant to guide, inspire, challenge, and provoke the priceless gift of restless inquiry. There should be as complete physical mobility within the school compound as there should be mental mobility in a freedom to disagree with the teacher without fear of reprisals. At times, within limits, an outlet for suppressed hostility should be permitted. Full development of personality, the widening of cultural horizons, the ability to function effectively in interdependence with society must be fostered in complete freedom, as to dress and hair style.

3. The Student Body

Size should be limited to 150 to 200 students; heterogeneous group with members of ethnic minorities essential, as part of the environmental factors.

Parental consent through a public relations educational campaign will be secured.

INSTRUCTIONAL STAFF

1. Instructional Staff, Graduates of Liberal Arts or Science Colleges Only

The teachers signify a major factor in the failure of our public school system. Unfortunately college curriculum is frequently totally irrelevant to the profession. The requirements are extremely low. Graduates often enter the teaching profession because they are unable to meet requirements of the other departments of college. Many teachers are poorly prepared, unable to inspire the student and lack the in-depth knowledge in the specific field. The gifted teacher is often unable to be innovative as any departure from the usual is frowned upon. Teachers in my project should be young, dedicated, well educated, willing to share and to learn from the students. They should be totally unrestricted in decorum, capable of utilizing every opportunity for teaching through unorthodox, pragmatic means. They should maintain an atmosphere of mutual respect based on a symbiosis with the student. They will be given twelve weeks of intensive training in the total education submersion method.

176

2. Personnel Involved in Project.

1. Coordinator.
2. Highly motivated instructors to be trained by Stern.
3. Secretary.
4. Bus drivers -- instructors.

EVALUATION

Nova University has agreed to evaluate the proposed project, throughly and objectively. An evaluation team comprised of two behavioral scientists and several Ph.D. candidates in behavioral sciences will conduct the evaluation. Dr. John M. Flynn, will lead the team.

Nova University has won acclaim in spite of its short existence as an outstanding institution of higher learning. Its contribution in behavioral sciences and commitment to behavioral research qualifies it uniquely. Nova's computer facilities and competence in statistics will enhance the validity of the scientific evaluation.

CHAPTER 16

The Head Start Program –
A Footnote to American History

In the spring of 1974, I was commissioned by the Child Development Service Bureau of H.E.W. to conduct a study of the Head Start Program. The authorities at the Department of Health, Education and Welfare had read my book, *The Making of a Genius,* and became intensely interested in my Total Educational Submersion Method, especially as it related to the early intellectual development of children.

Thus I embarked on this very significant assignment, summoning my best faculties, fully aware that my recommendations might bring a profound change in the structure of this most vital sector of the war on poverty. Likewise, I was eager to demonstrate the validity of my educational theories which emphasize the benefits of an early education.

My study took me to every classroom within the jurisdiction of the program – notwithstanding the warnings that the "roads are at times impassable" and a trip to the inner city might pose a threat to my life. I spoke to tens of thousands of children, teachers and administrators. In each instance, I conducted model classes, concluding the visit with a staff conference.

To my satisfaction, parents who were often maligned by the critics of the program expressed genuine interest in their children's progress, as well as a compelling desire to improve their own skills. At my press and television interviews, as well as at meetings with school officials, religious and community leaders, I stressed strongly the need for assistance in the form of volunteers, transportation and housing.

Surprisingly enough, the response was favorable. Lengthy newspaper stories following my visits brought a generous outpouring of clothing, blankets and food supplies to augment the children's nutritional needs and for better wearing apparel.

The study revealed that minority and disadvantaged children, in particular, are handicapped at an early age because of their environment and upbringing. Their education is neglected at home, adequate schooling is unavailable to them and the community offers little motivation or inducement for scholastic or academic success.

I reached the conclusion that the Total Educational Submersion Method can be highly effective with children of all races, creeds, colors, ethnic backgrounds or any social and economic status.

By utilizing the methods that I used with Edith and David, I knew that I could achieve quicker and better results with poverty stricken, educationally floundering ghetto children than the finest nursery schools available. For the most part, existing nursery and kindergarten schools are based on traditional, rigid, white middle-class cultural and educational standards.

The Office of Economic Opportunity accepted my proposals and I was commissioned to recommend improvements in the Head Start Program.

I delved deeply into its philosophy, its objectives, its principles and the operation of the government's multi-million dollar project. Much money, I found, had been misspent. But, on the whole, Head Start served a useful function in helping impoverished, neglected children get an early educational start in life, a start that might help them compete with more advanced children at a later date.

Among my recommendations, which I sincerely hope, for the sake of the children and their parents will be adopted, are the enrollment of children at the earliest possible age, even at the very early ages of one or two. I urged that classical music be used extensively in the total educational process, just as I did with Edith, starting when she was less than a week old, to have the students listen to the best music. Further, I advocated a closer interaction between parents, students and teachers and more stress placed on the development of verbal skills through dialogue and interaction between teacher and student. Of course, greater utilization of field trips is essential, just as it was in the case of my children. Indeed, the Head Start program can help create intelligent, well-adjusted, emotionally secure, highly motivated children who will value schooling and what it can bring to them in the future. Without motivation, children are doomed to fail. But I found in visiting the children in the Head Start Programs, that many are malnourished coming from poverty-stricken homes, with parents who lack the knowledge or opportunity to provide them with proper meals, who lack books or other educational materials in their homes, and who follow the pattern of least resistance, unable to see that an education may well prove the only sound way that their children can begin to climb the economic ladder and leave their own unfortunate life pattern of poverty and academic neglect.

The full report, as submitted to the Department of Health, Education and Welfare on July 10, 1974 follows:

A STUDY OF HEAD START PROGRAMS AND PROPOSALS FOR IMPROVEMENT OF ITS EDUCATION COMPONENT

One undergoes a most moving experience while visiting Head Start Centers during the lunch period. Unlike the bedlam which accompanies mealtime in a white middle class family where children have to be scolded to conduct themselves properly, at the Head Start Center, a serene awesome calmness prevails. There is dignity and decorum. Children wait patiently for their meal to be served, and with a truly remarkable skill, exhibiting dexterity and fine motor ability, gracefully handle the silver. One can well understand why it is so. Mealtime is the most important event of the day. It satisfies the children's physiological craving for food. Perhaps this is the only nutritious meal these children will have in the course of the day. When you are unable to obtain any response from a shy child, the reference to the meal will definitely produce some kind of remark, such as "I had bread, cereal, etc." It is quite clear to the most insensitive observer the tremendous significance which the children attach to the meal. This message is vivid and clear.

Children's yearning for learning and spiritual nourishment is equally essential to their development, a message which few of us have learned to decode or care to.

The titanic struggle of the oppressed minorities, chiefly black, for social and economic equality was enormously enhanced by the historical 1954 school desegregation ruling of the U.S. Supreme Court, monumentally augmented by the Landmark Civil Rights Act of 1964. This historical event, whose impact cannot be yet fully comprehended,

180

brought about the most profound changes (to be sure not without turmoil) to the American society. The changes are unprecedented as to their depth and scope in the annals of man. As a result, the role of governmental agencies, federal, state and city, has changed. No longer are they indifferent to the plight of the minorities, but to the contrary, armed with effective laws, these agencies protect minorities against discrimination, as it were, to compensate for the past abuses, by means of generous grants, quota requirements, in a sincere effort to launch a mass assault on poverty, prejudice and ignorance. (This is not to suggest that prejudice can be easily eradicated from the hearts of man.) No longer are members of minorities denied the dignity of public facilities, eligibility to jobs, admission to universities.

It is against this background that the magnificent coalition of progressive forces, nourished by a sympathetic government under the banner of the struggle for civil rights, accomplished this incredible metamorphosis, by peaceful means. Henceforth, the battle has to be conducted for social justice, a battle which must be aimed at uplifting the huge masses of people towards their integration into the mainstream of American society, with its enormous potentials during this stormy tide of rising expectations. The problem is no longer how to secure admission for a black person to a white restaurant, as this is guaranteed by law, but how to enable him to earn the necessary funds for the meal. No longer will there be a traumatic experience of a black student who is denied admission to a white university, (a conflict which once caused one of the greatest constitutional crises in American history resulting in a confrontation between a U. S. President and a governor), but rather how to find competent applicants for university admission, faculty positions and the many generous employment opportunities which opened up for minorities. The only way that this mass socioeconomic transformation towards a better and more gratifying life can be accomplished is through education. A gigantic assault on poverty with its ugly residue must begin with the infant.

Extensive research conducted by Bruner, Piaget, Stern, Hunt, Caldwell, Bloom and many other scientists strongly supports the belief that mental development commences at birth.

This report is based on Head Start Programs visited. Since the centers studied constitute an all black student enrollment (with the exception of one branch in St. Petersburg and a few in Dade County), this study deals with a group of children which is homogeneous in its racial and socioeconomic composition.

Although I have been commissioned "to recommend approaches for improving the quality of the Head Start Education component," I regard all of the Head Start components to be so intricately interwoven that it is impossible to analyze one component without considering the symbiotic relationship with the other components.

Dr. Arthur R. Jensen in the opening line of his 1969 *Harvard Educational Review* article states "Compensatory education has been tried and it apparently has failed." This is a view shared by Dr. Herrnstein, Dr. Eyseneck, a host of other psychologists, and the Nobel Prize laureate in physics, Dr. Shockley. Based on my observations, limited to the facilities visited, I found this conclusion totally inaccurate.

Perhaps the difference of opinion between the advocates of continuation and expansion (and I am one of the latter) of Head Start and its adamant critics is due to the variance of interpretation of the program objectives and especially of the criteria by which one evaluates the progress of the program. If our objectives and methods of assessment of the program are biased in favor of middle class white America, including a capricious and arbitrary interpretation of I.Q., then the program indeed must be regarded as a fiasco. On the other hand, if we accept the premise that the program is to provide children with a learning environment and varied experiences which will help them develop socially, intellectually, physically and emotionally toward the overall goal of social competence, then it is a success. Equally important an objective is to involve parents in the educational activites of the program, to enhance their role as the principal influence on the child's education and development and to assist parents to increase their knowledge, understanding, skills and experience in child growth and development.

In fact, I regard the Head Start Program as the most vital sector in the war on poverty. The benefits which the child derives from this program are manifold and crucial to his development. What has not been adequately emphasized is the profound effect the program has on the whole pattern of living in the family and its structure. In many cases which I have studied the program brought about a desirable transformation which enabled the families to part with welfare roles and establish financial independence for the first time in their lives. This has been attained through enlightenment derived from the Head Start educational opportunities which have been extended to parents mainly in the area of child development. This enlightenment ultimately has led, in many instances, to a teaching position within the program, giving the mother the opportunity to embark upon a vocational training course while the child was being provided with care.

For example, one of the most dedicated teachers in the Jacksonville Center was a former welfare recipient. She familiarized herself with the Head Start Program through her daughter's enrollment. Recruited as a teacher's assistant, she pursued academic studies and finally became a full-fledged teacher. The educational director said she was "one of the best on his staff." Another mother in Jacksonville described her experiences in the following manner: "Parents are motivated through the Head Start Program to continue education. I have finished high school after many years of interruption." Still another mother said, "Head Start has been a help to me economically inasmuch as I am learning a trade. It has helped me to understand my family better as well."

Undoubtedly much of the vigorous attack on the program is due to lack of understanding of the many faceted aspects of it. A typical enrolled child comes from a broken family residing in substandard housing, lacking basic nutrition, and what is equally tragic, dental and medical care. The Head Start Program provides wholesome food, which is very important for the child's general development and which is necessary for his physical well-being, particularly if we should assume that he will not obtain proper nourishment at home. Also, he obtains expert medical care, proper clothing, and an educational program which enriches him culturally, fosters his socioemotional development, and improves his motor ability and dexterity in an atmosphere of love. These are goals which are usually taken for granted in the affluent suburbia society but which are remote by astronomic distances from the bleak existence of a ghetto child.

Given these inputs, which are not directly compensatory education, the significance of the Head Start Program cannot be overlooked. There are many examples of the program changing a child's life. For instance, Mary, five years old, came into this world at a most inopportune time. The family, crowded into three rooms, derives its meager income from welfare. The father abandoned the family when Mary was only two months old. Since Mary's mother had her hands full with six other children, who were one year apart, she apparently did not notice that Mary was unable to run well and that she tired easily, nor did her condition attract the attention of the examining public health doctor during his routine examination. When Mary, at four, was enrolled in the Head Start Program, an alert teacher noticed the unusual pattern of behavior of the child. A pediatrician's examination revealed a heart abnormality. Finally, a cardiologist diagnosed a congenital disorder and a small hole in her heart was surgically repaired. Mary, who would have been destined to live as an invalid for no more than 15 to 18 years, now should lead a normal and full life.

In Broward County, Florida, John seemed to be a normal child, but, as was the case with Mary, a large poor family, white or black, cannot afford expert medical care, nor can an overburdened mother lavish too much attention on one child. Upon enrollment into the Head Start Program, the teacher quickly recognized John's learning potential, but when the child attempted to copy the alphabet, the letters appeared to be grotesquely distorted. An opthamologist's examination revealed an unusual pathology, which if untreated could have caused total blindness. Presently John wears corrective glasses and happily demonstrates his mastery of the alphabet.

These and other similar cases, illustrate that many of the benefits of Head Start are not directly educational. Dr. Benjamin Fine, in the *Stranglehold of the I.Q.* puts it very succinctly: "Youngsters whose physical defects undoubtedly would have gone undetected, get the necessary help in Head Start Programs, to have at least a fighting chance for success at school."

On the educational side, I was also impressed. For example, during my meeting with the parents, a mother said, "My youngest son, attending Head Start Program, is by far better developed than his older brother when he was his age, but who did not attend the Head Start Program. He is better able to get along with other children and he possesses better developed verbal skills."

In order to demonstrate the feasibility of en masse successful deployment of my methodology, and effectively rebut the bitter attack on compensatory education for culturally deprived children, I have conducted educational experiments in a few centers visited. Each visit to a classroom was accompanied by either a director of education or his designee. None of the visits was announced in advance. Furthermore, in no classroom did I spend more than two hours; usually my visits were limited to one hour and twenty minutes. For scientific validity, my experiments are all well documented.

At a St. Petersburg, Florida center, using a simple game, "Simon says touch the," I enabled four year old children in twenty minutes to identify twenty parts of human anatomy such as elbows, eyebrows, eyelashes, temple, etc.

In Broward County, I worked with a group of four and five year old children, who according to the teacher, were never able to build complete sentences in the past. I had them respond to questions such as "what did you eat for breakfast?" and "what would you like to play with?" After forty minutes, only three children out of sixty failed to reply in full sentences. In the same center, three and four year old children mastered the ability to count up to twenty by counting members of their class and finally counting boys and girls separately.

In Jacksonville, I told a group of five year old children a story and then solicited a more detailed inquiry regarding the number of children and the color of their attire, etc. Soon enough four of the children gave me their version of my story in a very satisfactory manner. In almost every instance, children who were not able to count at all or had difficulties in counting up to five benefited substantially from a simple device of walking with me in the classroom while loudly counting the steps. All of these events took place in an atmosphere of excitement, joy and informality.

In St. Petersburg, I was particularly pleased with my efforts with one three year old boy, from a broken family, who was very timid, shy and withdrawn. He seldom showed emotion. Yet, during the visits to the class, when I asked for volunteers to count my steps, Michael volunteered at the teacher's suggestion. After a second try, he correctly counted eight steps to the amazement of the teacher and classmates.

It is noteworthy that the communities which I visited are deeply concerned with the program and stand ready to assist generously. The news media gave my visits prominent and sympathetic coverage (as the enclosed testimonials will show). They were most helpful in targeting on the specific needs of the centers such as transportation, appeal for volunteers and improvement of physical facilities.

Likewise, community leaders whom I met have shown a willingness to assist constructively. The community concern and awareness are an eloquent testimony to the effectiveness of the Head Start program. This is a positive factor inasmuch as the administration of the program is delegated to the local authorities. This vastly improved climate must be cultivated through involvement, better and more effective public relations and closer ties with parents.

In the course of my visits, I met many teachers and was favorably impressed with their enthusiasm and dedication. I spoke to parents who sincerely hope that their children will break loose from the chains of poverty. I have seen the sparkle in the children's eyes following a suspenseful story, their zeal in brushing their teeth and scrubbing their hands, their rhythmic cadence of a song sung in unison, their animation and laughter on the playground, posed against the grim specter of ghetto, and it is against this background that Dr. Jensen's pronouncements appear to be heartless.

Proposals

My mandate states, "The specialist is requested to recommend approaches for improving the quality of the Head State Education component. These approaches shall focus primarily on actions that can be taken within the existing resource levels." Consistent with this, I can only propose the following recommendations, rather than the sweeping reforms based on the "Total Educational Submersion Method" which in my judgment, would revolutionize the early child development.

1. Many studies, including my own work with my daughter, have demonstrated that intellectual growth and development begin at birth, and that the most receptive period for learning absorption is from birth to 10 years of age. This coupled with the significance of the environment to the learning process prompts me to propose that the Head Start Program enroll children at the age of two and if possible, at an earlier age, and that the children attend classes for a period of eight hours. The earlier enrollment would enable the child to develop in his most formative period in an atmosphere conducive to learning. Likewise, his nutritional as well as his medical needs, so crucial at this stage, would be better met. The longer session would substantially increase the learning experience. Also, from an economic standpoint, the longer day would enable the parents to pursue either vocational or academic training in their quest for self-sufficiency.

2. The children must be protected in their formative and impressionable age from any form of violence. The parents should be enlightened about the harmful effects of violence on TV or any other form of entertainment.

Ghetto congestion coupled with a high unemployment rate gives rise to bitterness and frustration, resulting in areas with the highest crime rates. Quite often a member of the youngster's family collides with the law, be it as a drug peddler or minor offender. Demographic studies reveal that the size of a family is most often in direct proportion to its financial

186

status, that is, the poorer the family, the more numerous it is. Sociologists cannot agree on the reason for this.

Under these circumstances, crowded apartments give rise to conflicts within the family, with the children taking the brunt of it. During one of my visits to a Head Start Center in Central Florida a teacher complained that many of her children "lazily indulged in lounging on the makeshift beds beyound the allocated hours." Obviously the teacher failed to understand that many of the children lack a bed of their own at home or perhaps share one with two other siblings. Thus, resting in an air-conditioned room alone in a bed perhaps gave the child the only opportunity for rest.

If these bleak circumstances are not enough, the youngster spends many hours watching TV at home with many programs violent in nature frequently glorifying the villain. Don't we emerge from viewing "The Godfather" admiring the old man's loyalty, courage and resoluteness?

In the course of my numerous visits to centers, I found children seldom form sentences. The only ones which were frequently uttered were such as "Give me a gun so I can kill people." "If I go home with you, you will poison me." "When I grow big, I will be a policeman and arrest people." Undoubtedly, the impact of violence has taken a heavy toll on those innocent children. Let us alleviate this deep trauma.

3. Based on my own experience with my daughter and research conducted throughout the world, I believe classical music plays a constructive role in rearing a child. It engenders nobility of his character, gives him a sense of aesthetics and harmony, and develops his artistic values to an optimum. The advent of tape recorders and other inexpensive devices, such as the radio and phonograph, makes music accessible practically to all. I would, therefore, suggest that children in the Head Start Program be exposed to classical music as a background at all times. Additionally, I believe there should be a greater utilization of functional music in the curriculum, with the children's participation in unison singing.

4. In order to reduce the student-teacher ratio, I would urge the H.E.W., if necessary through legislative measures, to oblige colleges and universities which receive federal funds to assign their students in the fields of psychology and early child development to intern at Head Start Programs.

5. To enhance the quality and competence of the teaching staff, I would propose a system of incentives for teachers to receive continuous training through college and university enrollment. The Head Start Centers should intensify the recruitment of parents through training. Many mothers, because of their familarity with life in the ghetto, possess the finest potential as teachers. In fact, some of the most dedicated teachers are ghetto dwellers. Also, I believe every effort should be made in recruitment to attract male teachers, assistants, and volunteers. The frequent absence of a father in many families probably leaves a psychological scar on the children.

6. The program should broaden the liaison with parents. No educational program can be successfully implemented without parental enlightment and participation. In order to assure a closer cooperation, increase visits to homes and invite parents to participate through incentives such as plaques for the most dedicated parent, post pictures on bulletin boards, and institute other forms of awards. Furthermore, the aid that can be rendered to parents in terms of guidance and general enlightenment is a vital objective of the Head Start Program as a vanguard in the war on poverty.

7. Greater reliance should be placed on field trips to places such as zoos, libraries, police and fire departments, and even shopping centers. Community resources should be utilized whenever possible so that children will not be isolated from the ongoing life of society. These should be instructional visits made in conjunction with the topics under study and the availability of facilities. Each trip should be well planned in advance to obtain the maximum educational advantage. Depending upon the availability of transportation, at least 2 visits should be made weekly, to be followed up by discussions with the class.

8. There should be greater stress on verbal skills and communications. Many children are being referred to speech therapy when actually they suffer from no pathology. They simply have never been introduced to proper diction or heard proper sentence construction at home. I share the view of many sociologists that the major deterrent to the black man's socioeconomic progress is his dialect. Verbal skills are the tools by which people can communicate thoughts, feelings, grasp concepts, translate symbols into spoken language. Undoubtedly the area of verbal skills appears to be the Achilles heel of the Head Start programs, one which requires the most intensive work. Due to the culturally deprived environment in which poor people often live, communication is poor, and abrupt. Furthermore, children are not encouraged to be talkative, they are to be seen rather than heard. Consequently the child has little stimulation.

Significantly enough, I found the majority of the teaching staff woefully lacking in this area. Every effort should be made to stimulate sentence construction in the very early stages.

9. Replace teacher's monologue with a dialogue to assure children's participation. Children's span of interest is brief. The dialogues should be carefully planned.

10. The teachers should be truthful and candid. They should utilize every opportunity for teaching, such as the birth of a baby or even a death in the family. They should discuss daily current events within the community as well as the nation such as hurricanes, space exploration, athletic events, etc.

In general, the teachers should utilize every event for educational purposes, such as counting all objects, discussing the nutritious value of the food served, etc. They should have their classrooms stocked with plants, shells, rocks, aquariums when possible, etc. They should attempt to give correct answers without evasion. They should regard themselves as the children's friends and relate to them by sitting on the floor when they do, clapping hands, dancing and singing as they do.

In summary, I believe that the Head Start program is an extremely valuable vehicle to improve the lives of the children it serves. Indeed, we owe these unfortunate children an opportunity for physical and mental growth at this crucial stage of their life on moral grounds. But since morality is less persuasive than economy, it would be well to remember that it costs the state $12,000 per annum for each inmate at a correctional institution. Surely, if the ghetto children, at a fraction of this cost are not assisted by means of compensatory education, many of them will turn to crime at a great cost to society.

I believe that teaching in a Head Start program is one of the most noble endeavors in our society, for there can be no greater fulfillment and joy than to see poverty stricken children, predestined to a secondary role in society, develop their intellect and overcome the adversities of their social position.

My final report obtained wide recognition in the nation's press, under prominent headlines. "Education Ideas said Better than Upper Class Schools" was the headline of a United Press International five hundred word story emanating from Miami on July 27, 1974, ending with the following remarks:

189

"... His study was submitted and accepted this month at about the time that the White House demanded and received the resignation of Alvin J. Arnett as director of OEO, the controversial command post of the remnants of the 10-year old War on Poverty. Arnett said he was told that President Nixon does not want OEO, and he was accused of fostering it. The President has refused to request funds for OEO in the budget..."

As is customary, a flood of mail accompanied this publicity, most of it commending me for the advocacy and the strengthening of the Head Start Program.

My astonishment reached the zenith when one caller introduced himself as a close associate of President Nixon. Since the television was blaring and I had no pencil at my disposal, coupled with the unusual excitement, I was unable to write down or later remember the surname of my caller. Fortunately, I remembered his first name - that was easy - it was John. Now, John advised me that he was calling with the President's authority in urging me to "come to Washington in order to accept an important governmental appointment." My excitement gained momentum.

For the moment I forgot Watergate and current issues. Collecting my thoughts, I replied as calmy as I could:

"I would like to think it over."

"Very well," came the answer. "Here is the phone number - call us back without delay."

Subsequent to the phone conversation, I began to speculate about the proposed assignment. The caller's polite remark at one point that "your work with the Head Start Program impressed us deeply," made me aware that it had something to do with the newspaper stories. My suspicions were fully confirmed within the next two hours as I called back Washington. This time I reached John directly.

However, another person frequently broke into the conversation. His heavy German accent resembled the voice of Rabbi Korff, President Nixon's close associate and friend. The following is my recollection of the conversation:

"I'm glad you called. The President will be ready to see you at once.

Make sure you bring along the proposals that you have submitted concerning the Head Start Program and its effectiveness."

At this point, my suspicions that I was to be used for political expediency deepened. Any White House official could easily obtain my proposals in Washington from the OEO office of the Department of HEW. It was obvious to me that time was of such great significance that my arrival and delivery of the documents would expedite the matter at hand.

"You will be appointed Director of the Office of Economic Opportunity to replace Mr. Arnett," came the bombshell statement, stunning me momentarily.

Before I could advise the caller that I had no administrative ability, no political ties, the White House spokesman persistently inquired:

"How would the liberals greet your appointment? Would the black leadership trust our initiative in the resurrection of the OEO? How about the Senate?"

I realized that President Nixon, whose impeachment in the House brought the final stage of the battle to the Senate, was desperately courting Senatorial votes, during the heat of the last ditch battle. I thought that probably the newspaper story about my Head Start report caught the eye of a Nixon cohort. This, coupled with the reaction to the imprudent dismissal of Arnett, to be sure, called for drastic action.

"How many votes will the President win in the Senate as a result of a revitalization of the OEO program?" was more than I could bear.

"I don't know nor do I care," was my chilly reply.

"Furthermore, I refuse to be used for the purpose of manipulating public opinion in such a crucial moment of our history."

An angry reply on my caller's part terminated the conversation.

With relief, I looked up at the blue Florida sky and felt proud of being an American - free to resolutely oppose for the second time in my life, a President, when I considered him to be wrong.

This was a lesson in civics and statesmanship that both David and Edith would enjoy and applaud, I knew. And I was right.

CHAPTER 17

Stone Age Tribe – Tasaday Infants

A unique opportunity exists now to subject my Total Educational Submersion Method to its most acid test. An untouched by civilization Stone Age tribe called Tasaday has been discovered in the jungle of the Philippines. This gentle tribe has been living for hundreds of years in total isolation from the rest of the world. Its life-style is reminiscent of our ancestor of 2000 years ago.

It is against this background that as a finale to my life-long research I would like to adopt two Tasaday infants and expose them to my pedagogic methodology. I believe that under my tutelage these children would be reading at age two and would become geniuses by the existing standards before reaching adulthood. This, I believe, would once more document that environment rather than heredity determines the individual's intellectual growth and mental development.

As a matter of fact, so confident am I about the outcome of my project that during my lecture tour at Berkeley, California, I have invited the man who occupies the opposite of my spectrum, Dr. Jensen, to head a panel of scientists to evaluate the progress of my pupils.

Although officials in Washington with whom I spoke, in my search for support, gave me their moral blessing, none would offer financial backing. Furthermore, roadblocks were placed in my way by the Philippine government, which felt that it would be unwise to take small children out of their natural environment. But I am not discouraged. I still feel that some way can be found to bring members of the Tasaday Tribe here, or failing that, for me to go to the Philippines and attempt to educate them in their native setting.

If no financial support is forthcoming, I am willing to foot the bill myself, in the interest of science, if only the Philippine Government will allow the children to come here. My wife, Bella, and I are prepared to turn over one of our three bedrooms, in our North Miami Beach, Florida, home to the Tasaday children. I do not anticipate a major financial outlay, since Spartan conditions are part of the training in which I engage.

I want to test my educational theories on children from the remote Tasadäy Tribe, discovered by the outside world in 1971, because I believe their Stone Age culture would be internationally recognized as a raw base — the lowest point on the genetic totem pole. Anthropologists are in agreement with me that the Tasaday Tribe is among the furthermost removed from technological advances.

They are genetically enough remote from the Anglo-Saxons to serve as a dramatic example to refute Jensen theories, according to Dr. Jay Ingersoll, a professor of anthropology at Catholic University and a specialist in Southeast Asian primitive tribes. Even though my experiment might not remove the bias against blacks and other minority groups, a dramatic demonstration would be useful. Professor Ingersoll recalled that French anthropologist Claude Levi-Strauss successfully had conducted a similar experiment by adopting a girl from a primitive Brazilian Indian tribe who subsequently graduated from the Sorbonne.

My theory assumes that intellectual growth begins at birth and ends at death. It involves the utilization of all resources. You may recall that when Edith wanted to go to the park, I took her past a construction site and she learned about physics. If we passed by a union strike, she learned about civics. I would do the same with the Tasaday children. These children of a Stone Age culture will develop mentally in their new environment. I will take them to the golden, sandy beaches where they will learn infinity from the vastness of sand. I will point to the stars overhead and they will begin to understand astronomy.

Those who object to my bringing Tasaday children here are fearful lest our climate, our environment, our food and our culture harm them. However, the similarities in climate between Florida and the Philippines would work in their favor. Also, since I plan to raise the children in the atmosphere of my home, this would help reduce whatever traumas the children might suffer in being separated from their family and tribe.

Although my project might not produce statistical evidence of my educational theories, nonetheless it would take us a long step forward. There just aren't enough Tasadays to refute or prove anything statistically, but even one can be a starting point toward discovering the

193

truth in the nature-nurture controversy. I am not looking for statistics -- I want to see if I can take an uncivilized -- from our point of view -- totally unblemished mind and give it the dimensions of which Einsteins and Freuds are made. The number of such "untouched" tribes is rapidly decreasing. I am eager to undertake this exciting and challenging venture into total educational submersion.

When told of my project, Professor Ingersoll lauded its innovative nature, and said: "The only way science has made any leaps ahead is by threatening established wisdom."

A member of the United States Advisory Commission on International Educational and Cultural Affairs, Margaret G. Twyman, has said that my proposal to bring the Tasaday children here, or to go there in person is "fascinating." However, she took a realistic position and admitted that State Department support might be "remote."

I did get some help from Edmundo Libid, first secretary designate at the Philippine Embassy, who passed along my proposal, which he called "unorthodox", to the proper authorities in Manila. Mr. Libid thought that my objectives seemed to be to prove that there is no difference in the natural capacity of man. I assured him that this indeed was my objective. Then Mr. Libid, possibly unaware of the Jensen/Shockley controversy, and those who claim blacks are inferior mentally, added that he thought I was trying to prove what is already taken for granted.

"It's the same thing as trying to prove that water is wet,' Mr. Libid remarked.

True. We should accept the thesis that there is no difference in the natural capacity of man, based on his color, creed, national ethnic origin or economic status.

That is true in the best of all possible worlds, where all men are treated as equals, not only in theory but in practice. That is not the case today. Far too many people in our society, covering diverse segments from a noted Nobel prize laureate to a backward hillbilly in the South to a screaming fanatic in South Boston, believe that blacks are inferior, that ethnic origin does make a difference in mental ability.

I know this is utter nonsense. But does Dr. Jensen? Evidently not. Statistically he may be correct in his conclusions. But individually? Edith and David are not statistics. They are individuals, and should be treated that way. That is the trouble with education today. We educate the mass, not the individual. We are overwhelmed by numbers, not by actual conditions. We can twist and shape statistical evidence out of proportion, and reach the conclusions that we set out to prove. That is why in my opinion if I can get but one Tasaday child here, and show that his I.Q., as tested by any of the recognized criteria, is close to zero, but then, after I school him for six months his I.Q. approaches the genius level, the 150 plus mark, wouldn't that have some influence on our thinking?

On the other hand, we are constantly dazzled by the performance of one actor, the courage of one fireman, the plight of one migrant child, or the success of one genius, while we are not overly enthusiastic when we read about thousands or tens of thousands of children performing, or showing acts of courage, or starving in India, or in the sweatshops of South Korea.

Imagine the impact on the academic, professional, political, or scientific world when I bring forth a Tasaday Stone Age child and prove that his mentality exceeds that of ours.

CHAPTER 18

How I Altered the Life Style of a Call Girl

My TV appearances often elicit strange results. There were those who thought that they had an unfailing solution to the Middle East conflict and sought my support in putting their formula into practice. Disgruntled teachers and administrators offered their services in the event that I might establish a school geared to my Total Educational Submersion Method.

A woman allegedly possessed a formula for a chemical compound that would restore hair to bald people -- handed down by her esteemed Hungarian grandmother. A black woman claimed to be the first of her race to be invited to meet with General Franco's daughter to start a campaign in cancer research. She wanted me to join her on a trip to see the Spanish dictator's daughter and then seek an audience with the Pope.

And, of course, a legion of parents, students and teachers frequently call. Disenchanted with school mediocrity, they welcome an alternative school. I scrupulously return all calls, notwithstanding the inherent risk involved.

One caller provided a sharp contrast and a unique challenge. It was late Sunday evening in the autumn of 1971. On the other end of the line was 'the voice of a young woman who vigorously demanded my attention.

"What can I do for you?" solicitously I asked.

"Please meet with me," she replied. "I am in a mess. Having watched you on television, I realize that you have the guts to call a spade a spade."

"Precisely what can I do for you?"

"It would really be inadvisable to discuss what I have to say over the phone," she suggested.

Again, to clear up any doubts whatsoever, I said: "You surely must be aware that I am not in a position to secure a job for you or to assist you financially."

"My problem falls into another area, which, however, I cannot discuss over the phone." She appeared to be laboring under a strain.

Disregarding my wife's customary skepticism, I embarked upon a lengthy automobile ride to a distant and unfamiliar section of Miami. Gradually the neatly cultivated suburban houses gave way to dilapidated bungalows in the midst of which I found a relatively well maintained dwelling.

At the door appeared a young willowy woman in her early 30's. Her long hair freely flowing down from her graceful shoulders somehow harmonized with the warm blue eyes. She was attired in a short bathing suit.

The interior of the house provided again a striking contrast with what you would expect to find in this area. Neat furniture, utilitarian in nature, was tastefully blended with the reproductions of classics hanging on the wall.

"Won't you sit down?" she asked, a broad smile crossing her face, while a ferocious looking German shepherd licked my hand.

"Everything you see, I earned while flat on my back."

I looked up more in surprise than shock. Before I could respond, the woman, evidently seeing the expression on my face, broke it:

"Please don't tell me anything about morality. I want you to know that the roster of my clients constitutes a Who's Who in this community."

Gradually the cherubic face lost its charm as her tirade gained momentum. She tried to defend herself vigorously, not realizing that she did not need to apologize.

197

"What can I do for you?" I repeated.

"As you can see," she picked up the conversation, "life has dealt me a bitter blow. All my efforts to lead a life that society considers honest and dignified led to failure. My father, an alcoholic, beat me mercilessly; the school and my teachers bored me hopelessly.

"Finally, my marriage, with which I had hoped to end my misery, resulted in a divorce within two years. Thus, I was left with two babies and a meager alimony which ceased when my husband disappeared. My numerous jobs were financially unrewarding and emotionally unfulfilling.

"In my agony and despair I ran off to Florida, penniless, where I started my present lucrative career. Suddenly, everything turned to roses. I was able to acquire this house, purchase furniture and, for the first time in my entire life, I enjoy financial security."

"Why do you seek my assistance?" I interrupted her gushing monologue.

"Because deep in my heart I feel I can better fulfill myself if given a chance to go straight. Your own struggle in face of great hardships, Mr. Stern, convinced me that I might do as well if given a fighting chance."

There was no desire on my part to rebut the woman's argument. Her keynote statement that "everything I own I earned while flat on my back" closely approximated my own view of the system which rewards corruption, greed and decadence, mercilessly eating away the fabric of our society.

"Let me think about it. I shall call you in a few days. But before I go, tell me, in what ways do you think I can help you?"

She answered quickly, eagerly: "By providing me with reading material. By helping me to pass a high school equivalency test so that I can go to college. By offering incentives, motivation, the ability to make me want to continue with my education."

"I shall call you in a few days," I said slowly, as the enormity of what I had been asked to do gradually began to sink in on me. Usually prostitutes do not want their minds broadened or enlarged -- nor do they want to get an education that does not relate to the body. "Let me think about it."

With this I left abruptly. On the way home I tried to sort out my impressions. The prospect of testing my educational theory in such a different situation provided me with an enormous challenge. On the other hand, the risk of involvement with a prostitute, innocuous as it was, frightened me. However, my insatiable desire to test my theories and to be of service overcame all obstacles.

After two agonizing days, in which I weighed the pros and cons, the value to the girl of getting my help, the dangers to myself in possibly destroying a world-wide reputation, I phoned again.

"Very well," I said. "I am willing to assist you on your difficult journey, provided that you adhere to the guidelines that I will lay down for you. As you might expect, your transition will require a drastic decline in your style of living, which may affect you brutally."

Then I admonished her to do her best. I could hear an enthusiastic cheer on the other side of the phone.

"You bet, I'll do my best," she uttered softly and almost apologetically. This kindled my hope for success in this most bizzare and exotic undertaking.

Our next meeting was much longer and took up most of a working day. A discussion of a general nature revealed that the woman was well informed about current events, and truly eager to learn. Gradually her hostility towards society gave way to a child-like enthusiasm for learning.

"I suggest that you phase out your business operation, starting immediately," I urged. "I know that it calls for sacrifices on your part, but this is the most vital part of your rehabilitation. You will soon acquire skills which will enable you to earn a living with dignity.

"Insofar as your educational program is concerned, I shall lend you a set of Encyclopaedia Britannica. Study history, geography and recent developments of mainland China and determine whether, in your opinion, it is wise for the world to seat China at the United Nations."

That very evening, I reflectively suggested to my wife: "Imagine the bewilderment of Jean's clients when they find an open volume of the Britannica at her bedside!"

I found that Jean read and understood what she read. I had assigned

199

her a paper on the role that China could or might play in the 20th Century, either in or out of the United Nations. Her handwritten paper depicted profound interest, hard work, and an analytic mind. Its poor sentence structure and atrocious spelling did not diminish the reasoning power and deep thinking.

"The admission of China to the United Nations, in the light of its growing military and economic power is in the best interests of peace," is how she concluded her paper.

Now I knew that my battle had been won. A colleague of mine, teaching political science, after reading the paper, remarked: "How can one mature so impressively, without acquiring the rudiments of English: I would like very much to meet that student."

"I have no doubt that you would love to, Paul," I answered with a cryptic, sardonic smile. Paul had frequently indulged in extra-marital affairs.

During the following meetings my student frequently argued with me about the socially redeeming attibutes of her profession, and they truly made sense.

"There are so many men incapable of establishing meaningful relationships," she pointed out, "the widower, the divorcee, the unhappily married man. Sexual inhibitions on the part of wives, sexual incompatibility, the rising tide of sex crimes due to frustration which could be reduced by legalization of prostitution, all are mute witnesses for the value of my profession."

"This might all be true," I answered, "but it is my feeling, Jean, that you can fulfill yourself better and make a more dignified and worthwhile contribution to society by other means."

This argument remained my most effective weapon in the truly bitter struggle ahead for the soul and mind of a human being so crippled by an indifferent society. My educational tools were simple indeed. An abacus for the mastery of arithmetic. The scrupulous reading of *The New York Times* for current events and the improvement of English. Daily reading of the Encyclopaedia Britannica as related to the subject under study. which led my student to read every volume within one year.

To relieve my charge from the "yoke of slavery", I arranged for her to take an intensive course in steno-typing. Within eight or nine months I noticed a sharp contrast in the life-style of my student. Gone was her expensive clothing. An old car replaced the recent model. This more or less corroborated the information which I obtained from a neighbor. Said she: "Jean has not had any male visitors at all lately. I wonder why?"

Soon, Jean prepared for a High School Equivalency Test, which she passed with impressive scores. She was admitted to college with a large block of credits, obtained on the basis of college level examinations.

Thus, my student was launched on a full time college career. A woman relative took care of her children.

A lengthy speaking tour and my student's abrupt relocation of residence, terminated our contact.

Then, in the latter part of 1973, I conducted a series of lectures on the Berkeley campus of the University of California. One day, upon the conclusion of my lecture, which was given to a large class of predominantly graduate students of child psychology, a woman in a distant row of the auditorium raised her hand.

"Professor," she began, her voice confident, "What do you think of adult education? **Is it worth the effort?**" Can one retrain for another profession through it?"

I must have astonished my audience of teachers, students and community leaders when tears came streaking down my face. "Yes, I said, by all means, adult education is not only worthwhile but is the best hope for a strong democratic government. And, yes, of course, one can **retrain for another profession at any time, regardless of age. Motivation is the key word.**"

The question came from Jean. Her triumph from the bottom of degradation to the exalted heights of intellectual growth and maturity testified to the power of human perseverance and dignity.

After the lecture, I spoke with Jean. She was enrolled at the University as a full time student. She had embarked upon a course in social service, and was looking forward to serving as a social worker. I knew that this was the right profession for her. Her past experience, coupled with her present training and insight, had developed empathy, understanding, compassion and humaness within her.

She grapsed my hand and said softly: "Thank you, my good friend

Aaron Stern. You helped me when everyone else turned the other way, not wanting to get contaminated with my impurity. I am working my way through college -- serving as a waitress at $2 an hour. It's funny, but if I wished, I could get $200 an hour, my former fee. But I am much happier now. And I won't let you down. I want to be a credit to you and your ideals.

Filled with emotion I blurted out: "Would you like to have dinner with me?"

Total Educational Submersion indeed can succeed with adults as well as with children, with Jean as well as with Edith.

The truly formidable effects of environment on the human being, for good as well as evil, will be dramatically demonstrated in the following chapter.

CHAPTER 19

The Change of Guard
A Tragedy Averted

Unquestionably David's yo-yo like, stormy, dramatic   adolescence with its grim pitfalls fortifies more the validity of the Total Education Submersion Method, than the spectacular vertical ascent of Edith, who rose to unprecedented lofty heights, without the slightest crisis.

It all happened brutally and swiftly, David, who like his sister, had the advantage of intensive stimulation almost from birth, began to read at 2. He debated newspaper reporters at 5. Imbued with culture, he awed teachers with his erudition, actively campaigned for McGovern at 11. At 13, the child inspired a congressional resolution, citing him "for escellence in Marine Biology". However, at 14 he succumbed to the devastating influence of his peers which could have proven to be fatal. It happened at a time when my health began to deteriorate further, as my vicious heart spasm confined me for longer periods to bed, while the ever increasing demand upon me to deliver lectures grew. I have in the past observed valleys and peaks in David's progress, always directly related to the amount of stimulation that I could give to the child. It formed a perfect curve. This time the decline assumed a grave threat.

One day David insisted that I drive him to see a movie. Unfortunately, neither my health nor the type of this movie would warrant it. In anger he left the home to return late, same evening. Without any comment he went to bed. Next day, David failed to return home directly from school. This, too, went unnoticed. Little did we know that this seemingly unimportant event heralded great trouble.

Subsequently, the drama began to unfold at a frightening speed. My rapport with the child suddenly began to break up. There was a dismal change in the child's pattern of behavior. His eloquence and finesse were replaced by crude expressions. No longer would he articulate. His love

203

for classical music was sacrificed to the wild gyrations of Rock and Roll to the accompaniment of the body-twisting, grotesque as it appeared. The child's treatment of his parents, once based on mutual respect and love, was substituted by alienation if not outright hostilities. All my efforts to counsel the child were futile. At times communication with the family ceased altogether, as he moved in his shabby clothing erasing his neat appearance, among us. As it might be expected, David spent more and more time with the neighborhood kids, whose presence he hitherto ignored. Now he desperately attempted to adapt or imitate their deplorable conduct.

These middle class children, most of whom have already established police records due to acts of vandalism, truancy, petty larceny had won his total loyalty to the exclusion of his family . . . the mainstay of David's progress. David's devotion to social justice and morality was brutally displaced by racial prejudice. The child's insatiable quest for knowledge which I devotedly nourished from his infancy gave way to nihilism, comics and vulgarity. Yes, it all happened in a matter of days.

Significantly enough, the child's galloping decline was accompanied by a deep sense of fatalism bordering on resignation which may have been induced by usage of drugs, although my in-depth investigation ruled out hard drugs.

Soon enough David with several of his friends were charged with allegedly defacing the exterior of a neighbor's house and harassment of the owners. The charges could not be fully substantiated in Juvenile Court. However, David emerged from this experience triumphant, able to demonstrate "toughness" to his friends. This act of baptism as it were, made David more incorrigible, his actions more defiant. Without a shade of contrition he would disappear into late night prompting me to check hospitals and police stations for his whereabouts. The moral emotional and intellectual as well as physical wreckage of this child had the intensity of a hurricane.

As I realistically appraised this situation, I felt it was only a matter of time, at best weeks, before David would have been charged with a serious offense. The specter of my son, a victim of a ruthless environment, rotting in jail, as do many poorly motivated gifted children, tormented my soul. Indeed, I stood helpless, watching a horrendous cancer eating away the flesh of my beloved child.

It is against this background that my family reached a consensus. David had to be removed, without delay, from this environment at any cost. The immediate disposal of our house was impractical as the state of economy crippled the real estate market. The two viable alternatives were David's relocation to live with Edith or a boarding school anywhere in the world that David would consent to attend. Both measures had the enthusiastic support of Edith who would alone underwrite it. What a magnificent sacrifice on the part of a 22 year old sister. David adamantly rejected both solutions professing "unswerving loyalty to my friends. I'd rather go to jail than abandon them" he stated defiantly during our family meeting. "You may have to do just that in order to be with your friends," concluded Edith the heated dialogue as tears rolled down her cheeks while Bella stood speechlessly by.

It became obvious that drastic measures, commensurate with this emergency, would have to be taken to rescue David from the imminent danger.

Next day, notwithstanding the sharp protest of my family I arranged an appointment with a social worker of the Juvenile Court. With humility I faced my defeat, shocking the astonished young man who read frequent stories about the "genius maker" with my sad story uttered in a hardly audible voice I pleaded, "Could you please send a letter to David warning him that disobedience of lawful and reasonable demands of parents consititutes, on the part of a minor, a violation of the law."

"Surely, I will" replied the social worker deeply touched by my predicament.

"But with all due respect, so far I see nothing criminal on the part of David to warrant such despair. Your alarming attitude provides a sharp contrast with the obvious indifference exhibited by many parents whose children land here due to well documented criminal acts."

"Herein lies the tragedy of our society," I replied squeezing gently the hand of the kind man who sought to console me.

The following few days were faced with great apprehension as I awaited the letters fearing the reaction that it might cause. What will be my family's response to it? Couldn't it further enrage David who might decide to run away from home altogether. What will happen if the story leaks to the press, and will its impact discredit my methodology, were the thoughts which crossed my mind.

Finally, the day arrived. With trembling hands I accepted the letters from the mail carrier, one addressed to David and the copy to me. David at first refused to read it, then with a wry grimace suggested "let the pigs shovel it..."

Advised about the letter, Edith rushed home in the middle of the workday. The siblings locked themselves up in a room for a period of an hour's discussion punctuated by angry outbursts, as we the parents awaited with apprehension the outcome of this truly fateful event.

Finally, they emerged from behind the locked doors. "Well, I will live for a while with Edith," anounced angrily the boy as his pale sister emerged wiping the sweat from her face.

At this very moment I intuitively felt that my battle was over and a tragedy averted. Unable to restrain my emotions I embraced and warmly kissed David who appeared to be somewhat bewildered and embarrassed by my impulse.

The very same day, within hours, the siblings left for Boca Raton, and what proved to be a new and glorious leaf in David's life. His parting words were reminiscent of MacArthur's historic statement "I shall return to my friends whether you like it or not." Inasmuch as David's departure took place in the middle of the semester, I had to obtain school transcripts and what a sad task this was. The guidance counselor who assisted me in gathering the documents bitterly remarked "My God, it took extraordinary efforts on David's part to fail courses. Anyone who breathes and answers to a roll call passes." How unbelievable it appeared that this very student just a few months earlier scored scholastic triumphs truly effortlessly. Soon enough many of his friends dropped out from school, and one by one, faced court charges while our neighborhood saw an epidemic of house burglaries. Our neighbors who were once proud to have "a genuine genius" in their midst were relieved at David's absence.

Edith who undertook the Herculean task of rehabilitating her brother with every faculty at her command, lived then in a modest apartment adjoining a shopping center. Fearing that the lure of a shopping center might be detrimental to her brother, without delay bought a house on the outskirts with David receiving the largest room for himself.

Edith arranged an equitable division of labor with her brother's responsibilities encompassing house maintenance, cooking, gardening and shopping, in addition to studies, for which he was given a satisfactory allowance.

Contrary to the experiences of other siblings, these two got along excellently from the very start. The fact that during the last 8 years of David's formative growth Edith was away from home, makes their very harmonious relationship even more remarkable.

At once he embarked upon the laborious task of cataloging and sorting Edith's huge library, while he began to everyone's joy to fill his own shelves with university texts on Marine Biology and Ecology, to which he commits his total allowance.

Fully aware that peer pressure was responsible for David's problems, Edith introduced her brother to her friends. Both enjoy a rich social life irrespective of the age difference. Karate lessons, volley-ball games, scuba diving, boating, frequent trips to bookstores, libraries, occasional visits to Disneyland, football games and above all debates encompassing the widest spectrum, enrich David's background.

Since we decided that it would be wise for David not to return to his old neighborhood, our first family reunion was held in Boca. As it is customary Edith ran to greet us. Solemnly she stated, "Well Dad your pedagogic technique undergoes its most severe test here. Through creating the proper environment I will return my brother to his former splendor."

"You have already succeeded my dear in a way that supersedes my most optimistic expectations. David will emerge from his traumatic experience better able to cope with adversities." As the events proved later, I was right.

As in the past, David who could boast college credits at 14 is again a straight A student. His expertise in Marine Biology (especially study of sharks ranks with the top academicians). Likewise, his moral conduct is excellent. When quizzed lately about his social life by a reporter he replied, "I have few friends of my own age as I have very little in common with my peers. Thus, it is hard for me to relate to them." In the course of the same interview David remarked, "The only friends I am interested in are those with whom I can share the little knowledge I have or those I can learn from."

Yes, as for his former friends, the following comment can best summarize it.

"Regrettable as it is, those were 13 to 14 year old, pajama-clad, poorly armed but highly motivated Vietcong youngsters who crushed our military might in Vietnam, while their American counterparts in large numbers crowd Juvenile Courts. Something very drastic will have to be done to motivate our youth if this society is to survive."

CHAPTER 20

The Precious Value of Skepticism

One of the most precious attributes of an enlightened mind is a healthy skepticism toward personalities, authorities and institutions. In my education of Edith and David, great stress has been laid upon the quest for the abstract, for the broad horizons of free, independent thought uncluttered by unrealistic images and myths. This involves healthy skepticism because so many of the world's young people are brought up thoughtlessly admiring heroes instead of having strong beliefs in concepts or ideas.

No doubt there are psychological advantages in building personality traits of a youngster by stressing positive characteristics of a prominent person. But this "respect" should be sharply delineated from the more dangerous situation of substituting broad concepts with hero worship of a mortal who supposedly personifies this concept. This latter technique will of necessity be injurious to the truth, since much of what we are told about the so-called hero is exaggerated or outright contrary to the facts.

Of course, there is a limited socially redeeming value in the portrayal of great men and women in the best light possible. If intelligently presented, these lives can create models for children to emulate, thereby strengthening their moral fiber and social adaptation. Thus, youngsters will be inspired by the patriotism and martyrdom of Joan D'Arc, the fortitude and courage of Abe Lincoln, the devotion and charity of Albert Schweitzer. In many parts of the world, however, this has been and continues to be abused. This is particularly true in the totalitarian countries, where the government engages in intensive indoctrination of the young towards a blind obedience to their leaders who supposedly personify the leading party and the state. In these instances, this technique often becomes grotesque and contraproductive as the heroes of today become the villains of tomorrow.

A prime example of this were the millions in Germany whose Heil Hitler salute often denoted the first exhibit of motor ability. They were destined to lose their lives in a horrible slaughter from the frozen expanses of Soviet Russia to the burning deserts of North Africa, in a vicious senseless war unleashed by this madman. So were millions of Soviet people who glorified Stalin to perish later in the concentration camps erected by this despot.

From a pedagogical point of view, the hero worship technique is tempting to the incompetent teacher who evades challenge as it does not require dwelling on in-depth discussion of given periods, historical events or ideas. Above all, it must be stressed that learning constitutes an ever-lasting search for the truth and whenever the slightest departure from this guiding principle takes place, no matter how advantageous it may be to a given situation, the repercussions in terms of credibility loss will be formidable.

Despite the damage to the learning process, this technique is being widely employed on the elementary and secondary school level, leaving in its wake harm to the child's analytical skills. His power of reasoning becomes subordinate to a preconceived image of the hero and a pre-determined moral judgment of the event under study. This glorification is also responsible for the chauvinistic "my country, right or wrong" attitude which ranks as one of the greatest fallacies of mankind.

Analysis and appreciation of great lives should not be totally forsaken in modern education, however, but outright worship should be avoided. My education of the children in the Displaced Persons Camp after the Second World War illustrates a challenging and productive approach.

My objective in this unusual educational undertaking with these refugee children was to give them some measure of education, social behavior and interaction, and above all a sense of self-esteem and purpose. This had to be done in the shortest time possible, as our residence in Germany could be terminated at any time. Since six languages were spoken in the group, the struggle to establish a common language helped give the group an identity.

The attainment of these immediate goals was parallel to the importance of the three Rs in modern schools. It was as urgent as would be the training of an army facing a formidable adversary in battle. Determined to do my very best, I began to exploit the heroic deeds of Moses with the flair of a revival evangelist. The leading of the slaves to the Promised Land was a poignant analogy to the situation we were in. I could see the electrifying effects in their misty eyes as I vividly drew parallels between the exodus from Egypt and the contemporary one.

The account of the humble shepherd David scoring a victory over the wicked giant Goliath strengthened the morale of my students. The effects of this technique were truly remarkable. Although there was no opportunity in our Spartan-like environment to devote time to the broader plateau of social issues, my children have developed a keen sense of fairness and compassion which is attributable, in my judgment, to their tragic past, no less than to my pedagogic talents.

During the 1950's when the Southern Blacks emerged from the years of opression and neglect, in order to awake their pride, identity and self-respect I have recommended similar measures to the then segregated schools. The results were very reassuring as demonstrated by the childrens' improved social behavior and a substantial progress in the area of verbal skills. A general enthusiasm towards learning was also observed.

Two decades later the Head Start research project brought me again in close contact with culturally and economically disadvantaged black children. Notwithstanding the devastation brought upon them by the environment, my accounts of the meetings with Dr. King and references to Mohammad Ali brought a warm response from the most withdrawn children.

Those who might be appalled by what would appear to be an inconsistency on my part for scolding those who violate the cannons of ethnics by dwelling on hero worship, while I illustrate the panacea like results of the same method, should remember that drastic amputations unfortunately performed so often in the field hospitals, under enemy fire, should not be resorted to in a peaceful hospital setting, where conventional methods can save limbs.

When working with Edith and later David I have used the whole world as a text. The dynamic and often stormy events of post-war period, the rapid progress of science and the inexhaustible treasury of the past made their insatiable quest for knowledge, a joyful way of life. Great men and women of the past ages were a part of this learning process, but instead of being demi-gods, we regarded them as real human beings.

When studying the Jewish history we relied often on the fascinating Old Testament with its rich repository of metaphors and aphorisms, abundant in mythology and lore. Its heroes were always portrayed as mortals given to the shortcomings and imperfections common to humans. Thus while Solomon's wisdom impressed the children profoundly, his vanity and arrogance were not overlooked.

"Well, even Moses was a sinner," exclaimed the 5 year-old Edith defending Ben Gurion's acrimonius conflict within his ruling party in Israel. On the other hand when we related to contemporary personalities, my children formed their own opinion based either on personal contacts, as was the case with Albert Einstein whom Edith met, or based on their activities. Of course, the wave of assassinations claiming the lives of John and Robert Kennedy and Martin Luther King grieved them deeply, an expression of which can be found in Edith's moving essay "Martin Luther King - In Memoriam" included in this book.

David, while attending 5th grade, was once asked to write an essay on "My favorite hero." His schoolmates chose Washington, Lincoln, and Adams. David, who was by far worldlier than his schoolmates, chose our neighbor, a woman whom he knew. This woman, having been abandoned by her husband, had to work on two jobs to rear with dignity her five children. He concluded his composition with "Sarah's devotion to her children, in face of such a hardship, is truly heroic," which made me so proud of him. The teacher's comment, "Did no one ever inspire you more than this woman?" appeared to be truly lamentable.

Awe and hero worship, as every historian will testify, are the precursors of the worst calamities of mankind in its entire history. Blood thirsty, intoxicated by the overwhelming obedience and worship of their subjects, tyrants and despots such as Khan, Pharaoh, Caesar, Napoleon and Nasser embarked upon tragic adventures submerging the world in oceans of blood in search of conquest, glory and immortality. Even the 20th Century Shah of Iran maintains that he is divinely inspired to carry on his bloody reign.

Insofar as learning and mental growth of an individual are concerned, there can be no substitute. The method of suspended judgment and systematic doubt challenges the mind to be critical, analytical and above all inquisitive. Ideas and concepts must be incessantly scrutinized. An individual must continuously examine the moral and social issues of a constantly changing world. In order to maintain a constructive feeling of self-esteem and self-reliability, an individual must not view any other person, irrespective of his wisdom or nobility of character, as one personifying all the virtues for it is debasing to one's ego. It leads to abdication of one's rights and responsibilities, a feeling of subservience, unworthiness and general inferiority. This is not to suggest that some of us are endowed with great talents and genuine altruism. As a matter of fact, I have been deeply inspired by Einstein's greatness, the nobility of his character, his legendary modesty and shyness. But at no time did I forget that Einstein was a mortal, notwithstanding his remarkable attributes, a mortal given to certain weaknesses and imperfections.

Universal quality education is the only salvation for the tormented world, and its chief adversary is veneration of individuals, blind obedience with the residue of prejudice, hate and fatalism and resignation.

Some of my most inspired teachers could never reach the plateau of full professorship because of their unwillingness to bend as required. What often determines the greatness of a physician is the location of his office. If he is on the fashionable Fifth Avenue he is regarded as a "big doctor" and of course commands a high fee. His counterpart, due to lack of funds maintains a modest office in East Bronx is relegated to the role of an ordinary doctor and will command a much lesser fee. I have always admired the gallantry, valor and leadership qualities of Churchill until I saw a movie based on the British statesman's memoirs in which he simply pleads with his beautiful mother to advance his military career by somewhat less than ethical methods. Nor are particularly encouraging the lately proliferating books describing the promiscuous conduct of our presidents.

How easily we are impressed by the size of the company. "What is good for General Motors is good for the country" is taken by many literally.

Rockefeller's enormous wealth bestows upon him an aura of nobility, refinement and altruism as well as wisdom. Therefore, it is assumed by many that he would make an ideal president. Of course the disclosures of Rockefeller's meteoric rise abounding in ruthless manipulation of people in the pursuit of his ego has not dampened the enthusiasm of many. Not even the fact that he did not pay a single penny of income tax one year prevented him from reaching the lofty heights of Vice Presidency. The tragic death of President Kennedy and his brother, Robert, most likely prevented the family from leading America for generations as was the case with Roosevelts. As a matter of fact Senator Edward Kennedy is constantly being counted to be the Democratic Standard bearer. with

212

every political observer betting that he could defeat any Republican candidate. Why, we must ask, with all due respect for the devotion to public service of this family, must the United States, a vigorous nation of 220 million be governed for 3 to 5 generations by one dynasty? Don't we have in our midst other gifted and dedicated people?

On the other hand partly due to the merciless conditioning which accompanies us from infancy through the media, there is an uncontrollable urge to emulate to worship, to depend on and to admire individuals. This deplorable impulse expresses itself in form of idolizing movie stars, athletes, political figures, men of wealth and at times convicted criminals. It is the urge to abdicate responsibilities, the discomfort of making decisions, that prompts us to be led by others. In order to reinforce our faith in these leaders we attribute to them superlatives, and open ourselves to all forms of exploitation, demagogy by mass hysteria and disastrous wars. And yet, what sets man apart from animals is his ability to think, to probe, to judge, to envision, to soar freely on the wings of imagination.

It is education that fortifies a person's intellectual faculties for scientific inquiry and enhances his dignity. His sense of fairness stimulates his innermost desire to develop himself and to become more sensitive. The joy of learning is the eternal search for perception and above all the truth. Whenever we relinquish any of these God given faculties or delegate any of these functions to others, we open ourselves to material exploitation, psychological manipulation and any number of degradations.

CHAPTER 21

Mastery of Deceit

Another vital area in which we abdicate our vigil is advertising. In the constant battle waged for our hearts, minds and pocketbooks, we confront a formidable army of well equipped manipulators who urge us to buy products we don't need. These subtle, and at times rude, persuaders succeed by methods of coercion or cajoling or pleading, by appealing to our vanity by wrapping themselves in patriotism, so we will part with our funds, to relinquish our rights and freedoms for their selfish, self-serving motive. This formidable assault, comprising all forms of communciation media from the highway poster to the TV screen, eats away daily our dignity and self-respect.

Proponents of the advertising industry vigorously defend it on the grounds that it:

1. Enlightens the public
2. Stimulates the economy
3. Promotes consumer protection
4. Induces business competition

In actuality, notwithstanding these alleged lofty objectives, advertising constitutes the most sinister force in our society, seriously threatening our very survival and, indeed, that of the world at large. Since in reality the only true objective of the advertising industry is to create profits for its clients, the advertisers use every method at their command to induce the public, as it has been classically stated, "to buy goods which they do not need with funds they do not possess," thus playing havoc with the social structure.

214

In the relentless pursuit of their "lofty goals" the advertisers resort to the most diabolic techniques of fraud, dressed in flattery, appealing to the basest instincts, inhibitions, prejudices, and fears to peddle in many cases their worthless and often harmful products, such as cancer-causing cosmetics and addiction causing drugs. This perfidious assault on public intelligence is conducted by a highly skilled group of charlatans who are well versed in mass psychology techniques, to the tune of 60 billion dollars a year -- at the cost of $300 per annum for each of us in the U. S. A., paid by the taxpayer himself, inasmuch as advertising is tax-deductible.

To this, one should add countless sums spent on call girls, bribes and other questionable methods which business spends "routinely" and which, too, is deducted from income tax, tightening the yoke around the neck of the consumer-taxpayer. The late union leader, Mr. Reuter, compared this situation with Nazi mass executions, during which "the victims had to dig their own grave, pose for the firing squad and after being fired upon, fall neatly in, to be buried by the next formation of victims."

One of my professors fondly reminded his classes that in Greek mythology "Hermes was a God of merchants and thieves." Once he gave his graduate class an assignment "to find one single ad on T.V. which was not misleading and fraudulent." Not a single one could be found. It was this professor's contention that given a sound T.V. promotion campaign, anything smartly packaged (even polluted water) would sell.

My personal experience fully corroborates this. As a denture wearer, I have purchased several devices alleged to "clean the most persistent stains," as was colorfully demonstrated on TV, to realize that they fail to meet all of these characteristics. Today, twenty-two years later, these "products" are still lavishly being advertised on TV., suggest that the public buys them. To attain the best results, from their standpoint, the advertisers attempt to reach as broad a base as they can, cajoling, threatening and at times flattering the confused consumer, while perfidiously clothing their message in a mantle of awe-inspiring patriotism, altruism and piety and, above all, keeping him in a state of shocking mediocrity. They are fully aware that an enlightened public cannot be manipulated.

This explains the proliferation of crime stories on the air, appealing to the ugliest instincts of man, with a horrible price that society has to pay for it, in the form of ever increasing crime rates. Who can forget the pensively looking man dressed in a white doctor's gown, joyfully puffing a cigarette to suggest health advantages derived from smoking, at a time when there was mounting evidence that cigarette smoking causes lung cancer.

How unscrupulous are the priests of deceit by resorting to plain blasphemy by exploiting the noble aspirations of the women's liberation movement with the following catchy phrase, "You've come a long way, baby," to assure women equality with men in terms of lung cancer.

I recall a slightly embarrassing situation during one of my lectures during which I scolded those golden-calf worshipping actors who cheerfully advertised smoking knowing well that it is a leading cause of lung cancer. Succumbing to emotion I concluded, "I wonder whether these people can sleep well knowing that millions of youngsters will be hooked on this dangerous habit as a result, with many thousands suffering from lung cancer later" at which time Edith stood up and in agitation added, "Maybe there is poetic justice in Arthur Godfrey's suffering cancer of a lung. As you know, he was just operated on for lung cancer, after many years of advertising Old Gold Cigarettes."

Who will forget the pious advertisement by the oil industry urging the public "to conserve energy for the good of the country," which this very industry cleverly conspired with the Arab states to impose upon the oil crisis and thus reap huge profits while destroying the small independent dealer.

Perhaps the following example could sound grotesque, if it were not so tragic. A utility undertook an advertising campaign to the tune of $800,000 to "enlighten the public why the cost of electricity went up." A letter from a housewife published in a local paper suggested, "I know how you can save $800,000. Simply by not conducting this silly campaign." This finally prompted the company to terminate it.

My 12 year old David once remarked with regards to the deplorable give-away shows, "What indignities, in a circus-like fashion, these people are subjected to. They are ordered to hug, kiss and cry melodramatically on demand. What a sickening euphoria they create in the public, which is led to believe that they too, some day will be able to obtain gifts to the tune of 15 or 20 thousand dollars just by guessing.

"Oh, God, what a heavy toll this takes on the psychological equilibrium of these people."

With reference to dog food advertisement, he fittingly suggested "What a horrible contempt for the intelligence of the public, and brutality towards helpless animals. Any child could notice that the dogs have not been fed for days and that there is only one dish filled with food as they hungrily devour it. Finally, how do we know that the food consumed by the animals on camera is not the finest human gourmet dish."

Undoubtedly the most ghastly misdeed of Nixon, which unfortunately went unnoticed by the public and press and hopefully will be scrutinized by future historians, is his full reliance on a Public Relations firm in his bid for a second term. Mr. Nixon, in contempt of the American Public, chose Madison Avenue ignoring the legitimate organs of the Republican Party to pilot his campaign. Thus Madison Avenue utilizing the technique of the big lie which enables it to peddle sanitary napkins, panty hose or harmful over-the-counter drugs, brainwashed the country to re-elect an unworthy man to the most lofty office of the U. S. A. Thus unwittingly America, misled and manipulated, entrusted its and the free world's destiny into the hands of a cunning evil opportunist who at any moment could unleash a nuclear holocaust.

Who can forget the diligent public relations campaign from which the "God fearing, hardworking conservative Nixon" emerged. One who instituted prayer breakfasts in the White House, presided over by the venerable Billy Graham.

Who will forget the catchy slogan "law and order," who can forget the American flag adorning his lapel, while he and his cohorts were indulging in the most heinous crimes against this very country. Psychologists and sociologists have long ago established a causal relationship between social unrest, crime and the soothing advertising messages, "You can so easily own." Typical are the companies who urge you to combine "all large bills into one small payment and still have enough money left to spend leisurely." To be sure of the company's "altruism" their phone number is "freedom" in one locality and "justice" in another area.

How brutally typical is the following: A friend of mine was granted the treasured American citizenship in a mass rally 20 years ago. The next day, a letter arrived from a "respected" flag producing company, urging him and the many others like him, to purchase an American flag "to prove your patriotism." The poor man spent $12, as did many other new citizens, although he was not able to display the Old Glory as he shared a small apartment in the East Bronx with 3 other refugees.

217

How can one resist the temptation of adopting "a hungry Indian child" peering at you from the pages of a respectable magazine unless you know that 50% to 80% of funds are spent on administrative costs by the organization. The same idols that many Americans mindlessly worship endorse a service or product, sometimes worthless, which brings them huge sums of money and secures an almost instantaneous success to the sponsor. Watch for the clever slogans which are totally unrelated to the product or service, such as "for the young," which oftentimes might prevent the consumer from aging at all, inasmuch as the heavy content of sugar mght cause terminal disease. How about the propaganda campaigns by corporations through advertisement to influence public policies, foreign policies for the benefit of the industry, which is often inimical to the public good.

One should not forget that the main targets of this insidious campaign are the poor people who can least afford to be victimized and who do not possess the sophistication and judicious judgment to disregard it, and it is these poor people who pay for the enormous costs of advertising.

The advocate of advertisement industry will state that there are laws protecting the consumer, but industry blinks its eyes on these half-truths. There will be those who will attribute socially redeeming values as well as honorable truth in advertising. I challenge them as did my professor to give me but one instance.

It is noteworthy that in the course of my work with Edith and David I have strongly stressed consumer education by visiting department stores, armed with what proved to be misleading ads to document the fraud that is being perpetrated against the public. We have faithfully researched books on nutrition to rebut the misleading ads of soft drink companies. We have visited faith-healing sessions to learn about the mass psychology technique. Occasionally we would conduct consumer reaction surveys in shopping malls. One surprisingly revealed that headache remedy ads actually induced headaches in many people, at which Edith remarked: "you see how effective the power of persuasion is."

Once 9-year-old David sent a letter to AT&T asking "why do you waste millions of dollars on advertising, if as a monopoly you have a captive clientele?"

The letter was never acknowledged. Occasionally we would weigh pre-packaged bundles of fruits and vegetables in the stores, to discover discrepancies. I remember how once the 11 year-old Edith became outraged when after careful research at home she learned that penicillin under a trade name cost four times as much as under its generic name.

"I will have to call the police" said the alarmed pharmacist, "if you don't take her out." At the door she was still screaming, "how can you in conspiracy with the doctors, exploit the gullible public." On another occasion, David, age 8, realizing that a jumbo box of soap costs on a proportional basis more than that of a lesser size (a device cleverly employed to mislead the public which expects that the larger the package the less expensive the product) burned his leg from a broken bleach bottle which he accidentally broke as he heatedly argued his point with the store manager.

During a trip to Chicago, we visited a printing shop where we were shown by our host a huge order of price tags. The ordering chain instructed the printer to print a given price, cross it off and print below half of the price, to give the buyer the impression that she is saving 50% on each item. "This is routinely done, my little girl, on almost all orders" said the printer to the astonished girl. To this very day Edith remembers this lesson.

In my judgment consumer education should replace home economics in school. The instances I have just related show clearly that it should be granted the highest priority in educational programs for students of all ages, and developmental levels, starting with the very young. Only an alert and knowledgeable person can overcome the enormous pressures to which he's subjected in a relentless attempt to empty his pockets and at times to hurt him in the process. Furthermore, as an educational tool, consumerism spans such a wide area that it engulfs all fields of human endeavor and as such it constitutes an excellent vehicle for growth.

CHAPTER 22

Immorality – Flirting with Disaster

One day, during my never-to-be-forgotten chats with Albert Einstein, the great scientist, commenting on the hazards of cold war reality, suggested the following:

"I believe the world would be so much safer if the respective countries would be governed by academicians. Mind you, how much smoother would the U.N. function if professors rather than Machiavellian politicians were to face each other."

His beautiful eyes glowed as he elaborated on this idea.

Indeed, this was typical Einsteinian reasoning, profound and sincere and yet naive in the extreme. Knowledge can only be beneficial if it is in synthesis with its other component—morality. These two elements are truly indivisible. Morality without knowledge lends itself to exploitation and manipulation. On the other hand, knowledge lacking its other component becomes diabolic. In fact the history of man depicts as it were an endless chain of conquests of brutality and inhumanity of man towards man. The pyramids of Egypt, the Taj Mahal in India, the priceless jewels of archeology which are viewed as a testimony of man's ingenuity should remind us of the bitter exploitation of millions of slaves who from the dawn of time had built with their blood and sweat these monuments to glorify despots and tyrants. So are the conquests of Alexander the Great, Roman emperors, Crusaders, Khans, as well as Bismark and Napoleon. Hitler's and Stalin's campaigns brought in their way misery and tragedy to multitudes. The massacre of Armenians during the First World War, the Nazi genocide, the Stalin purges had their roots in the Spanish inquisition. Roman persecutions of early Christians and the plight of contemporary giants of intellect, courage and foresight such as Sacharow, Michajlow and hundreds of thousands of unsung heroes rotting in prisons and its newest version of persecution in mental institutions of USSR have a lot in common. The plight of political prisoners and modern slaves extends throughout the whole word from Spain to Chile and is quite similar to the martyrdom of the great beacons of light of yesterday, Socrates, Gallileo, Spinoza, Copernicus, Martin Luther and thousands of other thinkers who paved the way for progress of science and enlightenment in defiance of despotism and religious dogma.

As a student I was engaged in an intercollegiate debate; the issue was the hotly contested landmark Supreme Court decision repudiating the "separate but equal" concept in education. Notwithstanding my very vigorous and perhaps eloquent defense of the ruling which I based on morality and fairness, my opponent defeated me. Subsequent to which my professor scolded me unceremoniously "for not taking the bull by the horns. Your strategy was based on morality which constitutes a rather feeble argument. You should have stressed the staggering economic losses to the country due to not utilizing the black manpower which under existing conditions cannot secure the proper training due to the inferiority of the segregated schools," stated my indignant instructor. This reasoning proved to be convincing as I scored a decisive victory during the next debate dealing with the same subject.

Characteristically, the courageous opposition to our insane involvement in Vietnam on moral grounds fell on deaf ears as well. Not even the My Lai massacre, the polarization at home and the ever increasing American casualties deterred our government from escalation of this cruel war. Finally, the spiral of inflation, the economic dislocation and above all the reference to the staggering loss of $120 billion wasted in Vietnam prompted us to terminate our infamous role in defense of a corrupt regime.

Our national demoralization reached its nadir during the Vietnam War with the TV beaming daily pictures of incredible war atrocities, directly from the battlefield, through the miracle of satellite transmission into tens of millions of American homes, as families gathered at the table to enjoy their dinner with little or no concern for the needless human suffering. The reaction in my household was somewhat different. Whenever the camera during the 6:30 news turned to the Vietnam theater, an uncontrollable cardiac fibrillation would smite me in response. Although I have had a long history of an acute heart disease, none of my spasms could be predicted earlier. This prompted me to consult my internist, a rather liberal man. Nonchalantly my doctor urged me to visit a psychiatrist.

"You see no normal person ever reacts so dramatically to what appears to be an ordinary news broadcast." David who like Edith earlier accompanied me to the doctor on all my visits, usually restrained and respectful, now exploded in anger.

"Doctor perhaps it is the other way around. How can one endure the view of such an atrocity day after day without a trauma?"

"How about you?" pressed the doctor. "If you must know, I do suffer from nightmares" replied the 11-year-old boy.

Two weeks later David in an acrimonious debate vigorously supported McGovern in his bid for presidency. "You see," he heatedly argued, "McGovern has chosen the committee on nutrition which abundantly testifies to his compassion for the poor." The children rebutted him "Ours is the richest country in the world enjoying the highest standard of living. Why bother about a few hundred misfits?" "What a profanity . . . what an obscenity," protested David. A scuffle ensued. "Down with McGovern, elect Nixon; he will lead us to victory in Vietnam," screamed the youngsters as they punched the helpless child.

David came back from school upset, his bleeding nose providing a testimony to his courage. His statement "I am willing to lose a battle in defense of a just cause which ultimately will triumph" sounded truly prophetic.

With the rapidly rising crime wave which sweeps our country, the dreadful philosophy of "mind your own business" takes a heavy toll of our society. Perhaps equally shocking as the commission of crime itself, is the total indifference on the part of witnesses, who not only ignore the plea for help but with total disregard for the victim pursue their way without even notifying the police. Likewise, victims of accidents may lay helplessly on the highways for hours, with thousands of motorists merrily speeding by. At a recently attended sympsoium devoted to geriatrics a renown internist remarked:

"A major cause of fatalities resulting from heart attacks is attributable to the fact that many victims often collapse among strangers, who for one or another reason, do not bother to summon an ambulance."

Another shocking evidence of immorality and its devastating consequences follows. On February 2, 1976, the Miami Herald in an editorial scolded mildly the medical profession.

"27 per cent of the hysterectomy operations done last year in the U.S. were not necessary. The figure on prostate was 29 per cent, on hemorrhoids 17 per cent, on tonsils 70 per cent, on gall bladder removal 14 per cent. With so much unnecessary surgery done last year, the study concludes about 12,000 surgery related deaths were avoidable. Another 10,000 Americans die each year or suffer potential fatal effects from antibiotics prescribed but not needed." It should be stressed that these conservative figures resulted from a two-year study of none other than the College of Surgeons, hence the credibility and accuracy of this project is beyond reproach.

Of course, the enormity of these crimes defies comprehension, with the Nazi concentration camp doctors experimenting on innocent victims providing the only frame of reference.

What should also be stressed with alarm is that none of these white coated gangsters has been suspended from the practice of medicine. Nor has anyone been brought before the bar of justice. Thus, it can be assumed that in the future these criminals will be free with total impunity to prey upon their innocent victims, as a rule poor and helpless people. For it is well known that the rich and sophisticated usually consult several physicians before undergoing surgery. All of this crime will be continued with cold, calculated premeditation leaving behind death and indescribable suffering.

It is the height of irony that the only visible consequence of these shocking revelations is an increased volume of malpractice litigations, and the skyrocketing cost of malpractice insurance which, of course, in final analysis will be borne by the patient himself. Again, due to the lack of morality, the oceans of innocently spilled blood, the agony of pain and death are being equated with money. Who can place a monetary value on a human life and how can one explain the wanton murder, for a few silver pieces, committed, not by a destitute frustrated youngster who lurks in a dark alley, but by a physician whose calling personifies the most noble aspiration of man. And as it should be stressed in a materialistic society, by men whose earning potential is simply astronomical.

In the past military conflicts, no matter how savage, were limited, as to their scope to a region. With the advent of nuclear weaponry which a large number of countries possess, and which many more will acquire within the next 5 years, the possibility of the deployment of this frightening arsenal in case of a military conflict and with it a global catastrophy is truly real.

Moreover, what is being underestimated is the threat to life resulting from the vast proliferation of nuclear energy plants, the erection of which gained momentum with the worsening of the energy crisis. These plants are being erected by private utility companies where the quest for profit is the only consideration. These plants are often erected in close proximity to populated areas. According to experts they lack safety devices, which results from an effort to cut corners at times and of course is being aided by bribes of corrupt officials. What is more frightening is that we actually lack the knowledge to determine the harmful effects of the presence of these plants on man and vegetation. Some scientists believe that leakage in some plants has already been observed and that the consequence of it cannot be ascertained at once. It is assumed that the slightest accident, due to an act of God or a human error, could unleash a nuclear holocaust claiming millions of lives and a destruction of vegetation for many generations to come.

The erection of nuclear plants abroad and their management is under even less stringent controls. As a residue of proliferation of nuclear plants virtually throughout the world, the transition from peaceful use of the nuclear energy into military one, as was the case in India, is scientifically simple. This further increases the threat of a nuclear holocaust.

Last, but not least, political terrorists who wrought so much tragedy in the last decade, bringing governments virtually to their knees, will, with relative ease, be able to acquire these dreadful weapons, transporting them in conventional luggage anywhere in the world, terrorizing whole countries at will.

Corporations have never exhibited excessive concern for public welfare. Monopolies, with the aid of effective lobbying coupled with lack of labor laws, by dealing and wheeling have amassed great power in the relentless quest for money. From these emerged the legendary arrogant coal, oil, railroad barons.

At no time have the giant corporations otherwise known as multinationals been so inimical to the interests of our country and indeed of the countries where they operate. These huge corporations, irrespective of our national interest, move huge quantities of funds from one country to the other which has in the past severely depressed the value of the dollar. Because of the enormous economic and thus political leverage, they are able to subjugate governments. Cunningly, with the aid of multimillion dollar advertisement campaigns which are tax deductible, they wrap themselves in a patriotic mantle. In actuality many commit bona fide treason in the pursuit of their greedy objectives, as was the case with the oil companies which were ordered by the Arab governments during the oil embargo to deny the U.S. Air Force planes supplies of oil. This treacherous order was dutifully carried out. Likewise, during the Angola Civil War, Gulf Oil made substantial payments to the pro-Soviet faction thus aiding and abetting our adversaries. One corporation was stupid and arrogant enough to offer the CIA a substantial sum of money in exchange for its assistance in toppling the government of Chile, a country with which we maintained diplomatic relations.

The Watergate scandals revealed huge illegal contributions to the Nixon campaign in exchange for shady and crooked deals and concessions on the part of so many huge corporations.

Finally the incredible disclosure of the multimillion dollar bribes on the part of Lockheed, a company which was rescued by the taxpayers from imminent bankruptcy, as well as other corporations further proves my point. The effects of these scandals have literally destabilized our closest allies Japan, Germany, Holland and other countries playing directly into the hands of our adversaries.

It is not uncommon that the legitimate interests of the United States as represented by the State Department are being sabotaged by the shady activity of an American corporation abroad.

The possibility of a military conflict into which we might be drawn because of the shady machinations of corporations is being acknowledged openly. So serious is this matter, that the United States government was compelled to seek United Nations assistance to curb this affliction. It is obvious that unless something drastic is done, these unscrupulous giants in the pursuit of almighty profits will involve us in international conflicts, undermine friendly governments and through their corrupt influences pave the way to Communism and chaos.

In the past, a slick salesman would sell cure-all tonics from a covered wagon cheating a few gullible people, however causing no harmful effects, as the tonic consisted of distilled water or perhaps diluted alcohol. The enormous progress in pharmacology resulted in an array of life saving drugs, as well as an assortment of over-the-counter remedies which profess to cure colds, headaches and just about any other ailment. The government scientists possess sufficient evidence to expose most of these claims as simply fraudulent. Many of these so-called drugs are actually harmful. Aided by mass media of TV reaching tens of millions of people these advertisements depict wholesome neat families residing in peaceful little towns praising these drugs which allegedly overcome insomnia, headaches and colds, and just about all other afflictions. Apart from the fact that these remedies are worthless and often cause serious harm, these messages create a euphoric feeling that one can rely on pills for every problem, which explains the enormous increase in the consumption of over-the-counter drugs with its tragic residue.

Our wasteful economy which has so wantonly depleted our national resources, polluting the air, the rivers, dangerously upsetting the ecology in search of more profits for the few, has indeed brought us to the brink of disaster. The alarming increase of cancer in all forms makes my message strikingly poignant. Yesterday we desperately searched for a clue to cancer. Today, the unscrupulous charlatans cheerfully manufacture tons of carcinogenic agents for human consumption in the form of food dye, food additives, cosmetics and animal nutrition.

All profit-making enterprises including banks and loan associations are eager to have you believe that their only concern is "to build and to serve America." Actually, their only objective is to make money. This is not always necessarily synonomous with public welfare.

The steel companies pollute the air and waterways, for it is the most inexpensive way to make money. Likewise, the TV networks pollute the air waves as the junk mail destroys the vital postal system, without the slightest concern for public welfare.

The slick land company salesman who, in an effort to con you into buying an Arizona desert lot, tells you that "the Almighty God has produced just that much land and no more," appears to be religious for the simple purpose of softening your resistance. Likewise, the clever manufacturers who produce toilet seats and coffins bearing the American flag, supposedly as an expression of their patriotism to celebrate the Bicentennial, use cunningly this opportunity in a vulgar and obscene manner to make money.

In the same spirit, a politician who dons a skull cap to be photographed with Jewish Yeshiva children in New York, simply does it to court Jewish votes, as there are no Arab voters in the city that could be offended. So does a politician who vigorously blasts Castro's Cuba in Miami in an effort to win the Cuban vote, for there are few pro-Castro Cubans in the U.S.A.

In the same vein will a non-Irish office seeker lead a St. Patrick's Day Parade in New York City, while scolding the British for their suppression of Northern Ireland, for there are no British voters in New York but there are plenty of Irish.

As a matter of fact, not only is business void of any patriotism in the pursuit of its single objective, which is profits, but when its activities clearly become harmful to the public welfare it will by no means capitulate. It will, by methods of bribe, fraud and propaganda, prevail in pursuing its activities, overcoming public censure, indignation, and even legal restrictions.

How many manufacturers do you know who have ceased production of "Saturday night specials," or stores which have ceased selling them in the face of mounting evidence that these weapons are responsible for the rising tide of crime? How many tobacco manufacturers do you know who have terminated the production of cigarettes in face of irrefutable evidence that smoking causes lung cancer? How many stores do you know which have removed tobacco products from their shelves? To the contrary, you will recall how bitterly these people fought the prohibition of cigarette advertisement on TV. So do the manufacturers of cyclomate, food additives and dyes, cosmetics, and an infinite number of products which are linked to cancer.

For example people owning a coal mine by and large postpone as long as they can the installation of a safety device, fully aware that lack of it might result, and often does, in tragic accidents.

Do the activities of business contribute to social progress? As long as profits are high it is fine with management. However, should a choice have to be made, then profits will come first. If the U.S.A. should be involved in a war, the defense industry will promptly mobilize all its resources to meet the challenges. Of course, it would have to be watched for overcharging and fraud. In this case, the effort would be in the national interest, as well as self-serving, for it would generate huge profits. On the other hand, when there is peace, the managers of the idle war machines will meddle to create conflicts, as President Eisenhower amply warned us when speaking of the "threat of the military industrial complex."

Similarly, when a company occupies a strong position in an industry, it will tolerate weak competitors. However, when it is in its interest to get rid of competition, it will do so by legal or illegal means, for again its only objective is the insatiable quest for profits. A company will employ an advertising message rich in socially redeeming values, when it is in its interest, such as a life insurance company promoting health habits to prolong the lives of those that it insures. It does so neither loving nor hating people. Simply, it is in the company's best interest that the insured live longer and pay more premiums. Similarly, a leading encyclopedia, in order to promote its business, may extol the virtue of learning, so that people would buy its publication and contribute to the company's profits. Likewise, a publisher will reprint Shakespeare, Tolstoy, Dostoevski. On the other hand, when it becomes more lucrative to proliferate trashy literature, he will do so without having any regards for the public welfare.

A manufacturer of cereals, fully aware that his product has no nutritional value, as it often consists of 50% sugar content, will, with the assistance, I might add, of the TV network, extol the "nutritional values of its product," aiming at youngsters, with the aid of a violent show. It will do so neither loving nor hating youngsters, simply attempting to make a buck. If, in the process, it hurts little children who get accustomed to poor nutrition, so be it.

One day during my travels in Colorado, I visited a junior high school class in a small mountain village whose students, according to the principal's assessment, "because of the village's distance from Denver, are not too wordly". Yet, my conversation with them revealed alertness and a keen interest in the turbulent events of a world in crisis.

As we discussed the oil embargo, one student stated with perfect clarity, "We could in a matter of 4 to 5 years cease totally our dependence on imported oil. Simply, we can build cars which will give us 35 to 40 miles per gallon. From an engineering standpoint, this can be done without any obstacles. Since the average life span of a car is 5 years, our dependence on imported oil would cease in this period of time. Furthermore, having small cars on the highways would reduce the traffic congestion."

To my astonishment, all experts whom I consulted in related fields have agreed with this perfect solution. However, what this logically thinking student overlooked is the greed of the automobile and oil industry. Namely, it is in the interest of the oil industry (which so piously professes a commitment to oil conservation) to sell huge quantities of oil, as it is in the automobile industry's interest to build large, consuming huge quantities of gas cars, for there is less profit for them in building small economy size cars. Consequently, the country has to suffer the dire consequences of the skyrocketing prices of oil with the pathetic dislocation to our economy, and the enormous suffering in the form of massive unemployment, as a residue.

As it has been observed lately, giant companies have "cornered the market," having "placed the consumer over the barrel," resulting in shabby craftsmanship, appliances which don't last long, and warranties which are not worth the paper they are printed on. This enables the manufacturer to produce more, thus creating artificial demand and with it more profits.

To illustrate more vividly my argument, let me mention the hundreds of thousands of cars which manufacturers are withdrawing as unsafe, in consequence of a bitter crusade of one honest young man, Ralph Nader, just to mention one industry.

In the past, no automobile manufacturer would ever acknowledge any shortcoming of his product, always blaming drivers for all accidents. And of course the public, as well as the judiciary authorities, were led to believe that it was so.

How many other lifesaving devices have been introduced spanning the whole gamut of our economy from toys to drugs, from water purification to the current campaign to alert the public about the radiation hazards of the nuclear plants thanks to the efforts of Ralph Nader.

Of course, one should not overlook the incredible malice to which this courageous man has been subjected by General Motors, maintaining ironically enough, "What's good for General Motors is good for the country."

If a single man in course of a decade or so brought upon us profound improvements of such a magnitude, one can easily see how serious the consumer abuses are, how corrupt the business community is and how imperative is the need for ombudsmen to protect the public.

When a company is genuinely interested in producing something that would be sturdy, this is being done, and I might add, par excellence. The telephone receiver will last 15 to 20 years, because the phone company lends us it for the length of our subscription. This apparatus lasts, notwithstanding the frequent abuses which it is subjected to by children. It requires no repairs for a period of 20 years and longer. What is the explanation for it? Simply, the telephone company builds receivers in a sturdy manner. Were they inefficient they would have to be repaired or replaced at the company's expense, and this is contrary to the telephone company's interest.

If we accept the premise that this economic system resembling as it were the law of the jungle, is the only workable one and, therefore, the best we can have, let us then police it for the good of society and the consumer.

To be sure, the business community plays a vital role in the production and distribution of goods and services. Police and other branches of the law-enforcing sector, perform a vital role also, but they, too, have to be strictly supervised for the good of society. Otherwise, excessive unchecked police power may lead to totalitarianism; and, of course, Watergate reminds us what happens when political power is unchecked.

But, above all, let us not allow the self-glorification of the business community as epitomizing all the virtues and morality, ordained by a higher power to rule, to pontificate us, to pose as our loving benefactor, for it is not true.

Those who would conclude that I am anti-business are wrong, for I am neither anti- nor pro-business. My task is to enlighten the public without malice or prejudice as to the true objectives of business. Thus, beware of those who subscribe to the belief "that the business of government is business" or that government "should be run by businessmen and in a businesslike manner." What we actually need is a compassionate, well functioning, government close to its people. Awareness of the true nature of business can make it more usable to society.

But above all, let us protect the public from the merciless onslaught of vicious propaganda. Let every advertisement be scrutinized for the truth. Justice Holmes ruled that screaming "fire" in a crowded theatre, when there is no evidence of fire, should be regarded as a crime, for it will cause undue panic and, as such, cannot be protected by the First Amendment guaranteeing freedom of speech. Misleading advertisement is just as serious, if not more serious an offense, and should be curbed in the strictest sense for the good of the consumer and the good of society.

The lack of scruples or concern for the people that these corporations have exhibited causes not only deceptive advertising, but also the danger of man's possible destruction; therefore, it is imperative that we develop new concepts, new forms of relationships, a dedication to high moral standards in government as well as in the private sector, a dedication to sanity and tolerance through intellectual and spiritual growth or else we shall perish.

At one of my recent university lectures a grey-haired pensive looking man succinctly summarized the public frustration by stating:

"To be truthful, I was much happier not to be made aware of how precarious our very existence is as I can do nothing about it."

And as my lecture was to be terminated on such a sour note a young black man stood up and with a fervent zeal and resolution replied:

"The filth, decadence and moral decay encompassing the whole world will be swept clean when the torch passes from the old generation to the young one, united by a common desire to break loose the chains of political doctrine and hate."

A thunder of applause drowned his last words.

CHAPTER 23

The Bleak Ravage

Undoubtedly our nation's external enemies, armed to their teeth with nuclear arms, pose a lesser peril to the survival of this society than does the innocuous-looking TV set. For one thing, the clearly identifiable adversaries confront a formidable deterrent in the form of our own defense forces, as well as those of our allies. Moreover, the realization that both sides in the conflict possess sufficient resources to destroy each other fortunately has resulted in a detente, which, for the near future at least, alleviates the spector of nuclear annihilation.

On the other hand, the TV's relentless assault on our intelligence, decency, and sense of propriety and its tragic impact on its young, helpless victims is devastating. With no one making an effort to curtail this horrible air pollution, the commercial TV networks dump a barrage of garbage, consisting of violence, mediocrity and trivia into 98% of American homes for a period of 18 to 20 hours per day. Thus, day after day from the cradle to the grave, this miraculous media, which could be a source of blessings in our endless search for spiritual enlightenment and advancement of our culture, becomes a ferocious villain, fanning the fires of hate and violence, exploiting the dormant morbid curiosity and appealing to the prurient instincts. So effective, so shocking is the conspiracy of all three networks that whenever a viewer becomes extremely incensed with a particularly appalling program glorifying crime and in search of relief turns to the other stations he will find a similar program in progress. A recently conducted study revealed that for a period of three months, 64% of all crimes committed by young people aged from 16 to 24 were literally based on plots unfolded over TV, including even the most minute technical details. At times, as many as five crimes commited in different parts of the country have replicated the same TV program.

The TV not only triggers the interest but actually provides an excellent source of instruction for the would-be criminal, as well as for the untroubled youngster as to the intricacies of ballistics, the shortcomings of the law enforcing agencies and the leniency of the courts. My conversations with judges, lawyers, criminologists, and youthful offenders, fully corroborate this observation.

Of course, the networks pledge faithful adherence to the television code adopted by the National Association of Broadcasters, pledging ironically to adhere to programs which "reflect a high degree of creative skill, deal with significant moral issues." As for children, the programming "should include positive sets of values which will allow the child to become a responsible adult." Insofar as commercials are concerned, the following pledge is truly a supreme mockery. "Their advertising messages should be presented in an honest, responsible and tasteful manner".

When hard-pressed network executives do reluctantly confess their sins with a plea for understanding, they argue that ours is a violent and mediocre society, and that TV entertainment faithfully reflects these two components. Of course, both are a patent lie. For we Americans are a peaceful and compassionate people, deeply rooted in the Judeo-Christian tradition of charity and justice. We, as do other people, become violent after years of systematic brutalization by the infamous military adventures and by the merciless assault on our minds by violence on TV, movies, and trashy literature. Likewise, a country as creative and ingenious as ours, setting a model for the world in productivity and resourcefulness, nourished by the ethnic diversity of its people, is anything but mediocre but, here again, the persistent environment of trivia, which is being so skillfully cultivated by the media, is taking a heavy toll on us.

One might wonder what laws govern TV, if any. Why do the networks fail so appallingly to provide cultural programs? Why is it that those who sponsor the shows in order to promote the products tolerate this trivia? Why are the commercials so vulgar and offensive? Is the entertainment really free to the public, as it is stated? I shall endeavor to address myself to these issues, which in my judgment are very crucial indeed.

Many of us may not be cognizant of the fact that the air waves, like the air we breath, constitute one of the most precious national assets. And, as the air must be oxygenated and pure to enable our lungs to function well, so should the air waves become a powerful force for good in providing enlightenment to the broadest masses, in bringing culture to the most remote hamlet at a minimal cost.

The government licenses for reasons of "public interest, convenience, and necessity" a network for the purpose of broadcasting. This license must be renewed upon presentation of proof that the given station serves well the needs of the community. Theoretically, and unfortunately only theoretically, if a station fails to do so, the license may be revoked or not extended.

Of course, these stipulations sound like a farce, as all three national networks violate this covenant from the time they commence early broadcasts until they sign off late into the night. And, of course, the contributions of the TV networks to the cultural life of the country appear to be as impressive as is rampant inflation to an economic stability.

Strange as it may seem, the networks described by the former commissioner of the FCC, Mr. Minnow, as the "vast wasteland" deliberately fill the air waves with trash with the consent of the advertiser. Their appeal to the lowest common denominator, by glorifying crime and indulging for hours in melodramatic soap operas, assisted by the canned laughter machines, rigged contest shows, trivial and vulgar talk shows, is clearly designed to erode our intelligence and to lower our self-esteem. One would be hard-pressed to find one socially redeeming feature in this programming. Of course, if anything matches this disgraceful conduct in the depth of insults, venom, obscenity and vulgarity, it could only be the commercials, during which children convey affection to their parents on toilet tissues, coffeemakers reconcile broken marriages, toothpaste restores virility, and women express ecstasy over panty hose.

This concerted assault on our intellectual faculties, aesthetics, as well as prudence, is designed to make us receptive, by disarming our defense mechanism, to purchasing goods and services which often are superfluous, and at times downright harmful to our health.

Had the networks utilized the enormous talents which our gifted people possess, had they stimulated interest in our great novels and fine music, had they inspired racial understanding, advanced consumer education, political maturity through intelligent debates, our sophistication as consumers and citizens would have been enhanced. This is contrary to the interests of those who prey on our naïveté to dispose of the mountains of inferior goods and needless services.

Another patent lie, which provides a shield of last resort to the defenders of the air rape, is the often heard argument that TV is free to the public in the U.S.A. and, therefore, should be gracefully accepted in its present form.

While it is true that British and French people pay a subscription fee for their access to TV, the price which we pay is far greater; for, in addition to the moral devastation it causes, our financial contributions are substantial. Namely the lavish, extravagant shows, running into millions of dollars, are to the sponsors tax deductible as advertisements. The U.S. Treasury, in order to meet the budgetary requirements of running the government, must take a heavier tax bill on our income, in addition to which the cost of the products which we consume is in direct proportion to the advertisement expenses. Thus, they too, go up substantially.

232

Not to sound overly pessimistic, I should like to mention the true glimpse of hope that is Educational Public Television. It attempts, often successfully, to redress the abuses and harmful impact of the commercial networks on the nation. Of course, as the programming is geared to stimulate cultural pursuits, it provides by doing so a sharp contrast with the three commercial networks. However, recent surveys reveal that mainly the upper socio-economic group avails itself of this source of enlightenment. Hence, those who need it most in order to develop themselves, the blue-collar sector, are lured to the "glamour and splendor" of the commercial TV station.

The Educational Public Television derives its income from government, foundation, and public contribution; hence, it is not subjected to the same pressures as is the commercial TV station sponsored by advertisers whose interest lies in lowering the standards of the public. However, the management of the public stations is recruited from "pillars of the community"; staunch supporters of the establishment. And, as such, it, too, curbs the free flow of ideas and talents coming from the outside, from minorities, from women, and those who would like to air controversial issues.

Consequently, this dedicated group of crusaders fired by genuine enthusiasm and zeal to serve the public has been transformed into a well entrenched bureaucracy, worrying about security and prestige. Gone are the vigor and spontaneity of the early years. Hence, more and more money is being spent on administration and fund-raising, and greater becomes the reliance on nationally syndicated programs to the exclusion of local talents and community issues.

At the risk of being repetitious I must stress again my conviction that it is impossible to envision a more powerful, effective vehicle of enlightenment than the media of TV could have been. Its wide penetration and low cost could uplift man's dignity to the loftiest heights. Through true education, it could melt the curse of prejudice and hate. Its added video dimension of color could make the process of learning so much more meaningful. Unfortunately, none of these dreams has materialized. To the contrary, widespread TV viewing brings in its wake decadence and stagnation.

I recall, during my visit to Harvard University in the 1960's, a meeting with a South African high official of the Ministry of Education. Inasmuch as my lecture there dealt with the dynamics of school integration, a major issue of the decade, I thought I would slightly needle the man who represented a regime which I abhorred because of its apartheid policies by asking him: "What is, in your judgment, the most pressing problem in America today?" "The deep devastation which the TV has wrought upon the young. We in South Africa are most reluctant to introduce TV, fearing its impact on the youth and on our moral values," was the reply which caught me in astonishment. As it is known, South Africa resisted most vigorously for years the invasion of TV, but just a few years ago finally succumbed to the demands for introduction of it. However, its broadcasting is limited to a couple of hours a day.

The other day, I read a proposal of a California education task force, which was described as "revolutionary in scope." It proposed "that college students should not get their degree, unless they can read and write, especially write." My thoughts turned to the introspective man from South Africa, whose assessment tragically enough proved to be correct.

CHAPTER 24

Edith Speaks

SHORT ESSAYS WRITTEN AT AGE 7, 8, 12, 13, 16
A BROADER VIEW AT AGE 14, 24

I have been frequently asked what impact did the publicity have on Edith? Has my intensive work with her denied Edith a happy wholesome childhood? "Why not let nature take its course?" asks a child psychologist. Often I am reminded by eminent scientists such as Professors Jensen and Eyeneck that genes determine intelligence and intellect rather than environment. Of course, I vigorously disagree with these views and submit to scientific scrutiny this perhaps most important experiment ever undertaken in the area of child development.

At any rate Edith, who has won international acclaim in the area of cybernetics, speaks for herself. So does David (in another chapter), who at 13 inspired a congressional resolution for his excellence in marine biology.

Edith Stern
Age 7
Why Not Dignity?

My father took me yesterday to see a beauty contest, at which young women in various stages of semi-nudity paraded to the cheers of male spectators and the warm approval of the women present. And what a tragic sight this was, so reminiscent of a dog show at which the physique of the pure bred animal is being admired. I can well understand the sexual urges of a male and how such a spectacle stimulates him. However, what I don't understand is how girls capable of developing their mind and intelligence to the man's level and beyond resign themslves to be sex

235

objects to men and employ their body gyrations skillfully to arouse a male sex response rather than develop their mind to be creative, and contribute to the progress of humanity. How deplorable it is that women who constitute more than 50% of our population allow themselves by their consent and approval to be governed by men in Congress and our national economy, the professions and in practically every field of endeavor. Oh, how sickening it is when girls look forward to marriage as an ultimate fulfillment so as to be dominated by a strong male, to obediently giving him children and rearing them as he sees fit, to keep his house in a slave-like manner, to lose one's identity by accepting his surname and often his first name. How tragic it is that a girl from her infancy is led to believe that she is little, weak, that her clothing must be always neat, that the games she is to play must be lady-like, how dolls are thrown into her hands to remind her that her supreme goal is to bear children. How tragic it is that in every segment of our economy the women are at the bottom of the economic ladder always earning less money than men for equal work. They are never or very seldom allowed a promotion. This discrimination is being conducted at a time when we are involved in a bitter struggle with Communism for the hearts and minds of humanity. We could so easily double our resources without increasing the size of our population by encouraging women to develop their minds, to compete with men. Furthermore, would not the productivity of women enrich the lives of both sexes rather than to see it wasted on trivia, vanity and long outlived conventions.

Edith Stern
Age 8
Service is Our Only Motive

When Mrs. Jackson goes to her neighborhood department store to purchase a modest dress she is being enormously flattered. As soon as she decides on a dress the obliging saleslady suggests solicitously, "is that a charge or cash?" And without much imagination, Mrs. Jackson could detect that the saleslady would be much happier to sell the dress on a charge account.

What a moral uplift this is. After all, Mrs. Jackson is not a wealthy woman. The $120 per week that her husband earns in the steel mill is hardly sufficient to raise a family of four children. Therefore, it is tempting for her to delay payment on the dress in the face of mounting expenses.

Furthermore, Mrs. Jackson, a relatively poor woman, derives genuine satisfaction from being regarded as trustworthy. Had she inquired at the credit office what the charges were, the answers would have been evasive.

236

The clerk would have politely answered, "it is only 50 cents a week. As far as the percentage is concerned, I really don't know."

Perhaps the clerk really does not know — her job is to process credit applications. This is what she is trained for and this is the extent of her knowledge. But in the elegant surroundings of the Home Office, the receipts of Mrs. Jackson's are neatly added on a computer. They are vigilantly being watched, for they represent 20% profits per annum. This makes mighty good reading on the annual stockholders report.

Consequently, everyone is happy. Mrs. Jackson has a dress for which she can delay payment, thanks to the "courtesy and accommodation of the friendly department store." So are the management and the stockholders of the chain for they all can "unselfishly serve the public."

Edith Stern
Age 12
Demagoguery at Its Best

President Lyndon Johnson, the proud Texan and a skillful demagogue, encounters a lot of trouble. Shot to pieces is his grand strategy to win peace in Vietnam. His generals' victory pronouncements turned unfortunately sour. His inability to subordinate the Congress puts the country on a collision course. The polls show a catastrophic decline of his popularity. The poor man is even unable to address himself to his fellow Americans due to fear of a hostile demonstration. Be that as it may, Lyndon the knight on the white horse is adamantly determined to win the war in Vietnam, even if it takes the killing of every Vietnamese in the process, the destruction of every hamlet south or north of the demilitarized zone. For Lyndon the Texas wonder boy does not retreat from the chartered course. Lyndon Johnson, the President of these United States, is also a skillful politician, an expert on rousing the emotions of the masses, and one who values highly the tools of mass communication. To mend his fences and obviously fences must be mended, President Johnson chooses the decoration of a wounded captain to strike a devastating blow at his war critics. The stage is set for the drama, a young captain wounded halfway around the world, accompanied by his proud parents appears before the cameras at the White House. The President in an emotion choked voice pontifically addresses the nation.

"My fellow Americans at this time doubters among us sow seeds of defeatism thus giving comfort to our enemy. The brave Captain Jackson unselfishly and heroically sustained a grave wound in battle defending freedom and liberty. No argument can be more eloquent in refuting the demand for cessation of bombing. Our determination and fortitude will prevail. An honorable peace will be won."

Whereupon Mr. Johnson with tears flowing down his cheeks proceeds with decorating the proud captain; a warm handshake seals the event.

At the other end of the TV sets redblooded Americans become indignant. They shake their fists; feelings of pity, pride in the flag and the hate for the enemy rises. Mr. Johnson has skillfully accomplished his job. But a careful, logical analysis will prove that he spoke a lot and said nothing. For the mere fact that a young brave American lost his limb in battle proves only that hostilities are in progress in Vietnam. It does not prove that our presence in Vietnam is justified or warranted or prudent. Nor does it suggest in the least that suspension of the bombing of the North will not lead to peace talks. Least of all does it prove that opponents of the war are unpatriotic as his speech implies. But logical analysis is being conducted on college campuses only and Mr. Johnson directs his appeal towards the millions of Americans who are aroused by flag waving, for this is the most effective tool in persuading masses throughout the world, no matter how unjust or illogical the cause may be. Indeed, Mr. Johnson scored one more victory. Again, he has set American superpatriots' hearts on fire.

Edith Stern
Age 13
Public Welfare

No issue in American life stirs more controversy than public welfare. Anything pertaining to it is being hotly debated and often successfully employed as a vehicle to secure public office, to defeat civil rights legislation or for any other political advantage. Welfare is at the heart of the Negro problem. Its wide scope embraces the whole spectrum. The simplest means to define welfare care in a pragmatic way, consistent with the limited space of this article, would be the following: public welfare is a government effort to provide assistance to its citizens who for reasons of poor health, lack of skills or unemployment cannot adequately support themselves.

In a broader sense, the welfare concept is at the heart of every legislative accomplishment since the depression, such as aid to schools, social security, medicare, medicaid. Its administration in various forms is conducted on every level of federal, state and city government. The opponents of welfare advance the following argument. American society is based on rugged individualism and free initiative. Hence, every person in our affluent society with little effort can secure for himself a decent standard of living. It is argued by these people that welfare tends to undermine man's initiative by providing readily available financial support. Thus it kills the incentive for self-support. Welfare recipients tend to rely fully on support, hence their children, by and large, tend to rely in maturity on government handouts. The administration of welfare is poor, wasteful and bureaucratic. On the other side of the issue, the proponents state the following: the primary objective of government is to assure welfare for its citizens. Its main objective is redistribution of income, so as to assure a larger measure of equality. It is our humanitarian obligation to the less fortunate. The failure of welfare recepients to obtain gainful employment is the fault of society, since adequate schooling was not offered to them. Since a large percentage of welfare recipients are members of the black race and other minorities, prejudice plays an important factor in the inability of the recipient to secure adequate schooling and employment.

Irrespective of the merits or demerits of the welfare concept, the main facts are being totally overlooked. Namely, the most vocal militant opponents of welfare, the conservative and affluent strata of our society, benefit most from government subsidies in one or another form which for all practical purposes constitutes welfare.

It suffices to mention the huge subsidies extended by the government to industries running into billions of dollars, such as oil depletion, subsidies to ship builders, airlines and railroads, junk mail which mostly promotes swindle and deception, mainly responsible for the huge post office defict. How about tax free income from municipal bonds and above all the huge complex of government employees from the President down, for they too, obtain their livelihood from government funds. Who for example can determine the value of a government servant. It is not determined by the labor market and hence this group, too, benefits from the redistribution of the national income. They, too, are for practical purposes on public welfare.

Edith Stern
Age 16
Dr. Martin Luther King — In Memoriam

A vicious bullet cut short the life of Martin Luther King. Eulogizing the tragic death of this great man, one cannot comprehend the magnitude of his accomplishments as well as the nobility of his character.

Martin Luther King with a truly invincible spirit and an unswerving love and dedication was committed with his body and soul to free his people from the chains of oppression, darkness and humiliation, leading them to the Promised Land of equality and self-respect and racial harmony in this land that he so dearly loved. This was a fulfillment of the highest humanitarian ideals which he truly personified. Perhaps the loftiest goal of Martin Luther King was the salvation of the soul of white and black America rent by prejudice, hate and the frustration of affluence and moral decay.

Perhaps it is too early in this hour of sadness, bitterness, shock and frustration to assess the life of this great man. This will be done by future historians. Indeed it would be inaccurate to regard the late Dr. King a great black or American leader only.

Dr. King like Gandhi and Tolstoy belongs to the world. First and last Dr. King was a man of God and a great humanitarian. Unlike President Kennedy, whose rise to prominence was smooth and orderly, though to be sure remarkable and inspiring, Dr. King the grandson of a slave won the world's love through a bitter and courageous struggle. From the famous Alabama bus strike which ushered in a decisive phase in the blacks' battle for equality, Dr. King ceaselessly and methodically through his Southern Christian Conference focused the conscience of white America and the world on the Negro tragedy. Faithful to the concept of passive resistance, Martin Luther King chose endless jail sentences to dramatize the plight of the blacks. His numerous protest marches, often in face of provocation and police brutality as well as unruly, riotous conduct of the demonstrators, were inherently dangerous. Therefore, Dr. King could no more be blamed for the violent outbursts and looting than Moses could have been blamed for the erection of a Golden Calf in defiance of God. Martin Luther King the mortal was never given to bitterness, anger or disillusionments, although no other man has been more maligned. Martin Luther King did not value worldly possessions; the proceeds from the Nobel Prize and from his books were quietly donated to charities. The painstakingly agonizing marches which he led in ever present danger, in his many scholarly lectures, numerous publications and the endless search for understanding. Martin Luther King, the leader, humanitarian and minister, aimed at the salvation of the soul. His objective was harmony and brotherly love which may sound Utopian but finally will prevail. Unfortunately, he was not destined to lead his people to the Promised Land, not unlike another great leader some four thousand years ago.

Edith Stern
How I View The World At Age 14

It is with a great deal of reluctance that I confront the limelight into which I have been thrust. Gone are the privileges of obscurity and anonymity. Now I am told that the eyes of more than the educational community follow my progress. Once a king asked his most learned advisers to relate a phrase to him which would be appropriate for every occasion. Their efforts yielded the following — "And this too, shall pass."

On the other hand, I sincerely welcome the opportunity to participate in the debate which surrounds the educational methods employed by my

240

father. It is to these methods that I owe my modest achievements. Indeed, I regard his pedagogic concepts as revolutionary. For they provide the only alternative to the sterile dogma of complacency prevailing in our school system. They have achieved unparalleled success in my case as well as my brother's.

To be succinct, my father maintains, and I believe justly so, that

1. Educational processes should commence at birth and cease at death only.

2. A child should from infancy be exposed to as much information as she can absorb without regard to chronological age.

3. Recreational activities (toys, games) must stress and stimulate intellectual growth.

4. Molding the traits of character so essential to the development of a personality can be best accomplished through personal example. These traits include, of course,

    a. Abhorrence of violence

    b. Commitment to the ideals of social justice

    c. Non-conformity

    d. Active involvement in the affairs of the community

    e. Self-discipline

    f. Self-restraint and

    g. Humility

5. Total permissiveness with regards to non-essential factors, such as etiquette and conventions.

I believe that the above are his basic premises.

Too often I read in newspaper accounts and the voluminous mail which I receive the erroneous allegation that "her father stole her childhood and forced her into responsibility and premature adulthood." This I resent strongly for it is, to say the least, inaccurate.

My childhood was not stolen from me. In fact, I am confident that I had more of a childhood than most other youngsters. Indeed it was richer and more meaningful. I too played with dolls and blocks, but they conveyed a rewarding message. The dolls depicted a family structure and the blocks introduced me to gemoetry. I played with other children, but grew at a faster pace than they did. I built castles on white beaches, but also learned of the infinity of numbers from the grains of sand. I read Hans Christian Anderson's tales and enjoyed them immensely. I marveled at the serene beauty of the ocean, while learning about the role of the gravitational force of the moon in the formation of the tides. I was overwhelmed by the blue firmament, but learned astronomy from it. Since my infancy, I have enjoyed music, but it was Rachmaninoff and Chopin. Above all, as far back as my memory can reach, I have always had books. These were and are my most precious friends.

It is true that my material possessions were not overabundant. But on reflection, perhaps this made me a person better equipped to cope with hardship.

I was taught to abhor conquest and violence. Today I resent deeply any manifestations of brutality. I learned at an early age about the genocide practiced by the Nazis through my father's research in this field. Now, I sympathize with every victim of prejudice and bigotry from the sunbaked shores of South Africa to the Arctic freeze of Siberia.

At the age of four, I followed with great concern the brutal suppression of the Hungarian Revolution.

I learned during infancy, about the martyrdom of my grandparents at the hands of the Nazis. Today, I regard the assassination of Martin Luther King and the Kennedys as a personal loss.

I have learned from my father to search for intrinsic values and to perceive intellectually. Today, I despise symbolism, ritualism, regimentation and cliches in any form or shape.

I learned from my father the sanctity of life and the dignity of man. Consequently, I am bitterly opposed to the war in Vietnam, not only because it is not in the national interest, but because it is immoral.

I learned from my father to treasure spiritual values above material ones. Consequently, I chose college teaching as my field of endeavor, a career that does not command great financial rewards.

My father's concept of women's emancipation inspired me to match or supersede a man in creativity. I shall never be transformed into a housewife since my father has instilled in me the insatiable yearning for growth, improvement and perfection. I shall always endeavor to attain it.

I chose mathematics although I attained a straight A record in all my liberal arts courses. My father completed college in thirteen months. I was then determined to supersede him. Perhaps I have.

The next question which inevitably arises is, "Are you happy in an adult world?" Very much so. My admission to college at the age of twelve signified a full social and intellectual liberation. The chronological gap, which horrified so many people, presented no obstacle. I was fully accepted and respected. In contrast, it was not so prior to my college matriculation. Then, I was ridiculed and maligned by my chronological peers, while school authorities were appalled by my "audacity and impatience."

I am frequently asked what I think about the young generation. I sincerely believe (and my father fully agrees with me) that ours is the most promising generation the world has ever known. The social conscience of our youth can best be measured by the spectacular success of Senator McCarthy's election campaign and the vital strength of the late Senator

Kennedy which was nourished by the uninhibited vigor and dedication of young people throughout the country. The disenchantment with the hypocrisy, nihilism and expedience of the older, "respectable" generation which turns over to us a society divided, decadent in its sickening affluence, rent by racial hate, "dripping in its own fat," is well justified.

The new generation of purposeful young people dedicated to the ideals of social justice constitutes a sharp contrast with the carefree college "elite" of yesterday whose favorite pastimes were crowding into telephone booths, staging panty raids and participating in goldfish eating contests.

Insofar as the gap between generations is concerned, there is none between myself and my father. Perhaps this will serve as the most eloquent justification of his methods, since at all times he was honest and sincere with me.

For it was not my father who preached sexual morality while indulging in promiscuity. My father did not instruct me to derive strength from empty symbolism and the mechanic ritualism of dogmatic religion. My father did not seek the euphoria of alcoholism, the comfort of racial superiority, the virtue of shiny cars, and the quick buck. I have, therefore, no cause to rebel against him.

This is not to suggest that there is no difference of views between us. This is precisely what he opposes. I was taught by him to have strong convictions and an independent judgment. This may explain why I have chosen mathematics. Perhaps it was to sever the umbilical cord, to blaze my own trail. After all, my father is a liberal arts professor who knows little about mathematics.

Often I am asked, "Do you have compassion? Will you be able to function in a mediocre society?"

Definitely, I have no compassion as interpreted by the "soap operas." I do not read the "Woman's section" of newspapers. I shed no tears over Ann Landers-type "victims" nor do I select movies for a "good cry."

But I respond wholeheartedly to the plight of the blacks for social justice. I'd gladly give a pint of blood when called upon rather than parade in a "candy striper's" uniform. I shall strive to erase poverty through legislative processes rather than indulge in charity balls by featuring a dress or a hairdo for the sake of publicity. I deplore tokenism and crocodile tears. For it is our duty to bring hope where there is despair; to build rather than "beautify"; to reform rather than preserve; to oppose rather than ignore; to act rather than "bless"; to identify oneself with a cause rather than nonchalantly to suggest.

As to the latter part of the question, my father was once told by an editor, "either you write on a seventh grade level to be understood by the public or seek the seclusion of an Ivory Tower." His reply was, "it is my duty to elevate the public's standards rather than to descend to their level."

Similarly, I shall endeavor to contribute rather than appease; to be creative rather than be successful.

Invariably, I am asked what effective steps can be taken to eradicate the causes of violence.

A society which destroys its best men is destined to disintegrate. Unfortunately, we all bear a collective guilt for the tragic assassination which shook the world as well as the riots which only summon our attention when they affect us economically.

Then, naively, we pose a question, seek a panacea, and appoint commissions. Isn't it well known that ten percent of our population, the overwhelming majority of our blacks, by deliberate neglect and at best indifference, remain virtually outside our prosperous industrial society? Isn't it true that Mississippi children suffer from malnutrition, while we lavish billions on a lost cause in Vietnam?

Can we deny the fact that our foreign aid is often channeled to corrupt and shaky governments, enriching dictators and despots while essential needs of Americans are being neglected?

Aren't we, notwithstanding our "breast beating," obsessed with bigotry and prejudice? Don't we have a climate that nourishes violence and assassinations? How hard is it for anyone to secure a lethal weapon, irrespective of his age and state of mental health? My father likes to remind me how I, at the age of four, once sneaked out to a neighbor's apartment and saw a TV Western in progress. Whereupon I asked him, "How did they ever build the West if all they did was kill each other?"

Indeed, approximately 70% of the prime viewing time is occupied by shows abounding in crime and violence, which quite often glorify the villain. Doesn't this influence people?

Aren't we collectively sick when we reward the President's assassin's widow, Mrs. Oswald, with hundreds of thousands of dollars, transforming her into a millionaire. To be sure, she cannot be blamed for her husband's crimes. On the other hand, isn't this "outpouring of generosity" pathological at a time when thousands of other widows suffer hunger and deprivation.

The press reports that Speck, the accused assasin of thirteen nurses, received donations and marriage proposals.

The recent assassin of Robert Kennedy is likewise being described by the press as a "religious, serious, withdrawn, young man." It is stressed that California "has abolished the death penalty." How many would-be assassins derive comfort and encouragement from it? Regrettably, I must conclude that all these facts suggest that we are sick.

What remedies would I suggest? Complete abolishment of violence on our airwaves (which belong to the people, not to the broadcasters) by voluntary restraint or legislation. Prohibition of all weapons, with the exception of armed forces and law enforcing agencies.

Will this constitute violation of constitutional freedoms? No. It is a matter of national preservation and the transition from a raw frontier civilization to a twentieth-century one.

We must strive for peace in Vietnam and a major investment of the released funds must go to a frontal attack towards education, vocational training, negative income tax and a vast housing program.

In many letters, I am asked, "How do you envision the future of the world?"

I am extremely optimistic. That is, if the present rulers don't blow our globe to pieces. I am of the opinion that young people the world over have a common bond of hopes and aspirations. A student at Columbia University can well understand his counterpart at Charles University in Prague. Nor does a Sorbonne student share the unrealistic illusions of de Gaulle. No less does a Madrid University student resent the bloody dictatorship of Franco. To the same extent does the student of the Lomonosov University (in the Soviet Union) care about Marx's dogma. There will be differences but they will be resolved, not by "wars of national liberation" or "interventions derived from treaty commitments," but by pacific means consistent with logic and prudence.

The spectacular progress of science will bring a cheap supply of water into the thirsty deserts, thus transforming them into blooming gardens. Nuclear science will provide an inexpensive source of energy to the poor regions lacking national resources. Oceans will yield nutritious food. Education will melt prejudice. Swift transportation will shrink the world, replacing parochialism with universal brotherhood. Medical progress will conquer heart disease, cancer and mental disorders.

The new dawn will melt the rigidity of political doctrines and Machiavellian intrigues when the torch will pass from the tired, discredited old generation to the young one.

For either we shall learn to live together or we shall perish together.

And Here is what Edith Says at Age 24

My whole life has been marked by joy, inner happiness, and peace. Hence, it is with self-confidence and optimism that I look forward to the exciting challenges ahead.

I grew up in an atmosphere of Spartan-like simplicity, nourished by the tender love of parents who, in the midst of bleak poverty, carved out for me a magnificent temple of culture, amidst the everlasting flow of classical music.

Inasmuch as spiritual values, dedication to the ideas of social justice and the insatiable pursuit of knowledge signify my father's life philosophy, I have been soaking up these values in an environment of total freedom, uninhibited by conformity, greed, prejudice and trivia.

Father's preoccupation with the expanding of my cultural horizons did not in any way prevent me from wholesome recreation and play with children.

Presently, my consummate pursuit of intellectual endeavors does not interfere with the genuine pleasure which I derive from swimming, hiking, bicycle riding, playing tennis and bowling.

To be sure, I abhor mediocrity and regard it the greatest threat to the survival of our society. I treasure the love which prevails in our family and also enjoy a rewarding social life rich in affection. Owing to the healthy atmosphere in which I was raised, I emerged an emancipated female, suffering from none of the frustrations and alienations so common among the young.

Of course, I am delighted with the truly superior education which my father offered me in the face of almost insurmountable adversities, and attribute my few achievements solely to his dedicated work with me.

An old adage has it that "As the twig is bent, so goes the tree." Nowhere is there more evidence of this than in my own life. An early environment of life-as-learning from classical music to flights of fancy scientifically molded by personality. My father's educational methods were never obtrusive. I never realized I was being taught. In my world, learning was a normal expectation. Logically, the best way to ensure that child will grow to be a reasoning, thinking adult is to teach the child, at the earliest possible age, to think and reason. Total educational submersion is the way in which I was taught.

I completely agree with my dad's methods and plan to raise my own children, whenever I may have them, in accordance with his technique. Perhaps by that time that will be the traditional methodology of education.

The joy of learning begins at an early age, just as its distaste may begin in the cradle. The only way to inspire children to learn is by example. Unless the parents are imbued with a love of learning, unless they show this love through reading good books, going to art exhibits and museums, strolling through botanical gardens or walking leisurely in the park, the child will not be motivated to do any of these things.

When I was very young my father was with me all the time, and my mother whenever she could get away from her work. They gave me the support and set the example that a child needs to develop into a happy, confident individual. I doubt if any child can be happy to sit in his room and read unless he sees his parents doing so.

246

Frequently I am asked: Did your father take your childhood away from you? That is rather a silly question since my father gave me a happy, contented, self-fulfilling childhood, one that I thoroughly enjoyed. I would not trade it for any other.

Ironically, the following aided my development. During my early childhood, my family rarely stayed in one place for more than a year. We moved quite a bit, because of my father's ill health, coupled with his iconoclastic views colliding with those of the universities that he lectured at, and with his responsibilities as an educational consultant. That meant that I didn't complete more than one year in the same school. The experience of traveling, getting to different sections of the land, meeting different kinds of people, helped me a great deal. This made my educational upbringing most interesting and stimulating.

Although I listened intently to the advice and direction given me, in no sense did I become a robot. Quite the contrary. As soon as I could talk and walk I developed a mind of my own. I wasn't always right, nor did I get conceited over the fact that perhaps I was somewhat brighter than my classmates. My independence on occasion got me into trouble.

I recall one incident when I was 8 years old. My nominal bed-time was 8:30, and on special occasions 9:00. But, unilaterally, I decided that this was way too early for me. I wasn't sleepy at 9:00 in the evening, so I thought why I should be forced to go to rest against my will and better judgment. Besides, I had better things to do, so I developed my own little routine to circumvent the parental restrictions. I said good-night and went to my room, closed the door, and then to escape detection I stuffed a towel against the bottom of the bedroom door so that the cracks of light would not show. Feeling safe and secure, I usually read until midnight, going through one book after another.

Eventually, I got caught. I think my mother decided to go into my room to give me some cough medicine, as I had shown symptoms of a cold that day, and that is when my little scheme was revealed. Both my father and mother gave me a lengthy, spirited lecture on the value of sleep for growing children. I disputed that, pointing to articles that I had read in several magazines which suggested that the need for 8 hours of sleep was still undetermined, and that it varied with each individual. I also pointed out that my self-examination revealed that I was three inches taller and 12 pounds heavier than I should have been at 8.

My parents remained unconvinced. I promised that henceforth I would obey the sleeping formula established for me — and I kept my promise.

To turn from reading, which is my favorite pastime, far above any other, I love music. I remember listening to music all day long.

My schooling, to be sure, was somewhat unorthodox. When I had completed the ninth grade in junior high school, my father, realizing that I was bored, asked me whether I would like to take a college summer session. I thought that would be an excellent idea, so I took a battery of tests and scored in the upper five percent, and soon after I was admitted for the summer session only. I did not realize at the time that there was a serious controversy raging as to whether I should be admitted as a regular student. I knew that I could compete with the other college students, even though I was only 12 and the others were 6 to 8 years older.

Finally, with the reluctant permission of the authorities, I was enrolled in two courses and passed them both with A's, after which I decided that I did not want to attend high school at all.

My father, determined as he is, persuaded the authorities to accept me as a freshman at Miami Dade Junior College — the youngest one, I later learned, in their history. At this time, I did not think of my age either as an asset or a handicap. The summer session had convinced me that I could readily do the course work assigned to me.

The worst problem which I encountered in the course of my Dade Junior College career was the commuting. From North Miami Beach where we lived I had to take two buses each way — one mile from our home. I walked this distance morning and afternoon, but didn't really mind the trip. Although the distance to the college from our home was only nine miles and could be negotiated by auto in less than half an hour, the double bus ride, plus waiting time, added up to almost four hours each day. But, it was worth it by far!

As I had thought, Miami Dade Junior College presented me with no challenge. In fact, I completed the two year program and received my Associate in Arts degree in one year and a half. What then? I was still under 14 and of course attending high school, which my peers were now entering, seemed ridiculous, so I enrolled in Florida Atlantic University in Boca Raton, Florida, some 40 miles from our home. I stayed in the dormitories, but came home on the weekends. Of course, once again I was the youngest. At first I kept my age a secret, as I suspected that my classmates, in learning that I was only 14, might regard me with suspicion or awe — and I didn't want either. Actually, the only ones who knew my age were my teachers, as they had access to my records.

Before long, I rebelled at my own hypocrisy realizing that if the only way I could retain friends was to conceal my age, they really were not worthy of my affection. So, I freely revealed my age to those who inquired. I guess going on dates proved somewhat embarrassing — to the boys, not to me. I felt quite at home with students 10 years older.

One amusing incident relating to age occurred earlier. I had an assignment in my English class requiring the presentation of a paper that would be comprehensible to a 12-year-old child. I read my paper to the class, at the request of my professor. The major complaint by class members was that certainly no 12-year-old could comprehend what I had

248

written or understand the significance of my point of view. It was with difficulty that I restrained myself from revealing my true age.

In looking back at my development, I do not think that anything could have been done differently to have helped me more. Academically, the only lack I felt was in chemistry and physics. In college I took both of these subjects and did very well in them. On completion of my undergraduate studies at Florida Atlantic University, I entered Michigan State University, where I pursued my graduate studies at the age of 15. As I understand it, I became the youngest university instructor in recorded history, teaching higher mathematics.

Neither the distance from home, the cold climate, nor the other major changes which I had to undergo had any affect on my morale, self discipline, or conduct as an instructor. Notwithstanding the fact that most of my students were 4 to 6 years older, I encountered no disciplinary problems and truly enjoyed my work. Consequently, I would like to fortify my father's thesis regarding the significance of the mental age as opposed to the chronological in child development.

On the personal side, I am frequently asked about the relationship I have with my mother, as well as my father. My father was quite ill when I was very young and my mother had to work to help support us. Of course, it was not by choice that she was out of my academic development but by dire necessity. Despite that, I had a very good relationship with her and always will have and, needless to say, I love very dearly my father as well. Whenever she could, my mother spent time with me, walked with me in the park, and read to me as a child. I recall that every Tuesday on her day off we would go to the book store, where I was permitted to select a book, which was very rewarding.

Since my father felt so strongly about books, I developed the reading habit at an early age, almost from the time I could talk. I went to the library each week and carried out the maximum number of books allowed — ten per visit. I would read each one, sometimes two or three times. When I was a child, we didn't have a television set — and to this very day, I would much rather read than do anything else. Too many people have lost the art of reading, because of television.

Another question I am often asked: "Since you have had so much publicity, does the attention affect you? Has it changed your life-style?" And my answer: "Not at all." I know that the newspapers, magazines, press syndicates, radio, television, and other forms of mass media have all been over-generous to me in their praise and in their coverage, but it doesn't affect me one way or another. At first I rebelled when I was asked to appear on television or sit for a press interview. Now I shrug my shoulders and say: "Oh, it's just another one of those things." After a while, you can get satiated with publicity.

Still, I have gotten some special advantages. That is, I got a free trip to the Lion Safari Country Club when I was 14. I had a trip arranged for me to go to New York to appear on a television show.

I don't want any more publicity, nor did I particularly care for it as a child. I got tired of seeing the many papers written about my foibles and idiosyncracies, my goals and ambitions. I have been lately asked to appear on various television shows, but usually I turn them down.

My father's critics, who spilled oceans of crocodile tears allegedly worrying about my emotional well-being, should be pleased to learn that I am truly happy. The pursuit of my satisfying career does not in any way deter me from enjoying sports and outdoor activities, parallel to my love for books and music. My social life is rich and full.

My advice to parents: If you want your child to be a reader, then don't spend every night watching television. If you want your child to like art, then don't sit back and play bridge or gossip with your neighbors when the time could be better spent visiting a museum or art exhibition.

You can't expect even an ideal school to train and teach the children during a five or six hour period, five days a week, while you have them at home for the balance of the day. It is essential that parents as well as teachers take an active interest in the child's education. Don't assume that the school is going to do everything. Remember, most of the child's time is spent at home.

Not every parent has the time my father had in being with me hours on end, helping, guiding, advising, comforting, showing me the difference between right and wrong, good and bad, true culture and pseudoculture. But, surely every parent should pay more attention to the educational needs of his child, to the improvement of his or her skills, to the imperative need for early instruction and supervision. In this way, the school and home will blend. That would be an ideal state.

Finally, I am always asked by well-wishers about my future. I refuse to draw a map. I go along as I please, turning where I wish. There is a multitude of things I would like to do.

In any event I shall always seek challenges and, of course, I am determined to contribute all I can to the betterment of the society and to the alleviation of the dismal misery plaguing a major part of the world.

CHAPTER 25

David Speaks, Age 16

As Edith's brother and Aaron Stern's son, I am invariably regarded as in the public domain. At times it is annoying, since I would like to develop my personality without a preconceived yardstick and public peeking.

On the other hand, I am fully aware that there are scientific benefits from a study of me as a product of Stern's educational methods, but it probably will surprise many who oppose my father's philosophy that I am not by any means a product of a pre-arranged mold.

As a matter of fact, my interests, hobbies, study techniques differ radically from those of my sister.

I, too, was constantly stimulated by my father to explore, to think for myself and withstand relentless peer pressure and to have the courage of my convictions in an atmosphere of Spartan simplicity. My father instilled in me a commitment to ideals of social justice, giving me the aesthetics of life, the preference for spiritual values over the material ones. I am told that I learned the rudiments of reading and writing, and commanded 2 languages at 4, and that I was able to defeat adults in a game of chess at 5. I, too, was involved in endless debates with my father, ranging from political theory to agriculture.

My dad often posed as a devil's advocate to broaden my cultural horizons, enhance the power of my logical reasoning, and deter me from cliches. He taught me to doubt but to have faith in the basic goodness and dignity of a human being.

Like a skillful orchestra conductor, my father expects me to achieve perfection in the instrument that I have chosen, rather than the one which he, my mother or society would select for me.

Thus, no views were ever imposed upon me. I have total freedom to do as I please in contrast with the conformity which society expects you to adhere to, as long as I am willing to develop my intellectual potential to the fullest. My father resents trivia, mediocrity and apathy.

Since I was a little boy, I was fascinated by the mystery and abundance of the oceans, which will, within 30 to 40 years, provide the major source of nutrition to a hungry overpopulated world. Consequently I study diligently marine biology and can boast a vast collection of fish.

I am frequently asked whether I don't envy my sister Edith, who was able to enter college at 12. Of course, I would have been happy to attend college. However, one must remember that Edith's transition from junior high school to college resulted from my dad's bitter fight with school authorities, which he ultimately won. Since then his heart disease has seriously worsened; another conflict of this magnitude would probably be, according to his doctors, fatal.

So to be stoic, I do my very best, considering school but a small part of my learning process which engulfs a great variety of experiences.

Two years ago, I attended an eight week study program in Israel sponsored by the Dade Board of Public Instruction, Greater Miami Jewish Federation and Israeli Ministry of Education. Its scope was wide, encompassing Jewish History, Western Civilization, Archeology and Israeli History. The classroom experiences were blended with almost daily field trips which constituted a beautiful synthesis. How fascinating and realistic were the archeological excavations with the layers of various civilizations piled one upon another which we were able to examine subsequent to our classroom study. This indeed is the most eloquent application of my father's Total Educational Submersion Method. Small wonder that in the course of the short eight weeks our group matured spiritually, emotionally, as well as physically. The academic workload which we absorbed is equal to two years of high school with some members of our group earning six college credits. En route from Israel, our plane was unsuccessfully attacked by Arab terrorists at Orly Airport, Paris. This traumatic experience deepened our understanding of the Israeli tragedy.

It is my belief that intellectual and mental growth will stimulate physical development and general well-being. In fact one complements the other.

I enjoy life to the fullest. I love tennis, baseball, football, bicycling, hiking and scuba diving. All this does not interfere with my desire to research deeper into marine biology, my love of good music, and my interest in reading, chess and a good debate.

Unlike some of my friends, based on love and mutual respect I have a good relationship with my parents and sister. My social life is also full and rich and I can boast many friends of both sexes.

CHAPTER 26

A Message from the Mother

I am frequently asked how does it feel to be the mother of a genius? I really don't know how it feels to be the mother of a genius, but I do know how it feels to be the mother of a very wonderful person. As a daughter, Edith is just marvelous. She has not been spoiled by her early upbringing. For a time I was afraid that she might be. In fact, I opposed Aaron's efforts to give Edith the early training that she received.

But I must hasten to add that my imprudent stand was motivated by what appeared then to be the best interests of my children. I feared that they would suffer from emotional instability if they continued to receive the accelerated mental growth, so skillfully nourished by their father. This fear was instilled and inflamed by the so-called experts who pronounced, in sonorous tones, that there was an inherent hazard in a horizontal and vertical growth of such magnitude. Utter nonsense, as I subsequently discovered.

The sharp division between my husband and myself over how to raise our children caused friction at first, but it survived the most gruesome challenge. Now we can see that the dedicated labor of Aaron has borne fruit, superseding his most optimistic expectations.

Apart from their incredible scholastic achievements, our two children Edith and David, are happy, affectionate and well-disciplined.

As a mother to whom the supreme goal is the happiness of her child, and as a woman who is in full accord with the aspirations of the woman's liberation movement, I take great pride in Edith and in David.

Cognizant of the platitudes which govern our lives, I am fully aware that there are those of both sexes who will define the role of a woman in this society as one who should share the burdens of her husband by raising children, keeping the house in order and gracefully accepting domination by the head of the family.

This widely shared anachronistic belief is based on the premise that a member of the weaker sex cannot and should not compete with the male whose intellectual superiority, physical strength and driving energy have destined him to command.

Edith's achievements fully invalidate this "truism."

I have heard experts in education or psychology attribute my children's progress to genetic superiority. Yet they have expediently forgotten the unholy crusade which they led against my husband for "subjecting his mediocre and uninspired children to a cruel educational program, one which will steal their childhood and transform them into maladjusted individuals."

The truth is that Edith and David did not, in their infancy, show any trace of greatness, nor can they boast genetic perfection.

To the best of my knowledge the only advantage which my children had over other youngsters was that their father, disillusioned with a decaying school system whose underlying philosophy has long outlived its purpose, was determined to dedicate all his energy and strength to molding perfect human beings. He did this with a passionate commitment to social justice, fully developing their intellectual potential and creativity so that they might successfully meet the challenges of a dynamic society to come.

Even his most ardent critics cannot deny that this he accomplished well.

Too many parents are beset by their children's alienation, drug addiction, promiscuous sexual behavior, lack of goals, meager aspirations and a dependency on their parents to map out a purpose in life for them. These are widespread maladies which pose a real threat to the survival of our society. We should remember that a major portion of the blame must be shared by the parents' lack-luster interest in their offspring's upbringing, and above all by a school system which fails to guide, inspire or develop basic skills. We are grateful that none of these problems exist in the Stern family thanks to the direction given by Aaron.

My husband's total educational submersion method is predicated upon a firm belief that the pre-school age is the one most conducive to learning. I am convinced that my children owe a major part of their academic success to the training which commenced at the earliest stages of their lives.

Those who advocate erection of elaborate school buildings must remember that a successful education will only be attained through the comptence and the dedication of teachers, in concert with a proper home atmosphere where spiritual and moral values and parental examples can be emulated.

I am certain that many parents, mainly mothers, would like to ask me: "Are you really happy with your children? Had you been able to start all over again would you raise them differently? Are they truly affectionate? Has their childhood been marred by endless hours of study? Are you worried at the prospect that Edith won't be well adjusted in later life? Because of her scholastic excellence, will Edith be able to establish a meaningful marriage relationship?"

To all of these questions – and I know they are reasonable ones – I can only answer: Indeed, my children are truly happy. So am I with them. Looking back, I deeply regret my attitude, which, coupled with the hostility on the part of the educational community against my husband's methods, made his task so much more difficult.

Yet, the relationship between my children, and between us, could not be closer by any standard. My children enjoyed a richer and much more meaningful childhood and now, in the case of Edith, an adulthood, than do their peers for they learned as they played and they played as they learned.

I am confident that when Edith marries – she is 24 already – her relationship will be based upon mutual respect, equality of responsibilities and genuine affection. For unlike many other girls, she will not consider marriage for the sake of comfort, security or expediency. She is financially self-sufficient now. Her mate, therefore, will have to offer something more than economic security. He will have to be intellectually compatible and beyond that, to quote Edith: "My children will be raised exactly the way I was." For that I am grateful.

As a mother, woman and a human being, I sincerely pray that my children's accomplishments will provide a source of inspiration to those who seek knowledge for the sake of peace and progress of mankind.

I have been close to my children. Aaron did not push Edith away from me. She always came to me with her aches and pains, as well as various personal problems.

I know that Aaron carried the burden of Edith's early upbringing and her education. Actually, because of my outside job, I was rarely home during the day. As it is known, I worked ever since she was a tiny baby, and still work. Accordingly, since Aaron did not have a 9 to 5 job, but did accept various lecture engagements, he was with Edith far more than I was.

Much has been written about Edith, but I want to stress that publicity has not gone to her head. She is a very warm and compassionate person, always ready to help as much as she possibly can, in any way that she can. I don't mean·financially, although she does that, too, but in many other ways.

When I read news stories about Edith, or watch her on television, I am very proud. Naturally, I have reason to be proud. Not everything that has been written about her is the truth, however, I see her in a different light. She is much nicer than some of the stories describe her. For example, one of the reporters described her as being a chain smoker. But she is not. Other little things, about her appearance, her dress, her relationship to her family, are not quite accurate. She is a devoted girl, and has strong family ties. Edith's relationship with David is simply marvelous.

For the past 2 years David has been living with Edith. They get along very well. They both attended scuba diving classes together. Both of them graduated from the course. They go bowling together, and have many interests in common. They spent many, many happy hours playing three-dimensional chess, or just talking about their hobbies and their plans for the future. Edith has helped David in selecting his tropical fish, one of the boy's favorite hobbies.

They enjoy each other's company very much. David doesn't resent the fact that Edith gets so much publicity and he only gets mentioned in passing as being Edith's brother. He knows that Edith herself does not want to get the vast amount of publicity that she continues to receive.

Edith doesn't want to be bothered with interviews. In her opinion, there is nothing unusual about her. She is just a normal human being. Perhaps she understands a little more deeply than her peers do, and she enjoys her reading more. As Edith likes to say, with books she can stay in her room and travel all over the world.

In my opinion, too, there is nothing unusual about her. She's just a well developed, well adjusted person. Of course, I know that she is bright. All you have to do is talk with her for half an hour and you will see how superior her mind is, and how well she has developed intellectually. And I also know that she is called a genius. I accept that, but then I ask myself, what is a genius? What are the criteria employed to classify a genius? She's bright. She's creative. She's doing well in her professional career.

Whether she's a genius or not, she's extremely bright, well read, knowledgeable in various disciplines, and tremendously alert. Aaron did something right, that is certain. Actually, if he only did one thing — and he did many more — that of increasing the level of her reading, and endowing her with the joy of reading, the joy of learning, that alone would be worth everything.

As I have indicated, when Aaron took over the training of Edith, and announced in the hospital, while the child was still in the crib, not more than a day old, that he would create a genius, I resented that attitude. Then as he continued to play music constantly for her, to read to her when she could not even pick her head up from the crib, to speak in full sentences to her, and give her a wide variety of educational experiences, my resentment remained.

But that has disappeared long ago. I now see that the earlier you start the child on an educational program, the better it is. Children are capable of so many things that one cannot even imagine their potentialities, their capabilities, their strivings. I do know now, and this has been brought out forcefully by Aaron, that the earlier you start teaching a child the better off he or she is. A child retains concepts much better when he is young, when his mind is flexible, when he can grasp and retain knowledge.

If I had permitted Aaron to use the educational submersion method as intensively on David, as he did with Edith, David would have become a "genius," too? David is extremely bright. He has a very sharp mind. He is several years ahead of his age group in school. He is taking advanced college math this year, although he is only 16. He is also taking advanced science. I know that David is ready now to spurt ahead, to do marvelous work in school, and he, too, will make a name for himself in the academic world as well as the professional one. It would be ironic if, in time, Edith becomes known as being David's sister. That is entirely possible, when you see how bright David really is.

What advice, what message can I give. Parents should accept children for what they are, and not consider that brightness is the sole criterion of acceptance. I would, however, plead with parents to offer their children as much educational guidance as they possibly can.

Children should start their schooling at a very early age. Aaron's survey of the Head Start program has proven that the earlier education begins the healthier it is for the children. Schools should admit children when they are 3 years old and provide them with the three basic R's – reading, writing and arithmetic. Beyond that, though, home training should start virtually at birth. Children should be exposed to good music, to good literature, to good family examples. I believe that a child should be spoken to, even when still a baby in arms, on an adult level, and not in baby language.

Edith never heard baby talk. The goo-goos, and paddy-pats, the bow-wows and moo-moos were out as far as our children were concerned. We talked to them in an articulate manner looking into their eyes, smiling and nodding our heads as though they actually understood what we were saying – and I believe Edith, at 8 months, could understand Aaron when he discussed the advantages of classical music over that of jazz, or the poetic sounds of good literature over that of cheap comics.

Although I did oppose Aaron, in the early days when I felt that he was wrong, I did, however, act as a counterbalance. Aaron concentrated on her academic growth and training but I was on the other side of the scale. I attempted to smooth out whatever rebellious attitudes developed in her. And at times she was rebellious, not against Aaron but against everything that seemed to frustrate her.

For example, when she entered college at the age of 12, she was at first frightened that she would be unable to meet the competition of campus life. After all, she was still in junior high school. She did not want to disappoint her father. I spoke to her for hours and tried to convince her that if she were not able to do the college work, nobody would hold that against her, or consider her to be a failure. I stressed that she could always enter high school, if after sampling college, she found that she was not quite ready for this drastic educational move.

"There's no shame in going to college and then finding out that it is more than you can handle," I told her, being as sympathetic as I could. "You'll try, and if you do not make it, then you won't make it, that's all."

Evidently I convinced her, because she entered college and did marvelously there. But Edith is a perfectionist and didn't want to disappoint her father.

We now see that the end result of Aaron's program is truly amazing, truly marvelous, beyond our expectations. Where will you find a daughter who is so warm to her family that she will come home each weekend, traveling 100 miles, just to spend several hours with you. Of course, she has her own schedule, her own friends, her own appointments, but despite the many other things she does, besides working, she travels from Boca Raton to visit with us every Sunday, if only for several hours. As I look about me at other families, that is something unusual today.

As for her social life, she has many friends. She goes to parties, goes out on dates, enjoys the company of men, engages in lively conversations with her friends of both sexes. I never pry into her private life, and Edith respects me for that. I listen to her, and if she tells me, that is fine. But I don't ask her for details. At 24 she doesn't have to worry about her future social life or her marital status. She has a good head on her shoulders and whatever she does, she does what is best for her, her family and the community at large.

Although she isn't considered a "beauty," she is a fine, sensitive girl, attractive, well groomed and physically fit. She has an aversion for the beauty parlor. "What do I need that for?" she asks. I have no answer because I don't go, either.

Some critics have told us: neither you nor Aaron made Edith into a genius through your educational methods. They insist that she probably had inherited our genes, and that you cannot take a child who is born with normal or mediocre genes and make him bright, let alone a genius. They point to Professors Jensen, Herrnstein or Shockley, to name a few, as persons who believe that intelligence is inherited, at least up to 80 percent of it, and that environment can play only a minor role, only 20 percent. But I don't believe it. I am of the opinion, based on my observation in the field, particularly as related to Edith, that environment plays a far more important part than heredity.

I maintain that environment has more to do with a child's ability than heredity. An intelligent child with a normal background can be taught almost anything if it is done in the right way. The child must be motivated, but not pushed. You teach the child as you go along. Aaron's illness, which kept him in the house so much, was our misfortune but Edith's fortune. When Edith was young, she had her father with her constantly. I know that this is an impractical situation for most parents, but at any rate, they can spend far more time with their children.

Our travels helped Edith's education, too. We went from one state to another. As we passed through a state, Aaron would tell Edith as many facts about it as he possibly could. She learned the agricultural products that it had, what kind of people lived there, why they settled, the population, their political and religious preferences, and when the state was founded, by whom, and when it entered the union. He answered every question that she raised. No question, no matter how trivial or unimportant it seemed, went unanswered.

Aaron served as the catalyzing agent. He just started Edith off, and then she went on her way. She would pore through the encyclopedias that we always carried with us, Information Please almanacs as well as other studies and reports in the field. I listened intently, and as long as Edith was content, I was too. Any rebellion would get my sympathetic attention, and whatever the situation, we managed to smooth it over.

The college enrollment was, of course, a major event in Edith's life, as well as in ours. Suddenly, the world took notice that here was a 12 year old, still in junior high school, jumping over a required high school program and ready for college. Then, if ever, Aaron was vindicated! All the abuse he had taken from friends and critics alike now evaporated. But I played my part, too, Edith said to me: What will be the students reaction to having in their midst a 12 year old girl?

My moral support was very helpful.

Her worries, it turned out, were unjustified. She enjoyed college very much, and later the university. Since she lived in the dorms at Florida Atlantic University she was totally on her own. But she made many friends. In fact, she still sees and visits with a number of these friends.

Edith has pronounced views on world problems. She has profound philosophical thoughts. But we keep our discussions on the lighter level. We go shopping together, and we both enjoy this. However, she doesn't care much for clothes. At least, she didn't until recently. Now, evidently, she has become somewhat more clothes conscious. She likes to dress well, but simply.

Another big event in the life of the Stern family was the day she received an invitation to teach at Michigan State University. She was really scared, poor baby.

Here again I told her: "Look, the students will come to class to listen to you. They will have to do what you tell them. Their grades depend on that. So don't worry about your age."

She taught several years, giving courses in mathematics. She did extremely well, gained confidence in her teaching ability, and thoroughly enjoyed her work. Teachers are evaluated by their students each semester. She received a glowing evaluation report, and was later told by her chairman that it was among the best given to any faculty member. Evidently the students liked her, and she liked them. She is a very good teacher.

Edith loves teaching. She plans to do it again, although she also enjoys the highly important position which she now holds.

Edith is well taken care of on her way to glowing success. David is next. I'm not going to influence his choice of career. In fact he wants to be a marine biologist. The ocean appeals to him. That is why he is a scuba diving buff and why he keeps several tankfuls of fish in the house. We kept his fish alive and healthy while David spent two months in Israel. He came back filled with enthusiasm, excited and stimulated by what he had found there.

But he's only 16 years old, and I'm sure he'll make career changes before he decides what is best for him. He has a long way to go before he makes a firm decision. We'll offer suggestions, guide him, direct him, but we won't make up his mind for him. For his age, David is very mature. He thinks clearly, knows exactly what is going on in the world, and I'm confident that whatever his final decision may be, it will be best for him and fine with us.

My advice to other mothers is simply this: Be yourself. Be natural. Have faith in your children. Give them an opportunity to develop to their fullest potential. Don't nag your child - or your husband if he has far-out ideas in child-rearing practices. I'm sorry I was angry and annoyed with Aaron. I see now how wrong I was. Fortunately, Aaron did not listen to me when I urged him to give up his ideas and permit Edith to develop as a "normal" child. If he had listened to me, that's all Edith would now have been - a happy, normal, unimaginative child. Now she is a happy, superior, creative, imaginative young lady. She was the first born and I was worried lest her future be destroyed with experimentation.

It wasn't. I'm proud to be the mother of a genius. But I'm even prouder to be the mother of a warm, compassionate, loving, devoted, sensitive, friendly daughter. That, to me, is worth all the heartache and anguish that I underwent in the early days of Edith's road to intellectual success.

CHAPTER 27
Total Educational Submersion Method Mass Tested

The scientific community and the news media have followed my research in the area of early child development, spanning over a quarter of a century, with considerable interest.

To be sure, some widely circulated stories have at times painfully distorted my philosophy, causing anguish to my family and myself while they were warmly applauded by my critics.

However, one can assume with certainly that the continuous press coverage, frequent T.V. appearances, my numerous lectures and the respectable distribution of *"The Making of a Genius"* have had an impact upon millions of people, here and abroad.

Unfortunately, in spite of my extreme dedication to my lifelong dream, the establishment of a school based on my methodology or the introduction of it on en-masse basis, into the Public School System has not been realized. And I am doubtful whether I will see, within my life-time, this fervent hope of mine fulfilled. This indeed grieves me deeply. Yet, my bitter and lonely struggle has not been in vain, as one can witness by the increased stress on pre-school education, the granting of college credits based on "life experience", early college admission policy, intensive medical study programs, and above all the extensive research into early child development with findings corroborating my own theories. I also can take some measure of comfort from the reliance on my book as a reference source by leading universities.

Of course, the greatest gratification I derive from the huge volume of mail which incessantly pours in from readers. Literally, tens of thousands of letters, the bulk of which arrived since the publication of *"The Making of a Genius,"* testify to the deep disenchantment with the Public School System. Fourteen to fifteen thousand of my correspondents, few of whom, communicate with me regularly, have employed my methodology either vis a vis their own children or less frequently as school instructors on all levels of education with a high degree of success. Many of these persons regard their own educational advancement attributable to my methodology. This phenomenon provided an excellent opportunity for me to conduct a follow-up study to appraise my methodology at work. A detailed questionnaire which I mailed to obtain the pertinent data, has, for some unknown reason, met with a poor response. Having no choice in this matter in order to pursue my study, I had to rely on the flow of correspondence with the input determined by the parents, who might have been at times, less than objective. Due to these circumstances, this project, cannot be considered totally objective by strict canons of scientific research. On the other hand, my personal contact with some of the children, coupled with documentation in the form of news stories and statements by psychologists and educators often attached to the letters, give it a high degree of credibility. As a precautionary measure and in order to stress my objectivity, I shall refrain from tabulating the specific data and confine myself to general observations, empiric in nature, which, however possess a wealth of pertinent information.

All told, my study conducted in the course of 12 years deals with over 18,000 persons, mostly parents, at times guardians and in some cases teachers reporting progress of their students. Often more than one child per family was exposed to my methodology.

I have hoped to test my pedagogic theories, mainly on the culturally and economically underpriviliged children, whose need for educational advancement is the greatest, while the effects of my methodology would have been no less impressive.

However, over 15,000 of my correspondents were white, which constitutes 83.3%, as it could be determined either by direct reference to color through attached pictures or by other means.

The intellectual growth of children has the greatest appeal to educated and often well-to-do parents. This explains why the socio-economic inequality is being perpetuated, as the following diagram, dealing with the status of my correspondents, testifies.

	NUMBER	PERCENT
Correspondents	18025	100
Persons associated with university and college teaching	4205	23.3
Professionals (non-teachers) or pursuing educations towards a professional degree	4257	23.6
University, College graduates or attending school	14041	77.9

All told some form of information was obtained with reference to 22,575 subjects. This number excludes teachers reporting progress of their students at all levels of education.

Nearly 13,000, or more than half of this group, were less than 14 years of age. The following is a breakdown by sex of the group as was reported to me.

	NUMBER	PERCENT
Male	9310	41.3
Female	11035	48.9
Sex not determined	2230	9.8
TOTAL	22,575	100%

2,134 of the subjects were exposed in various degrees of intensity to my methodology, literally from the earliest infancy. This group shows the finest results in terms of intellectual as well as physical development.

Incredible as it sounds, 2,013 of these children, or 94.5%, read at age 4, while 412 mastered the intricacies of reading at age 3, as per chart that follows:

		PERCENT	READING AGE 3	
			Number	Percent
Male	903	42.2	155	36.7
Female	1078	50.6	249	61.2
Sex not reported	153	7.2	8	2.1
TOTAL	2134	100%	412	100%

So rarely do children read at this tender age, under prevailing conditions, that I was unable to find reliable statistical data to juxtapose my study.

In each instance the parents or parent report a more satisfactory pace of development as compared with the older siblings.

Almost in every case the child's progress is commensurate with the amount of time she or he, or both of them, devoted to the child.

Thus, children who mastered reading at 3 years of age enjoyed 5 hours an average of parental time in educational activities. Youngsters who began to read at 4 obtained 3½ hours of instruction.

Based on the information forwarded by parents, parallel to the intellectual development, there was an exhilarated physical growth of the child. None of the correspondents reported ill effects of my methodology on the socio-emotional maturation of the child. None has expressed regreat over exposing the child to an intensive course of learning.

In a small number of cases, work with children had to be relaxed, or terminated temporarily or permanently, due to congenital ailments or surgeries.

Harmony among parents is very important. About 2% of the infants had one parent with them, usually the mother, before they reached their first birthday. The proportion of one parent children, mainly because of divorce, is reaching nearly 4.5% at age 4. As one could expect, best results are achieved by children enjoying the care of both parents. Only about 2% of children reading at 3 had one parent caring for them, as contrasted with almost 4% of those who began to read at age 4.

In addition to psychological factors this is due to economics as well, since a mother compelled to work because of divorce, cannot devote much time to the child's development.

The vast majority of this group watched only 2 hours of T.V. daily, limited to educational programs. In some cases T. V. was totally absent.

Most children were exposed to classical music. The rest had a mixture of classic and popular music. Very few report rock n' roll. All parents regard music a very positive factor in childrens' growth.

1,400 children of the group have reached by now the age of 7, 1,117 of the group play some instrument, predominantly the piano. They constitute 79.8%.

2,010 of the 2,134 group of children attend schools, 1,875 of them are described as very unhappy with the school pace and this constitutes 93.2% of the group.

Only a very insignificant number of black and minority children was exposed to my methodology.

However, the number of black and minority girls reading at 3 appears to be proportionally greater than that of white and black boys.

The excellent results of the limited number of black and minority children exposed to my methodology reinforces my thesis about the significance of environmental factors in the intellectual development of a child, rather than his racial or ethnic origin.

The higher proportion of girls in the group dismisses the myth of male intellectual superiority.

The sight of happy, well adjusted 3 year old youngsters reading, thanks to the total educational submersion method, while some high school graduates are unable to do so, will simply awe you.

Parents of a few children, suffering from Down's Syndrome (mental retardation), an area with which I have no familiarity, report impressive success of the drill and repetition technique. Such method, these parents claim to be effective in improving motor ability and dexterity. These unfortunate children appear to be very responsive to music, mainly classic, which perhaps signifies the only autistic experience which they enocunter.

The balance of the general group, heterogeneous in nature, consists of persons from age 8 to 45. The application of my technique spans a plethora of activities, from academic studies to acquisition of vocational skills, from mastery of jet flying to the improvement of chess playing.

Ethnically it encompasses a great diversity from Vietnamese refugees in their effort to master English to the Indian reservation expatriates seeking vocational skills. The subjects report from the dingy cell of a penitentiary to the lofty heights of a university campus. In nearly each instance my methodology is credited in some measure in the attainment of goals and objectives of these people. One must be aware that some degree of exaggeration and-inaccuracy from proud parents reporting children's progress can be expected. However, based on the experience that I have had with my children, as well as my direct work with thousands of youngsters, I can recommend my methodology very highly as a viable alternative to the dismal stagnation of the Public School Systems. Excerpts of the moving letters follow:

Michael, a 37 year old, doctoral student whose vehicle enroute to school collided with another car, emerged paralyzed, the only survivor, leaving behind all 5 occupants of the 2 cars dead. Unable to pursue his job and studies he suggested a divorce to his wife "so that you might find happiness in marrying a healthy man, capable of supporting our children." His wife refused to consider it. The patient became a recluse, unwilling to communicate with members of his own family.

"One day, I read in our local paper about you and found a vague reference to your war suffering and the many surgeries which followed upon your liberation, something prompted me to buy your book to which the story alluded.

. . . Your stubborn struggle had a profound effect upon me . . . Presently I am putting my final touches to the Ph.D. dissertation, and like yourself, I have turned my liabilities into assets by doing research in the area of rehabilitation of the physically handicapped."

Irene's husband works in a car plant. The family relocated to Michigan from Mississippi in the 1960's in search of a secure job. However, because of its size, six children, the family lives from hand to mouth.

"One day I read in the Detroit Press a story about Edith's exposure to classical music and the beneficial effects it had on the child. After discussing it with my husband I decided to do the same with my 1½ year old daughter and her 7 week infant sister who shared the room with her. The radio played classical and popular music all day long . . . I am glad to report to you that my 12 year old Rose plays piano excellently and we hope that she will attend, with the aid of a scholarship, Julliard School of Music. Joan, her younger sister, plays the violin and takes ballet classes."

John read in *The Making of a Genius* about the series of tests which revealed that my intelligence was very low for my ethnic origin and that I was urged to become a welder. Yet I decided to pursue college and did rather well in spite of the "gloomy scientific prognosis." "I was then pumping gas for a period of 2 years, after my guidance counsellor suggested in 12th grade that I could do little else. Inspired by your audacity I, too, decided to challenge the wisdom of tests and entered Junior College. Last month I was admitted to the law school and hope to serve my black community in the crucial area of jurisprudence."

I have received this heart-warming telephone call, just before my book went to print, "This is Joe Smith from Cleveland. About 18 months ago we purchased your book. Since then my wife Beatrice and I faithfully implement your technique, with truly spectacular results.

"Gerald, who is 3½ years old reads rather well. He responds very favorably to classical music and shows good physical development as well."

"This is really gratifying but what prompts you to call me just now, I asked, slightly intrigued.

"You see, when I married Beatrice I pledged to honor her desire to have just one child. However, Gerald's remarkable progress prompted her to change her mind. As a matter of fact, she expects another baby in about 2 months. We have just decided, after consulting my mother, to name the baby after you. In case it is a girl, we shall name her Aarona."

"To what do I owe this honor?" I inquired.

"Well, you have acted as an antidote to the birth control pills which Beatrice ceased to take."

"Thus, I have, in a weird sort of way, made my modest contribution to the population explosion."

"This is precisely so," cheerfully added Beatrice from her extension phone.

Robert ran away from home at 15, leaving behind a girl friend who he thought was pregnant. His family made no great effort to locate him, as his mother, deserted by her husband, had to feed 7 children. His absence from home did not prevent her from obtaining the meager allowance from welfare for him. As a boy, Robert truly 'hated school,' as it was not related to real life.

Two years later, after a few encounters with the police due to petty larceny and a drug charge, he finally volunteered for Vietnam where he served in the Medical Corps. "My revulsion for this cruel war, coupled with the undescribable suffering caused by it opened my eyes. I became deeply involved in my work and perhaps for the first time began to contemplate the purpose and direction of my life. Soon enough I was seriously wounded and discharged. Three years ago I finished high school at night and entered college. Presently I am taking a pre-med course of studies while holding a part time hospital job. I wholeheartedly applaud your sarcasm with regards to I.Q. tests, for I, too, was told in the penitentiary by a psychologist once that my aptitude is dismal.

On reflection, I wonder whether the I.Q. and similar testing devices are nothing but an effective conspiracy aiming at preventing the minorities to advance themselves."

Indeed this thesis merits consideration.

CHAPTER 28

Lecture Circuit

The numerous lectures which I deliver, mainly on campuses, afford me great joy and fulfilment. Indeed, I am deeply inspired by our young people who, in their nearly evangelical zeal to purify our society, sharply reject the perfidy and hypocrisy of their elders. Unfortunately, the skyrocketing cost of education coupled with fears and doubts about the future, due to the economic decline with its ugly residue of unemployment, have taken a heavy toll of the student morale.

Yet, notwithstanding these formidable adversities one senses on the nation's campuses an impatient resolve to eradicate the blatant inequities prevailing in our nation as well as in the world at large.

The main thrust is directed against the social injustice, and the systematic destruction of our ecology.

Last but not least, one can observe the bitter frustration caused by an anachronistic educational system which obviously fails to prepare the young to cope with the complexities and the challenges of our dynamic society.

It is against this background that my lectures, mainly devoted to the Total Educational Submersion Method, meet criticism on the part of the school administration, while they generate a good measure of enthusiasm among the students and young faculty.

To illustrate my observations I have selected a few poignant episodes.

A few years ago at the completion of one lecture, the discussion which followed soon switched from education to Vietnam and to its alienation of the college students. A young man stood up and said, "Just to illustrate the hypocrisy in which we so comfortably indulge, each time an issue of morality is raised, invariably the public is more concerned about sex than violence. Isn't the pursuit of a needless war with its attendant cruelties more immoral than any sex act? We have grown accustomed to viewing nonchalantly on television acts of incredible barbarism perpetrated against prisoners of war while they are being interrogated and villages being burned to the ground. We don't make as much as a murmur of protest. On the other hand, when a report appears dealing with student premarital sex life, a tide of indignation sweeps the nation. Where are our moral values?"

Another student offered a rebuttal. "On television we see only acts of cruelty committed by our side. No publicity is given to the enemy's bestial terrorism."

The first student replied, "I don't dispute your statement. To begin with we don't know what the public reaction in North Vietnam would be had they viewed the brutality of their armed forces, but this is irrelevant to this discussion. I am concerned with the moral values of this country, founded on the Judeo-Christian concepts of justice and mercy. I am concerned with the indifference which has resulted from years of conditioning to atrocities and human misery. I am concerned with the total disintegration of our moral values."

During a visit to another university, I met an elderly Jewish instructor from Poland. He made a commentary on our moral values which was far more poignant because of his experiences. As we discussed our tragic experiences during the Nazi occupation, he said, "You know, Aaron, I must confess a sin. After liberation from the concentration camp, I passionately hated every single German for the Nazi atrocities. The assurances which many offered in their defense, that they personally had nothing to do with it, did not convince me at all. My question, 'What have you done to oppose it?' would be met with silence, or a vague, 'What could one do about it?'

"Now that our country is engaged in a bloody war in defense of a corrupt clique, a war which drains our financial, moral human resources, causing destruction and indescribable horrors to South Vietnam, which we claim to defend, what do I do as an individual? Nothing at all. As you see, I function normally, teaching, reading, and traveling. How will I ever face God? How will I ever atone for this sin?"

The concern was not limited to issues surrounding Vietnam. At a large, well-equipped college, I decided to devote a substantial part of my lecture to the major cause of the increasing welfare rolls, namely the failure of education to impart employable vocational skills to students who are either unwilling or incapable of continuing their academic work. My thesis was well accepted by the audience. One young man suggested that part of the welfare problem was due to the attitude of the welfare recipients, who have abandoned self-reliance and self-sufficiency in favor of a public handout.

In response, a black girl said, "True, it is regrettable that some of our citizens lack the dignity and decency to be self-supporting when they could be. However, the vast majority of the welfare recipients have no choice, due to poor health or lack of skills as Mr. Stern suggested, but to turn to welfare. On the other hand, I wonder how many of you realize that welfare in one form or another is being generously extended by the government to many other groups without protest from the public. For example, it is being given to farmers in the form of subsidies to prevent them from cultivating their lands at a time when farm produce is so expensive and some of our children suffer from malnutrition. It is being extended to advertisers in the form of cheap postal bulk rates and the advertisers then flood our mailboxes with junk mail while the post office operates at a deficit. It is being given to the oil industry in the form of oil depletion allowances, the defense industry, the shipbuilding industry, tax depreciation allowances to business, tax free income to holders of municipal bonds, and so on. So you see the unfortunate welfare recipients are not the only ones who receive governmental subsidies."

A young man had previously raised the law and order issue, and in rebuttal, the black girl continued, "Does the outcry for law and order apply only to the frustrated unemployed black boy caught in petty thievery, or does it apply equally to Bobby Baker, Billy Sol Estes, and corrupted government officials who amass millions of dollars by swindles, who deceive and bribe with impunity or at worst, with a token penalty? Who can say whether the violence of a rioter is more harmful to society than the denial of food stamps to an undernourished baby? Should the funds allocated to the poorly managed welfare projects be a greater cause for indignation than the quarter of a billion dollars of public funds spent to rescue Lockheed from its bankruptcy? Is not the incredible waste of life and resources in Vietnam more harmful to the nation's moral health and financial stability than are the funds given to welfare recipients?"

At most of my lectures, I dealt directly with the issues and problems of education. On one campus I antagonized a small but vocal segment of my audience by criticizing universities for emphasizing athletics, often to the detriment of academic pursuits. After the lecture, a middle-aged faculty member related to me the following experience.

"I had been on the faculty of a prestigious university where I taught classical civilization. Because of my linguistic skills and a broad scholastic background acquired at leading American and European universities, I was regarded as one of the best men in my department. Since my course was required for students seeking a bachelor's degree, I always had a large enrollment in my classes. My greatest problem in teaching was the athletes who in general did not excel in scholarship. Since I was aware of the significance which the school attached to athletics, I was rather lenient with the players and expected a bare minimum of accomplishment from them.

"Then one semester, Joe, the star football player, was in my class. At our first conference, I became convinced that he planned to do nothing in the course. He told me that he always got a passing grade. As the semester progressed, the student failed every test and did not submit his term project, dismissing my warnings with a smile. At the end of the term, I felt that I had no other choice than to give Joe an 'F'.

"After the grades were issued, I was summoned to see the president, whom I had never met alone before. 'So you failed Joe,' the president said. 'Are you aware that as the star football player, he constitutes our most important pillar? Apart from the prestige, the team contributes huge sums of money to the university budget. The failure in your class would require his disqualification from the team. Can you visualize the consequences of such a step?'

" 'Fully.' "

" 'Then please revise his grade.' "

" 'I'm sorry, but Joe made no effort to meet his responsibilities. He learned nothing, wasting his time as well as mine. I would be derelict in my duties if I acted otherwise.' "

" 'Is that your irrevocable decision?' "

" 'I'm afraid it is.' "

" 'Are you aware that people like yourself are expendable?' "

"At that point, I requested a sheet of paper and wrote out my resignation. You know, Mr. Stern, my salary is lower now, but I don't regret my decision."

At another school, a young admissions officer zealously spoke about the crisis in education. He told me that many of the high school graduates applying for admission to the college were unable to fill out a simple form and that he had to assign a clerk to assist them with their applications. In fact, some of the applicants were unable to read or write properly, let alone comprehend concepts.

At many schools I found students who complained about the educational process. At one lecture, I met a young professor of psychology. After we talked for a while, he remarked, "You make a lot of waves, antagonizing people without accomplishing much. Why don't you follow my example by working from within the establishment to bring about improvement?"

"The establishment simply doesn't want me," I replied.

"Well, I'm quite successful in my work. I enjoy fine rapport with my students and I know them quite well since I create an informal atmosphere."

"How well do you know them?" I inquired.

"Quite well. They seem to be happy with the school. Would you care to talk to my class?"

I delivered a lecture and answered questions. Afterwards I suggested that we reverse the process. I asked, "What was your impression of the high school you attended?" Not one student praised his school. The complaints ranged from mediocre to deplorable with accompanying explanations. Then I inquired whether the students were pleased with the college they were presently attending.

Nearly every student raised his hand. The comments included "Mediocre" and "An extension of the high school waste." Some students admitted that they smoked marijuana out of boredom. Others stated that their presence at the college was exclusively motivated by draft evasion.

"You know, Aaron, you have elicited some information which amazed me," the professor told me later.

"Well, students are usually frank with people outside the establishment," I replied sardonically.

At one high school the principal asked me, "How does one teach children who are unwilling to learn? They are incorrigible."

"Why is that?"

"Well, there is a group of youngsters in our school whose ages range from thirteen to seventeen. They are about to drop out, yet no one can reach or motivate them. Probably some experiment with drugs. We are quite sure that a few smoke marijuana."

I asked if I could meet with some of the students, and within an hour a room was set aside into which twelve or fifteen teenagers, mostly black, came in. I decided to interview them separately and privately. I asked the first boy, "Why don't you study? How will you be able to earn a living without a high school diploma?"

"I ain't got much to do here. It's so stupid, so boring."

"You have a fine school and dedicated teachers. Surely there must be something of interest to you."

"Not much really."

"What are you interested in?"

"I like cars. I would like to take them apart and put them together again to see how they work. But I can't do that here."

Another boy was equally critical about the school. "It really has no meaning. This is not going to help me in the future."

"For crying out loud, you must be interested in something," I said. "Your dad will not support you forever."

"I have always wanted to be a pilot. I love the wide open spaces, the clean air."

"Indeed, you must finish high school and then study aviation."

"I don't think I'll make it. I have only failing grades. I feel I'd better leave school before they kick me out."

"They will not expel you, but you must show some desire to learn," I warned him.

"I really don't care anymore."

Mary was equally disappointed. "There is no sense in wasting my time any further. I will get married and have children."

"That is fine. Suppose your husband will need you to supplement his income."

"Well, I'm good at drawing."

All of the youngsters I interviewed impressed me as bright, but woefully lacking in both guidance and motivation. Later I admonished the principal, "Here is a boy interested in learning about an automobile. What a splendid educational opportunity this is. It includes combustion engineering, kinetic energy, electricity, and a wealth of information which you can impart without sweat or tears. Likewise the boy interested in flying would be eager to learn all he can about navigation, electricity, and aviation instruments."

"Unfortunately, we are not equipped to do that. Furthermore, we must comply with our curriculum requirements."

"Even at the cost of losing these youngsters?"

"Cruel as it may sound, we have no alternative," he replied.

All of the problems which I observed in the schools were not limited to the teaching and the curriculum. In some cases the schools have ruined students' lives by other means. For example, I heard about Mary, an attractive seventeen-year-old girl, who, as have many other teenagers, experimented with sex. Unfortunately, she became pregnant. Unable to obtain solace from her parents, who were devout Catholics, she could

276

find very little sympathy from her sexual partner, from the other students, and least of all from the school authorities. Such are the facts of life. Many girls play the game, but the one who gets caught must suffer. Of course, the boy remains unpunished.

The school, unable to cope with the situation, was determined to expel her, since it regarded her presence as demoralizing. A faculty meeting was called to consider the problem. I, an outsider, was also present.

"In compliance with school regulations Mary will have to be expelled. We have no other choice," the principal announced.

Whereupon I asked, "Is it true that other high school students indulge in sex?"

"Undoubtedly, some of them do," was the reply.

"Is it true that none of them have ever been punished for their promiscuous activities?"

"We have no knowledge of their sex activities. None have gotten pregnant before."

"How about the boy who fathered the child?"

"We don't even know who he is. Had we known we could not take any punitive steps against him."

"Which means that he will go scot free?"

"Yes, it appears so."

"Well, how can you indulge so cruelly in double standards of justice? Here is a young lady who unwisely experimented with sex just as her classmates have, but they did it with total impunity. Because of pregnancy she now faces a traumatic experience which may never be forgotten. She faces hostile parents, an indifferent society that is not likely to soon forgive her sins, and ridicule on the part of the other students. She will have to give birth to an unwanted baby without the funds to support it. In addition to all this, you will expel her from school and thus will deny her a high school diploma which she will badly need to secure a job or enter college at some future time. Has she not been punished enough? Please permit her to remain for the balance of the term and graduate. I understand her scholastic abilities are excellent." Tears prevented me from completing my statement.

A dead silence greeted these remarks. The poor girl was expelled. An editorial appeared in the paper the next day under heading "Radical Professor Advocates Sexual Promiscuity."

At many lectures, people asked how I maintained the rapport with my children. At one college, a professor said, "Mr. Stern, I have read so many accounts of Edith's accomplishments. How did you motivate her?"

"Plain educational opportunism seizing every conceivable occasion for learning. There is nothing mystic about it. Motivate and challenge the child constantly whether it is play, rest, or recreation. And above all, don't lecture. Learning must be a dual process of discovery. A kind of an eternal dialogue."

"Well, you see I have this problem: I try to teach my students the fundamentals of government and history, but they insist upon discussions of *"Soul on Ice,"* student alienation, Vietnam, legalization of marijuana, etc. Mine was an entirely different experience at Duke University."

"Perhaps those were other times and the composition of the student body was entirely different."

"As I understand it there is just one way of learning. You cannot intelligently appraise the black people's struggle for advancement without familiarity with the Civil War, any more than you are able to bring about a legislative action without learning the government structure," he indignantly replied.

"I don't dispute it at all, but the important fact that you seem to overlook is that you have young people eager to learn. Most likely the current burning issues are by far more relevant to them. Thus, you have an option either to seize this opportunity for a meaningful course of study or lose rapport with the students altogether. It is as simple as that."

"I really fail to understand you," he pursued.

"All these topics represent contemporary history. Why not reverse the chronological order and start from the current events? Why not create

278

meaningful parallels such as the landmark Supreme Court decision versus Lincoln's proclamation, the disastrous effects of the Vietnam War and the infamy of the French in Vietnam? Why not explore the historical balances of the branches of government and the sharp divisions of the Congress and Executive Branch over the conduct of the Vietnam War? The paroxysms of the Catholic Church in parallel with the pre-Reformation period. Or why don't you explore student unrest as a world-wide phenomenon?"

"You make it appear so simple. How did you really motivate her?"

"My dear professor, I just outlined to you in detail my methodology."

At a junior college appearance which attracted a huge crowd, a professor of education inadvertently required his education classes to attend my lecture. Many of his collegues as well as faculty members of other departments were present.

This happened subsequent to the submitting of my proposals for the demonstration school to the State Department of Education. I read the document to the audience. I was warmly received by both the students and faculty. When the question and answer period followed, the students endorsed one by one my proposals. A petition addressed to the State Department of Education requesting its implementation was signed by the vast majority of the audience.

Then one young teacher rose to criticize my methods which in his judgment "would destroy our education system." The students and I rebutted his remarks.

Finally he rose again to say, "Your proposals are contrary to the American tradition, since they are similar to the Soviet Union school system."

"You are dead wrong, sir. It is the Soviet system which adheres to a strict regimentation in accord with a dogma. A child there is destined from his infancy to follow a course of studies consistent with the needs of the state, irrespective of his desires. In the Soviet Union a strict discipline governs the school life. Innovation and experimentation are not tolerated. On the other hand, my proposals suggest a school where children, unhampered by any restrictions, are free to develop their personality and their creativity. They are free to argue with their teacher without inhibitions or repercussions and to grow at their own pace without regard for chronological age. Isn't this a sharp contrat with our public school system as well as the Soviet System? Obviously both fail to meet the challenges of their respective societies."

A burst of applause drowned my words. A young black student then approached me. "Well, Mr. Stern, you must realize that people fear change. They will resort to any form of innuendo in an effort to preserve their status. The same applies to school integration, as well as the medical association's opposition to the national health care program." He then asked to be considered for a teaching position when such a school is established.

"I think your chances are remote. I doubt that the State Department of Education will approve my proposals." Unfortunately I was right.

Berkeley Campus, University of California

Apart from being one of the finest universities in America, Berkeley is the most vibrant, dynamic and vigorous that I have visited during my lecture tour.

Embedded in the foot of the mountain, the winding roads amidst ever-blooming flowers of the northern California climate provide a beautiful setting. If there is any way to determine political activism of all shades, Berkeley will definitely win the highest prize. On any given day as you enter the university gate, you will be impressed by the variety of signs, announcements and political slogans, almost daily demonstrations, some of which become acrimonious and the often bloody confrontations with the stick wielding police.

Radicalism of all shades, for which Berkeley is notorious, takes a heavy toll of the faculty as well; many professors are not on speaking terms with their peers, and often blend with students during the unruly demonstrations.

Yet, in contrast, other intense forms of political activity appear to be peaceful. In the vicinity of the Student Union Building portable tables manned by several students are loaded with political literature, and heated discussions make it truly a market place of ideas. Probably this is the only place in the world where a few men wearing skull caps, representing a religious branch of Zionism, exalt the position of Israel, while two feet away a dark-haired Arab, assisted by several other young men, hoarse from loud arguments, passionately defends the terrorist activities of Al-Fatah. Likewise, various religious denominations, with the

280

aid of religious symbols and musical instruments, attempt with equal passion to reclaim "lost souls."

The teeming community, noisy in its appearance, uninhibited by conventions, and repressions, gives its eloquent expression to all political shades, nurturing dissent, freedom of thought and action. It is said that even the university's janitorial staff possesses a political sophistication which enables it to distinguish the dozen or so socialist groups on the campus.

This is Berkeley, at times grotesque and bizarre but always exciting, boisterous and charming with which I fell in love.

It was here that the first and probably last time in my life I rejected an invitation to lecture, because it was issued by a homosexual student organization. It is here that a professor at the beginning of his lecture may instruct his students on how to combat a police detail during a planned demonstration, or what supermarket is being targeted for picketing in support of a Chavez grape boycott. It was here that a Jewish instructor, with a Trotsky-like flair for demagoguery condemned the "Israeli imperialism" to the dismay of a predominantly Jewish class.

It is also here that Dr. Arthur R. Jensen, the noted child psychologist whose contributions to the field of genetic studies made him famous, teaches. Although I vigorously disagree with his scientific conclusions, Dr. Jensen has my esteem for his intellectual excellence and integrity, for his depth as well as for his prolific writings.

For a long time, I had hoped either to challenge this man to a debate or to lecture at one of his classes. However, soon after my arrival at Berkeley, I was shocked and dismayed at the isolation and ridicule that he was subjected to by most of his colleagues and the vast majority of the student body on political grounds alone. For example, any reference by a racist government such as South Africa to his work would result in a series of innuendos against the author. Likewise, any out of context quote by a Southern reactionary or an opponent of busing would rekindle the storm. Regrettably, Dr. Jensen the scholar, is flagrantly denied academic freedom by his own peers.

Under these circumstances, like a prudent tourist trying to visit the whole of the Middle East by first judiciously visiting the belligerent Arab countries and towards the end Israel, for should he reverse the order, no Arab country would allow him a visa, I decided to postpone my contact with Dr. Jensen until the end of my stay in Berkeley. My lectures at the various classes of the Institute of Human Learning were warmly received. The sales of my book, *"The Making of a Genius,"* were brisk. Invariably, loaded political questions were fired at me and in spite of my impeccable credentials as a liberal, I was branded by some as an "imperialistic swine" for my refusal to condemn Israel as a "war monger" and for my innocuous lectures at the Pentagon. On balance, however, I won many friends and followers among the faculty and student body. Seldom could I walk on the campus unrecognized. Even the vendors at the entrance dispensing orange juice and other goodies, would at times offer me treats. The student paper, always involved in altercations with the university administration, interviewed me on four occasions, a record of sorts and a tribute as well.

Then the unexpected happened. One day I knocked at the door of Dr. Jensen's office and was ushered in by this congenial scholar to a book-crowded and almost furniture bare office. The unpretentious professor received me warmly and forthwith set a date for my lecture at one of his classes.

This news sent a shock wave, electrifying the campus. Hundreds of calls came to my hotel from well wishers who offered their "service in your defense" which I dismissed with goodhearted laughter. No one could recall Dr. Jensen ever allowing a visiting professor into his class. On the day of my lecture, a persistent heart spasm troubled me seriously. Yet in spite of the discomfort, with the aid of a police car, I reached the lecture hall.

The presence of a uniformed security agent at the entrance to the lecture hall reminded me of the event's somber reality. The hall filled to capacity, Dr. Jensen introduced me warmly as "a scholar whose views are remote from my own but whose thesis deserves profound analysis."

Deadly silence prevailed as I embarked upon my discourse, candidly stating that "Dr. Jensen's scientific conclusions are the antithesis of my life's work." At the end, a vigorous question and answer period ensued, at which frank inquiries were directed at me.

At one point a tall handsome, white student, probably in his early thirties, in a tensely emotional frame of mind fired at me the following questions:

"Are you of the opinion that ethnic and or racial origin determines to any extent a child's intellectual potential, or do you regard environmental influences as solely responsible for a youngster's progress or lack thereof? Furthermore, without commenting upon the validity of Dr. Jensen's research, do you believe that his views on this matter could justify a departure from the governments's resolute determination to integrate the nation's public school system?"

The effects of these penetrating questions were deeply felt throughout the hall, with all eyes nervously focusing, alternatively on me and on Dr. Jensen. It was obvious, that the students were wondering whether I would give a straightforward answer and by doing so drag Dr. Jensen into an acrimonious debate, a role so inconsistent with being a host, or would I instead choose an evasive answer.

Fully aware that my utterances would be scrutinized and perhaps taken out of context by the press which in the pursuit of controversy frequently attended my lectures. I paused and as it behooves an iconoclast proceeded as it were to "rock the boat"·

"Indeed, I regard environmental influences, especially during the formative period, the most crucial factor in a child's intellectual development. This conviction is based on my 32 years of research in the area of early child development.

However, should we for argument's sake accept, for one moment, the premise that whites do possess some genetic advantages over the blacks, a theory which I reject vigoriously, then such phenomena would lack practical significance. It is well known that whites as well as blacks develop no more than 10% of their brain capacity. Thus, our children's minds, due to the overwhelming mediocrity, are subjected to an atrocious atrophy, which is the world's greatest tragedy.

It is clear to me that schools, integrated or not, composed of bused children or recruited from local communities exclusively, will remain woefully inadequate, as long as we have an anachronistic school system, one which not only fails to stimulate the child, but by conformity and regimentation actually stifles the student's precious gift of intellectual inquiry. Of course, I advocate a total integration, socially, politically and economically of all minorities into the mainstream of our country. This of course implies total integration of the schools as well. However, I must at the risk of being repetitious state that the school integration will neither enhance the learning process of the blacks, nor will it in any way alter the education of the whites, as long as the school system remains so dismally incompetent." In the course of the evening, I tried to remain as objective as it was possible in discharging my delicate assignment.

A standing ovation which is not common in academia concluded the lecture, after which Dr. Jensen offered a moving tribute to me. On departure, as I shook hands with my host, I noticed his misty eyes.

"As you see, Professor Stern, contrary to what you have read or heard about me, the only thing I am searching for is the truth."

Lecture at a Medical School

My criticism of the nihilism, greed, cynicism and mediocrity which erodes the moral fibre of this country that I love, reaches its crescendo when discussing organized medicine.

From my earliest childhood, I have literally worshipped the medical profession as personifying the most noble aspiration of man. Indeed, what could be more fulfilling and spiritually rewarding than to heal the sick? Consequently, for many years I hoped to become a doctor, a dream that could not be realized in Poland which imposed strict admission quotas to medical schools upon the Jews.

I will never forget an incident which had a profound effect on me. It had taken place when I was a little boy. During an early spring day, as the sun was melting the snow, a man collapsed on the sidewalk not far from our house. Due to lack of ambulances and emergency services, the only way to secure prompt medical attention was to alert the nearest doctor. A little boy ran over to our family physician. The doctor, an elderly man, hesitated by asking "Who will pay me for my medical services?" And of course there was no one who would oblige himself. Meanwhile, the patient having not received any medical care died from an apparent heart attack. The news spread quickly throughout the town. The doctor was reprimanded by his peers. I wonder what kind of reaction would it awaken today, if any at all, as patients sometimes die in waiting rooms of hospitals due to bureaucracy, indifference and staff overwork. Eventually the doctor's license was suspended since the authorities felt that he had an obligation to respond to an emergency call, irrespective of whether or not he got paid. Subsequently, this issue was heatedly debated in town with many people defending the doctor on the ground that he was old and poor. However, I never forgave the physician who in my judgment betrayed his oath by not attending a stricken patient whose life might have been spared.

The reverence in which I hold this calling can best be depicted in my many efforts to persuade Edith to become a doctor. This, of course, never did materialize. I sincerely believe that had she, given her genius, diligence, and compassion, studied medicine, she would have made a major contribution to research, perhaps by alleviating a dreadful disease such as cancer or heart disease.

A few years ago, I received an invitation from a prestigious medical school to give series of lectures for faculty and students. I recall how 12 years prior to it, the parent university of the medical school had me as a participating scholar at a symposium entitled "What Should Be Our National Objectives?" As one would expect, I offered a passionate plea for "national medical insurance as a moral imperative." It was met with caustic remarks, uttered by a member of the medical school who stated that the "U.S.A. has the finest medical care in the world. Any attempt to nationalize medicine is a socialistic plot." To make matters more difficult, the 8 year-old Edith visibly agitated, argued with a professor of economics, who maintained that the U.S.A. has the highest standard of living, documenting it by our Gross National Product and per capita income. To which Edith replied, "In my judgment, infant mortality is a valid criterion to judge a stardard of living. Unfortunately, in this area we lag behind other nations. Here too, we fail in an appalling manner." The latter part of her statement proved to be prophetic since later studies revealed hidden pockets of bleak poverty with the residue of incredible malnutrition observed in the southern parts of our country.

This time I had to appear alone. Edith, my beloved companion, was teaching higher mathematics at the university. The reception that I received was reserved but cordial. Perhaps the most illuminating part was the question and answer period which was recorded for me as follows:

Question: How can we in your judgment improve medical education?

Answer: As I understand the admission requirements of medical schools in the area outside the prescribed quota for minorities consist of a four-fold process; (1) scholastic record, (2) personal interview, (3) applicant's summary, (4) letters of recommendations. I assume that your applicants meet scholastic requirements set forth by the establishment, which of course from my standpoint do not always reflect the applicant's intellectual curiosity, maturity cultural attainments and above all ethics. The applicant will try to impress upon you his devotion

285

to medicine in his interview as well as the summary. And of course he will profess his determination to be of service whenever and wherever called upon and his disregard for worldly possesions.

The letters will corroborate his story as they are obtained from people that he can depend upon. However, we all know that a large number of young people are attracted to medicine mainly because of the enormous financial rewards and the social recognition which the profession bestows. The first two years the student spends in the classroom. In the third year he is introduced to the hospital at which juncture quite often the authorities realize that the student doesn't care much for the patient, has no patience for him whatever. Whereupon we say, well, we spent so much money on him, the need for physicians is so great let him continue. Our student continues and the closer the contact with the patient, the more he resents him. We say anyway he will become a specialist, the less he is involved with the patient, the better a technician he will become and furthermore, the doctors are in a perpetual war with the patients where the mistrust is mutual. As a specialist, the doctor builds a cordon sanitaire from the talkative and boring patient. He must be "impersonal and aloof". Inaccessible during weekends and evenings, he justifies his extraordinary fees with the many years of study and expenses (it is noteworthy that most of the educational expenses incurred by the student of medicine are defrayed by the society which subsidizes the school). As for the length of his studies, they approximate many other professions. On completion, our angry doctor forms a professional association to save on taxes, becomes a co-owner of a hospital where he conveniently sends his patients. My God, what a profane parody of the Hippocratic oath, what a national tragedy!

In order to train compassionate as well as competent doctors, I would recommend the following. Medical schools should admit candidates directly upon graduating from high school or not later than upon graduation from junior colleges. They should be scrupulously screened. Premedical studies should be conducted at the medical school and they should consist of 5 hours of academic training and 4 hours daily in the hospital as orderly and nurse's aide. Let us see how much compassion the applicants have. Let us see whether they are well motivated. How well do they relate to the patient? Can they stand the smell, sweat and blood of a hospital ward? Do they bring succor where there is agony and despair? Only those who are genuinely motivated would be allowed to continue the five or six years of intensive work crowned by the highly esteemed privilege of becoming a doctor. This I would call total educational submersion. Total devotion to the lofty ideals of medicine.

I am confident that a graduate of such a system of schooling would not indulge in sabotaging social progress, would not commit the most heinous crime of subjecting a person to the hazard of a needless surgery in order to earn a few dollars (a recent study revealed in New York that more than 35% of surgeries performed were totally unnecessary). Likewise, I would urge law schools to direct their first year students to the departments of welfare to assist the indigent, the minorities, the poor consumer who is a ready prey for the slick advertiser and exploiter. Let us test the moral fiber of those who are to become the guardians of our freedom and justice. Unfortunately, most of our law students direct their eyes to the green pastures of corporate law, to the lucrative prospects of guiding people in the intricacies of tax evasion.

Question: What do you think about the pressures to which we are subjected to admit often poorly qualified minority applicants?

Answer: As you know, many universities and medical schools have established remedial courses for these people. On the whole, results are good. The stigma of the poor environment with its residue of cultural deficiencies is serious. However, notwithstanding the innumerable handicaps, it is being fought resolutely.

However, I noticed that the motivation of these students is very good, Having come from the bleak ghetto and poverty, the student's roots and loyalties are there. He is fully aware of his sacred responsibility to bring the expertise back for the betterment of the community. He easily relates to the patient, understands his problems.

One may argue endlessly what is more important in the practice of medicine scholarship or plain human compassion. However, we will all agree that only a compassionate and well-trained person in the art of healing can be a good doctor.

Question: Do you oppose the whole medical profession which in your judgment, I gather, lacks professional ethics?

Answer: God forbid. I regard you full-time professors and researchers as the true physicians engaged in the relentless quest for progress. You have chosen your meager salaries over the glitter of the flesh pots of outside practice with its shiny cars, and thickly carpeted offices. I am fully aware that there are practicing doctors who devotedly pursue their noble profession, loved by their respective communities. But as anyone will admit, their numbers are small. I know that your practicing colleagues ridicule you for they feel that you fear the hazards of the business world and escape it by seeking the shelter of the school. Herein lies the tragedy and your triumph. Medicine should not be a part of the business world, it should be a sanctuary and you remain the guardians of the holy torch.

With regards to professional ethics, no concept has been so vulgarly, so obscenely prostituted, reflecting the moral decline of medicine. Historically, professional ethics meant the highest plateau of morality, in serving the patient.

Today this meaning has a diametrically opposed connotation. It is a device to defend another doctor in an act of malpractice, malfeasance or criminal conduct. What a shame, what a national tragedy.

Question: How much should in your judgement a doctor earn, in fairness to him and the society?

Answer: I believe that a doctor whose contribution to the well-being of the community is enormous should have an income commensurate with his role, one that will enable him to live in comfort. He should charge a reasonable fee for his services, as long as any person, regardless of his financial status will, as a matter of right have a guaranteed medical care.

Metro College

Denver, at the foot of the Rocky Mountains, is undoubtedly one of the most beautiful cities. The awe inspiring, snow covered peaks tenderly kiss the skies in the background. It is perhaps this intoxicating splendor that builds Denverites upright and tall. Straightfoward in their speech, tolerant of newcomers, suffering from no poison of prejudice and crime which destroys their Northeast sister cities, Denverites love their skyline and the great unconquerable outdoors. The simplicity of their attire prevents you from guessing their life stations. Its young people flock into colleges, taking life seriously. If you venture 30 or 40 miles into the mountains you will find the 19th century U.S.A. where hard labor and old-fashioned virtues reign supreme.

During my lecture tour in 1973, Denver was the world headquarters of the "Divine Light Mission" headed by the 16 year old "Divine Master" Maharaji who claims direct descendency from God. His devout disciples who occupied the major portion of a huge building utilize the most modern methods of public relations to disseminate the "happy message" to the world. In the evening, they were being driven in poorly ventilated vans to their humble monastery to contemplate and pray.

The "Supreme Master" on the other hand, while in Denver, traveled in a luxurious Rolls Royce to his beautiful villa in a fashionable section of the city. A selected group of slick, smartly dressed executives skillfully managed the "Perfect Master's" financial empire. The movement yielded great financial strength, the origin of which was a well guarded secret. The bulk of his disciples were decent young people, disenchanted with the greed and decadence of their elders, desperate in their search for fellowship, simplicity of life and nobility of purpose. These young, eager, Boy Scout-like disciples could be spotted by their lapel buttons depicting their youthful master. Some of the Metro College students were either weekend adherents of the movement or fulltime "servants." During my stay in Denver, intensive preparations were under way for a "historical event," a huge crusade in Houston named "Millenium 1973" at which the Grand Master was to unfold his "plan for world peace."

A newspaper story in the Denver Post announced my appearances at Metro College. This is perhaps why the lectures were so well attended. My appeal to the young, to shed the chains of greed and prejudice instilled by the older generation was especially warmly received.

One Sunday as I was resting from an exhausting trip to Aspen, a phone call interrupted my tranquility. It was the desk clerk sounding rather nervous. "Mr. Stern, there is a 20 man delegation wishing to see you."

"Who are they? What do they want from me?" I asked half scared.

My apprehension disappeared as a group of youngsters filled my modest room, with many reverently standing in the hall. The spokesman, with trepidation in his voice, softly stated: "We ask you to become our spiritual leader. The hardships which you encountered throughout your life, the dedication to serve people, the courage of your convictions have inspired us. These are the attributes which Maharaji claims for himself. Deeply disenchanted with his hypocrisy, we ask you to lead us."

Touched by this eulogy, I remained speechless for a moment, surveying the group whose facial expressions depicted enthusiasm and sincerity. Then choked with emotion I stated, "This is probably the finest tribute ever given me. Indeed I am deeply honored." At this point I embraced and tenderly kissed a young girl who presented me with a bouquet of flowers.

"Dear friends, I really don't possess these attributes. Please don't glorify mortals, don't seek a panacea, for a change can only come through group efforts."

Whereupon the young people slowly withdrew, bowing their heads.

Oh, how important it is to give the young of our land ideals that they can cherish, services that they can render, rainbows that they can follow!

My enchantment with Denver gained further momentum next day, when I was able to demonstrate to Metro students my technique.

The Executive officer of the State Department of Education, took us on an inspection tour. The elementary school where we visited was located in an old building. The student body, very diversified, was comprised of Mexican, Indian, black, Oriental and other minority children. I was told by the friendly principal that this is a transitory school inasmuch as the parents, migratory workers, move into this negihborhood immediately upon their arrival to Denver. As soon as they can secure a somewhat better paying job, they relocate.

Consequently, seldom does a child attend this school for more than one year. In addition to this serious problem, many children are unable to speak English, and above all the building itself is poorly equipped, being the oldest school building in Denver. Thus, the authorities are determined to close it.

However, I was pleased with the neatness of the children, their good behavior and the cleanliness of the classroom, halls and lavatories. On my request, I was introduced to the first grade whose teacher gladly turned over the class to me. As I surveyed the group, I concluded that one could not find a more ethnically diversified class of children. Almond-eyed Chinese, dark-skinned Mexicans, broadcheeked Indians and Caucasion children were looking up at me with great expectation.

"Good morning, children" met with a cheerful chorus of voices. "How would you say 'good morning' in your home?"

Seven different versions were offered, one of which was the Hebrew "Boker Tov."

"How many of you watch T.V.?" Almost all hands were raised.

"What do you like best on T.V.?"

"Cartoons," replied a girl.

"Sesame Street," said an Indian boy.

Finally, a little black girl in the back row shyly said, "News, cause news tells you all about the world."

"Very good, children, let us talk about the news", I responded, very happy with this turn of events. Since the major events of the day were the war in the Middle East and the infamous deeds of Spiro Agnew, I immediately targeted the discussion into this area, to the astonishment of the teacher and my host. The little Jewish girl argued (as would Jews the world over) "The Arabs attacked Israel on Yom Kippur, when the Jews were praying. What a shame."

"Yes, war is bad. People get killed, my daddy told me" added a little Chinese girl. Soon enough I moved swiftly into the area of ethics, with the children quite maturely commenting on the brutality of war.

"No one should hurt another person, ever" concluded a little Mexican boy.

Subtly I switched to Agnew without being overbearing at all times attempting to remain in the background, so as to enable the children to express themselves freely. About 40% of the class knew who Agnew was. For the benefit of those who did not know him, I said "Agnew is the man who helps President Nixon to run the country", whereupon they all agreed that he should swiftly be removed from office.

"We should kick him and Nixon out," prophetically stated a little black boy, bouncing his fist on the desk. "We would like to have a nice president like Abraham Lincoln," he concluded, with the class warmly applauding him.

The school bell terminated the session. The children affectionately hugged me as I left the room.

"I never knew that my children were so knowledgeable," were the parting words of the teacher.

291

Denver University saw me in a very depressed mood. I was shivering in my tropical suit as the first blizzard covered the campus with a soft blanket of snow. The Middle East war took a heavy toll of Israel, whose very survival was in grave danger and with that, the survival of the Jewish people throughout the world. My host, a professor of psychology, in introducing me to the class, questioned the propriety of my method. "Who says we should all be geniuses? Perhaps it would be better if we didn't emphasize too strongly the intellectual growth."

Soon it became obvious that we were on a collision course, as he rudely with the disapproval of his own class, interrupted my lecture, at times posing irrelevant questions and provoking me into a bitter dialogue. On my request he desisted finally from interfering - so I was able to develop my theme to a truly spellbound class.

With deep emotion, I described the nearly miraculous behavior modification pattern of my students, homeless Nazi victims in post-war Germany. I had instilled in them a sense of self-esteem that they lacked, and thus they were transformed into fiercely dedicated Zionists craving for the return to their ancient homeland in order to live in peace and dignity for the first time in their lives. I stressed that their longing for a homeland was so strong that they wished to be known by their adopted Biblical names only. Eventually they all reached the Promised Land where many of the children attained great distinction in all facets of Israeli life including its defense forces.

Suddenly one student gently asked me, "Are you in contact with your students presently?" This was more than I could bear inasmuch as at the same moment waves of Egyptian forces were pouring across the Suez into the Sinai. Overcome by what non-Jewish sociologists call the Masada Syndrome, I succumbed to my fears and answered: "Not only are the lives of my students in danger, but so is the existence of the State of Israel, the survival of its inhabitants and the Jews everywhere in the face of a totally indifferent world which stood idly by as Hitler systematically annihilated some six million Jews."

The somber expression of the class, some of whom were touched to tears, conveyed the atmosphere. The class adjourned quietly. As I walked resignedly through the corridor I noticed a group of young people following me.

"Could we talk to you?"

"Of course," I answered.

"We have decided to volunteer for service in Israel."

"Are you Jewish?" Before they could answer, I added, "What prompts you to do this?"

"Our group consists of 7 students out of which only 3 are Jewish."

"Thank God," I replied. "You have restored my faith in mankind."

My inquiry at the Jewish Agency in Denver later revealed that these students had sought to leave at once for Israel and could not be shipped off due to lack of transportation. What happened later, I don't know. Perhaps some of them did get to Israel and fought for what they considered to be the principles of juctice and freedom.

WAKE FOREST UNIVERSITY FORUM

The invitation to participate in the "Challenge," a forum conducted by Wake Forest University, stated the following: "It is with great anticipation that I write to you this letter. . . I am much interested in your writings on total submersion precisely because your work is not romantic theory but actual experience. You lend a wholly distinctive air of credibility to an idea which Holt, Gardner and others seem to make look unrealistic." This constituted a triumph for simplicity over the curse of comercialism.

Contrary to convention, I have no ageat to represent me and reject anyone who attempts to mold a desirable image for me. Such were the thoughts that I entertained as the plane smoothly landed at Raleigh Airport during a crisp early spring day in '73. Wake Forest University, consistent with its proud traditon, invited 7 noted academicians encompassing the vast spectrum of sciences as well as public opinion, to debate the issue of the "Crisis in Higher Education".

Present were Dr. Max Rafferty, the former controversial superintendent of Public Instruction of California; Dr. Charles Hamilton, a prominent Columbia University sociologist; Jonathan Kozol, the revolutionary author of " *Death at an Early Age;* "; Donald Barr, the

293

conservative headmaster of Dalton School of New York City, author of
" *Who Pushed Humpty-Dumpty*." Dr. Harold Lyon of Health, Education
and Welfare, R. Kenneth Eble, a noted professor of English from Utah
University, and myself.

As is customary at such events, people of diverse views were pitted
against each other in debate. Therefore, it was small wonder that the
organizers of the symposium would "pair" me, a "certified liberal," with
the arch-conservative Donald Barr.

The debate was held in the new dormitory lounge, where an
overflow of students and faculty clearly favored me. The Winston Salem
paper reported the following:

"Stern called for some loosening up of traditional colleges, saying that
students should have full autonomy, let them run the university and
decide the curriculum. Let them do all in their power to bring a more
wholesome life. He said that professors should be an adjunct to learning,
emphasizing experimentation and teaching students to think for
themselves. Things change, society changes and schools must get that
across."

My opponent, Mr. Barr, defended the traditional structure of the
school. Judging by the students' response, corroborated by the letter
which I received from the University Radio Station which stated, "I
finally got in touch with Donald Barr and he does not want the tapes of
your debate released." I must have emerged victorious from this debate.

A major highlight of the "Challenge" was meant to be a lecture by Mr.
Kozol, whose book portraying the life of black children in Boston, won
him instant fame among the young radicals. The Baptist church was
filled to capacity as the young author in clear departure from the
designated lecture, in an emotion-filled voice bitterly attacked the "racist
America", the "capitalistic system" and the "religious institutions." He
worked himself into a hysteric frenzy, wildly twisting his body in a
"give them Hell" fashion, screaming "join me in the march towards the
destruction of capitalism through a world revolution" with which he
concluded his speech. The polite audience, deeply disenchanted with the
highly erratic conduct of the lecturer, peacefully dispersed. At the exit, I
met my host, Dr. Milner.

"What do you think about that?" he asked me straightforwardly.

"What a magnificent example of tolerance, democracy and academic freedom." I replied. "Here is a Jewish boy, in a Baptist church pulpit, attacking religion in the heart of the South. Defiantly he calls for the overthrow of the capitalistic system while aided financially by the pillars of the very system such as Reynolds Tobacco, Celanese Corporation of America, Western Electric and other companies which sponsored this very forum; yet all his excesses will not be met with any form of repercussion."

"You are right, Aaron, we take it for granted," commented Dr. Milner philosophically.

PENTAGON LECTURE

The Pentagon, the symbol of the ultimate in strength, the fortress of freedom or the instrument of American "regna et divide" as our adversaries depict it, is an unlikely setting for an iconoclastic pacifist. One into whom at his mother's breast was instilled the unsurpassed beauty of Isaiah's "they shall beat their swords into ploughshares" and whose spiritual mold was fashioned by the teachings of Tolstoy, Gandhi, Russell and Einstein, the nobility of their character and thei unswerving faith in the goodness of man. Nevertheless, the Pentagon resplendent with its shiny uniforms and stern looking military men pacing the labyrinthine corridors became my forum during May of 1972.

At the invitation of the congenial chairman of the all-important Armed Forces Educational and Training Council I met with the heads of the various educational agencies within the military super-structure to discuss my methodology. Contrary to my expectation I found many of the military men and civilians to be warm and at times critical of our presence in Asia. The stiff military facade quickly melted as we pursued in-depth discussions about educational techniques and objectives. The climactic event of my Pentagon assignment was a lecture that I had to deliver to the Council. The briefing which I received from the Chairman of the Council emphasized strongly the unusual significance which I am to attach to this appearance inasmuch as said   "Council sets all instructional policies and actually supervises the mammoth network of educational functions within the U.S. Armed Forces encompassing the whole globe wherever U.S. forces are located." In order to obtain optimum results from my presence, the respective members of the Council representing all branches of the Armed Forces obtained earlier a copy of *The Making of a Genius* so as to get acquainted with my philosophy.

For the first time in my career I was overwhelmed by the heavy burden suddenly thrust upon my shoulders as I drafted my outline for this fateful lecture. This was indeed an important milestone in my life since such presentation, I thought, might enable me to employ my theories on an en masse basis. Such an event could result in a profound improvement in the learning process of the widest scope. A brief but generous introduction by the chairman helped me to sort out my impressions and to compose myself as the assembled members observed me carefully. Subsequent to the in-depth discussion of my book I swiftly moved into elaborating my philosophy, enthusiastically unfolding, as it were, the limitless horizons of englightenment which I felt can be offered to enlisted men who for years remain at the disposal of the armed forces, practically for 24 hours a day. "What a unique opportunity that is" I continued "to compensate those who come from culturally deprived homes, to broaden their background, to stimulate their pursuit of knowledge, to equip this easy prey of fraudulent advertising techniques, with enough consumer knowledge to enhance their standard of living, to make them more alert citizens. These are worthwhile endeavors which in no way would weaken the U.S. Armed Forces posture in securing the safety of our country, the military preponderance, or maintaining, the precarious global military balance."

Finally, I turned my discourse to the vital issue of the establishment of an all voluntary armed forces. Here I stressed the moral imperative of introducing the total educational submersion method in order to enable without delay the members of ethnic minorities who by and large were lacking in education to qualify for officer training. "Otherwise," I stressed, "we will create an all white officer corps elite commanding an all black enlisted army, a situation simply unbearable to this country, so firmly committed to erase the curse of racial barriers. The relatively lucrative remuneration planned for the enlistees coupled with the economic disadvantages of the black man in the private sector of our economy will inevitably result in an enormous surge of black youth enlisting". However, what I could not predict then was the steep decline of our economy with its truly devastating effect on the labor market in 1974-76, resulting in a swell of white enlistment due to the lack of job opportunities. I have no doubt however that when the economy recovers my prediction will prove to be correct, unless we take immediate remedial steps to alleviate this disgrace.

My passing remarks about our imprudent involvement in Vietnam which became even more poignant on this day in which escalation of Hanoi bombing was announced, in order "to shorten the war" a wierd rationale-reductio ad absurdum- engineered by Nixon and Kissinger, were challenged by one of the participants. Unable to restrain my anguish, I pleaded, "for our complete withdrawal from immersion in a bloody war in Vietnam - one which cannot be resolved militarily. Our presence in this tortured country in defense of a corrupt and despotic dictator is inimicable to our national interests, for it needlessly kills and maims tens of thousands of our young, millions of innocent civilians, it erodes our moral fibre and mercilessly drains our material resources. Thus, no matter how much we resent the North Vietnam aggressive regime, there can be no justification for our precious young to shed oceans of blood halfway around the world in a futile adventure."

My remarks, uttered with deep emotion, astonished the audience. Having recovered my equanimity I answered the many questions as articulately as I could. A warm applause concluded the event.

"Paul, I hope I did not embarrass you with my impulsive remarks".

"Quite to the contrary, it was refreshing and enlightening. After all, this is a free country, and everyone has the freedom to express his views," answered the Chairman of the Armed Forces Educational and Training Advisory Council. As I walked through what appeared to be an endless Pentagon corridor a flood of warm blood surged to my chest - as an American I felt elated and exultant for I had just witnessed a splendid victory of democracy. Soon enough my euphoria was shattered as I related my experiences to a Jewish military chaplain at the cafeteria "You know," he said, "It behooves us Jews to maintain a low profile and abstain from criticism. After all, Vietnam is not our problem. Must we always be conspicious at the forefront of all crusades ." To which I replied, summoning every bit of sincerity at my command, "Precisely so, as I perceive it Judaism denotes prophets with the fierce dedication to peace and ideals of social justice. The meaningless symbolism and ritualism practiced by organized religions constitutes an obscene blasphemy. It is a moral imperative for every decent person, Jew or Christian, to defend these concepts, to advance this cause by any legal means. I regard myself a patriotic American and a decent human being for doing so ." I could easily read his thoughts, as my companion whose moral infallibility was probably never challenged, in anger left the table without saying goodbye.

On the day of my departure, the commandant of the Pentagon honored me with a military parade concluded with picture taking and the usual amenities. What a significant moral victory was that for decency, for it was a black high-ranking officer comanding the most important military installation in the world, honoring a humble pacifist for the "courage of your convictions."

A car was assigned to drive me to my hotel. The respect which was accorded to me, usually extended to important personalities, was not consistent with my modest clothing, simple demeanor and non-conformist attitude which puzzled the chauffeur a great deal. His quandry was soon relieved when he was instructed to drive me to Pennsylvania Avenue. Having reached the Blair House, he intuitively stopped, hoping that this was the destination of a "visiting dignitary." "Please continue two blocks south," I jolted him gently, whereupon the prestigious limousine came to an abrupt halt at the entrance of the YMCA with my driver barely audibly repeating, "My God how can one go from the sublime to the ridiculous, from the mighty Pentagon to the dingy YMCA".

"My son, simplicity of living is the highest virtue," I answered cheerfully.

For the record, the Pentagon did not implement my proposals.

CHAPTER 29

The Dawn

In my deep concern over the destiny of our country, I am reassured and deeply inspired by America's youth which represents a new hope. Our young people, those wearing long hair and those wearing short, have discarded fancy clothing and shiny cars to embrace the simple joy of life, are leading the way to a just tomorrow.

White youths, rejecting the prejudices of their fathers who stood by Wallace in denying university admission to a black man, now walk hand in hand with their black brothers. Blacks have been elected as student body presidents in many formerly all-white universities not because of their color, but because they possess qualities of leadership.

Our children have acquired a love of peace, a sensitivity of character, and a burning desire to obliterate the inequities which they have inherited. I am greatly moved by the young people who have turned their backs on wealth to serve the Peace Corps and in Vista. I applaud the thousands who have devotedly campaigned for peace candidates.

I can well understand the young men who have chosen to sacrifice their freedom or who have accepted exile rather than mutilate innocent people in a needless war. I admire the Vietnam veterans, who having fought bravely, then had the courage to admit the futility of their sacrifices in a passionate plea for peace. I esteem the young people who opposed the war because it was immoral, rather than uneconomical.

I see the young generation as virtuous, and motivated by idealistic goals unlike any previous one. Our young have rejected chauvinism, dogmatism, and conformity. They have a simplicity of speech which excludes cliches and platitudes. Medical students have chosen the altruistic goals of healing the sick rather than to amass great wealth. Law students provide dedicated service, helping the indigent, protecting the consumer, and maintaining ideals of justice instead of seeking lucrative corporate law practices.

Young girls, rather than seeking the financial comfort of marriage, are determined to attain skills in order to contribute as equal members to society. Young blacks, rather than be merely embittered by the inequities of society, pour by the thousands into universities to learn and uplift their people.

I love you, young America, all of you who have denounced the terror of extremism, the euphoria of drugs, the nihilism of pageantry, the worship of beauty contests, the empty rituals of fraternities, in order to pursue introspection and study.

I also love the hard-working young people who, not having gone to college, provide the goods and services upon which our nation depends. Indeed, you maintain the dignity of labor.

It is my unswerving hope that the vote which the eighteen year olds have gained will lead to a young, vigorous, and honest leadership, not only for the sake of America, but of the world at large. Through such leadership, we can hopefully divert our enormous resources from an insane arms race to a betterment of life by providing high quality education and by solving the problems of dying cities, a stranded ecology, hunger, poverty, and unemployment.

Let us remember that the only way to overcome despair and bigotry is through education.

I love you young people, the best generation America has ever had. You are our tower of hope.

Bibliography

Alexander, Theron, *Changing the Mental Ability of Children in the City*, Philadelphia: Temple University, 1968.

Anastasi, Ann, *Heredity, Environment and the Question How?* Psychological Review, 65, pp. 197-208, 1958.

Aurback, H. A., *Selected Bibliography on Socioculturally Disadvantaged Children and Youth*, Pittsburgh: Learning Research and Development Center, 1966.

Bayley, Nancy, *Research in Child Development: A Longitudinal Perspective*, Merrill-Palmer Quarterly Behavior Development, 11, 1965.

Berger, Stanley, *Development of Appropriate Evaluation Techniques for Screening Children in the Head Start Program - A Pilot Project, 1965.*

Bettelheim, Bruno, *Love is Not Enough*, Glencoe, Ill., The Free Press, 1950.

Bloom, Benjamin S., Allison Davis, and Robert Hess, *Compensatory Education for Cultural Deprivation*, New York: Holt, Rinehart, and Winston, Inc., 1969.

Blough, Glenn O., and A. J. Huggett, *Elementary School Science and How to Teach It*, 4th ed., New York: Holt, Rinehart, and Winston, Inc., 1969.

Brown, George I., *Human Teaching for Human Learning*, New York: McGraw Hill Book Company, 1970.

Bugental, J. F. T., *The Search for Authenticity*, New York: Holt, Rinehart, and Winston, Inc., 1965.

Coleman, James S., and others, *Equality of Educational Opportunity*, Washington, D.C.: U.S. Office of Education, 1966.

Conant, James Bryant, *Slums and Suburbs: A Commentary on Schools in Metropolitan Areas*, New York: McGraw-Hill, 1961.

Cutts, Norma E., and Mosely, Nicholas, *Teaching the Bright and Gifted*, Englewood Cliffs, N.J.: Prentice-Hall, 1957.

Deutsch, Irvin, Katz, and Jensen, *Social Class, Race and Psychological Development*, 1968 by Holt Rinehart, and Winston, Inc.

Dobzhansky, Theodosius, *Heredity and the Nature of Man*, New York: Harcourt Brace Jovanovich, 1964.

Eyseneck, H. J., *The I.Q. Argument*, Library Press, 1971.

Fantini, Mario, and Weinstein, Gerald, *The Disadvantaged: Challenge to Education*, New York: Harper & Row, 1968.

Fine, Benjamin, *The Stranglehold of the I.Q.*, Doubleday Co., Inc., 1975.

Fine, Benjamin, *Stretching Their Minds*, E. P. Dutton, 1964.

Fine, Benjamin, *Underachievers: How They Can Be Helped*, E. P. Dutton Co., 1967.

Fine, Benjamin, *One Million Delinquents*, Gollancz, Ltd., London, 1956.

Fuchs, Estelle, *How Teachers Learn to Help Children Fail*, Transaction, 5:45-49, September, 1968.

Gagne, R. M., ed., *Learning and Individual Differences*, Columbus, Ohio: Merrill, 1967.

Gordon, Edmund W., *Programs of Compensatory Education*, in Social Class, Race, and Psychological Development, 381-406, Deutsch, Martin, Katz, Irwin, and Jensen, A.R., eds., New York: Holt, Rinehart & Winston, 1968.

Gray, Susan Walton, *Before the First Grade: The Early Training Project for Culturally Disadvantaged Children*, New York: Teachers College Press, 1966.

Harter, S., *Mental Age, I. Q. and Motivational Factors in the Discrimination Learning Set Performance of Normal and Retarded Children*, Journal of Experimental Child Psychology, 5, 1967.

Helmuth, Jerome, *Disadvantaged Child*, Brunner Mazel, 1970.

Holt, J., *How Children Fail*, Pitman, 1964.

Holt, J., *How Children Learn*, Pitman, 1967.

Hunt, Kellog W., *Synthetic Maturity in School Children and Adults*, Monographs of the Society for Research in Child Development, 35:1, 1970.

Hymes, James L., Jr., *Before the Child Reads*, New York: Harper & Row, Publishers, 1958.

Jensen, A. R., *The Differences are Real*, Psychology Today, 1973, 7, 80-86. b.

Jensen, A. R., *Level I and Level II abilities in three ethnic groups*, American Educational Research Journal, 1973, 10, 263-276. c.

Jensen, Arthur R., *Genetics and Education*, Harper Row, 1973.

Jensen, Arthur R., *Education and Group Differences*, Harper Row 1973.

Jensen, Arthur R., *How much can We Boost I.Q. and Scholastic Achievement?*, Harvard Educational Review, 1969.

Jersild, Arthur T., *Child Psychology*, Prentice Hall, 1965.

Kamin, Leon, *The Misuse of I.Q. Testing*, Change Magazine, Vol. 5, New York, 1973.

Kohl, Herbert R., *Teaching the Unteachable*, New York: New York Review Books, 1967.

Kozol, J., *Death at an Early Age*, Boston: Houghton Mifflin Company, 1967.

Kozol, J., *Free Schools,* Boston, Houghton Mifflin, 1972.

Kvaraceus, W.C. (ed.), *Negro Self-Concept: Implications for School and Citizenship,* New York:McGraw-Hill Book Company, 1965.

Leonard, G., *Education and Ecstasy,* New York: Delacorte Press, 1968.

Likert, Rensis, *New Patterns of Management,* New York: McGraw-Hill Book Company, 1961.

Lyon, Harold C., Jr., *Learning to Feel, Feeling to Learn,* Charles E. Merrill Publishing Co., 1971.

Maltz, Maxwell, *Psycho-Cybernetics,* Englewood Cliffs, N. J.: Prentice-Hall, Inc., 1960.

Mann, John, *Changing Human Behavior,* New York: Charles Scribner's Sons, 1965.

McClean, G. C., & De Fries, J. C., *Introduction to Behavioral Genetics,* San Francisco: W. H. Freeman, 1973.

Mercer, J. & Brown, W.C., *Racial Differences in I.Q.: Fact or Artifact?* In C. Senna (Ed.), *The Fallacy of I.Q.,* New York: The Third Press, 1973.

Miel, Alice, and Peggy Brogan, *More Than Social Studies,* Englewood Cliffs, N. J.: Prentice-Hall, Inc., 1957.

Neill, A.S. *Summerhill, A Radical Approach to Child Rearing,* Hart Publishing Co., 1960.

President Nixon's *Head Start Report to the Congress,* February 1969.

Osborn, A.F., *Applied Imagination,* New York: Charles Scribner's Sons, 1967.

Passow, A. Harry, Ed., *Developing Programs for the Educationally Disadvantaged,* New York: Teachers College Press, Columbia University, 1968.

Perls, Frederick, Ralph F. Hefferline, and Paul Goodman, *Gestalt Therapy: Excitement and Growth in the Human Personality,* New York: Julian Press, 1951, (Paperback by Delta Books Dell Publishing Co., New York, 1965).

Piaget, J., *Play, Dreams and Imagination in Childhood,* W. W. Norton Co., 1962.

Piaget, J., *The Moral Judgment of the Child,* New York Free Press, 1965.

Piaget, J., *The Stages of Intellectual Development of the Child,* Bulletin of the Menninger Clinic, 1962.

Radin, Norma, *Some Impediments to the Education of Disadvantaged Children,* Children, 15:170-176, September/October, 1968.

Osborn, A.F., *Applied Imagination,* New York: Charles Scribner's Sons, 1967.

Reissman, Frank, *The Culturally Deprived Child,* New York: Harper and Row, Publishers, 1962.

Scott, Louise B. and J. J. Thompson, *Talking Time,* New York: McGraw-Hill Book Company, 1966.

Roberts, Joan L., *School Children in the Urban Slum*, New York: Macmillan, 1967.

Rogers, Carl R., *Freedom to Learn*, Columbus, Ohio, Charles E. Merrill Publishing Co., 1969.

Rosenthal, Robert, and Jacobson, Lenore, *Pygmalion in the Classroom*, New York: Holt, Rinehart & Winston, 1968.

Silberman, Charles E., *Crisis in the Classroom*, New York: Random House, 1970.

Skinner, B. F., *Walden Two*, New York: The Macmillan Company (paper-back), 1962. (First published in 1948.)

Skinner, B. F., *Beyond Freedom and Dignity*, Alfred A. Knopf, 1971.

Skinner, B. F., *About Behaviorism*, Alfred A. Knopf, 1974.

Smilansky, Sara, *The Effects of Sociodramtic Plan on Disadvantaged Preschool Children*, New York: John Wiley & Sons, 1968.

Stanford Research Institute, *Compensatory Education and Early Adolescence*, Educational Policy Research Center, Stanford, Calif. 1973.

Stern, C., and T. Gould, *Children Discover Reading*, New York: Random House, Inc., 1965.

Stone, James C., and DeNevi, Donald P., eds., *Teaching Multi-Cultural Populations*, New York: Van Nostrand Reinhold, 1971.

Taylor, Calvin W., *Creativity: Progress and Potential*, New York: McGraw-Hill, 1964.

Temp, George, *Test Bias: Validity of the S.A.T. for Blacks and Whites in Thirteen Integrated Institutions*, Princeton: Educational Testing Service, January, 1971.

U.S. Department of Health, Education and Welfare, Office of Child Development: *Case Studies of Children in Head Start Planned Variation, 1970-71,* Bureau of Child Development Services, Washington, D.C., 1972.

U.S. Office of Education, *A Chance for a Change: New School Programs for the Disadvantaged*, Washington, D.C.: U.S. Government Printing Office, 1966.

Vandenberg, S.G., ed., *The Nature and Nurture of Intelligence in Genetics*, New York: Rockefeller University Press and the Russell Sage Foundation, 1968.

Warden, Sandra A., *The Leftouts: Disadvantaged Children in Heterogeneous Schools*, New York: Holt, Rinehart & Winston, 1968.

Widmer, Emmy Louise, *The Critical Years: Early Childhood Education at the Crossroads*, International Textbook Co., 1970.

Wisniewski, Richard, *New Teachers in Urban Schools*, New York: Random House, 1968.

Young, Michael, *The Rise of the Meritocracy*, Baltimore: Penguin Books, 1958.

Remarks About the Author

". . .your daughter's upbringing and experiences are unique. . .Edith is the only extremely precocious female in mathematics or science about whom we have heard. . ."

> JULIAN C. STANLEY, Ph.D.
> Professor of Psychology
> Director of Mathematically and
> Scientifically Precocious Youth,
> The Johns Hopkins University,
> Past President of the
> American Education Research
> Association

"But perhaps even more important than the facts themselves, from the standpoint of my students' benefit from this occasion, I feel, were the interest and personal respect generated by your great enthusiasm and dedication, as well as by your intellectual integrity.

One of the most important and lasting aspects of a student's educative experiences, I believe, is in having some contact with intellectually and morally dedicated individuals, and in seeing them in action discussing the topics of their deepest concern. For this my students and I are deeply grateful to you."

> ARTHUR R. JENSEN, Ph.D., Professor
> Institute of Human Learning
> University of California, Berkeley

"His concepts of the educational process, and particularly the belief that anyone can expand his intellectual capability if placed in an intensive

305

intellectual environment, are extremely relevant to Today's Army. The method by which he has transformed his daughter into a 'genius' is directly applicable to the Army training-learning situation, and we in the Army should be exploring such innovative techniques and procedures."

CARL F. BERNARD, Colonel, Infantry
Professor of Military Science
Department of the Army
University of California, Berkeley

"His approach to education is both original and challenging, and my students were quick to perceive its value.

I expect to make this book one of the special text recommendations for one or more psychology courses in the following semester.

NELL G. FAHRION
Professor, Psychology
Division of Natural and
Physical Sciences
University of Colorado at Denver

"Stern, lives a life of dissent, in opposition to the compromise that characterizes many 'well-adjusted' members of American society. His lectures are spirited, colorful, and iconoclastic. They can be pedagogically significant. . ."

PAUL GOLDIN, Ph.D.
Associate Professor of Psychology
Metropolitan State College
Denver, Colorado

"His criticism of various aspects of our culture, are worth being reminded of - and he provides particularly forthright reminders. Also, the positions on child-rearing which are represented in the way he describes the upbringing of his own children should be carefully considered . . ."

JOHN L. HORN, Ph.D.
Professor of Psychology
University of Denver

"Your full involvement and enthusiasm for the learning process was quite inspiring to me personally. I feel that the same qualities were conveyed to the students attending the program. But above all, I was impressed by your strong moral commitments."

JOSEPH O. MILNER, Ph.D.
Professor of English
Advisor "Challenge 73"
Wake Forest University
Winston-Salem, N.C.

". . .I have read it with interest and shall attempt to use some of the techniques described with my own children. . ."

R.S. LAWRENCE, M.D.
Department of Family Medicine
School of Medicine
University of North Carolina
Chapel Hill, N.C.

"You have stated very convincingly - and most interestingly, I might add - a difficult theory on education, which seems to me both compelling and challenging to prevailing notions. I am struck by the apparent applicability of your methods of instruction to situations in which persons are culturally deprived. . ."

HORACE G. DAWSON, Jr., Ph.D.
Cultural Affairs Advisor
Program Coordination Staff
(Policy & Plans)
United States Information Agency
Washington, D.C.

"In this fascinating book Stern presents a vivid graphic portrayal of a determined man who set out to make a genius of his child and did just that. . ."

SPOTLIGHT ON EDUCATION
North American Newspaper Alliance

"A delightfully surprising thing for me about your book was the fact that, though the jacket material would suggest an autocratic punitive approach to education, you are quite humanistic in your approach toward nurturing the uniqueness of the individual child. . ."

HAROLD C. LYON, Jr., Ph.D., Director
Education of the Gifted and Talented
Department of Health, Education and Welfare
Washington, D.C.

307

". . .the only book which will inspire a 13 year-old child and challenge a professor. . ."

JOHN M. FLYNN, Ed.D., Professor
Educational Psychology
Nova University
Fort Lauderdale, Florida

Prof. Stern, 'the youthful thinker' has a passionate love for the young, who, disenchanted with the hypocrisy, greed and bigotry devouring many of their parents, have chosen simplicity of life and nobility of purpose, from which he hopes a spiritually revitalized America will emerge to fulfill its destiny. . . The Joy of Learning will remain a monumental contribution to the world of culture. . ."

BENJAMIN FINE, Ph.D.
Pulitzer Prize Winner
Former Education Editor,
The New York Times

"Often when one discovers something unique and unexpected which we find exciting there occurs within us a strong urge to share this experience with others. . ."

I was struck by the utter drama of his ordeal of survival which few of us can ever fully comprehend. But even more impressive to me was the totally unexpected focusing of all the energy generated by his ordeals into a lifelong crusade to teach others what he had discovered about the working of the human mind. His insights into thinking, learning and experiencing the stuff of life are at once profound and moving. . ."

STANLEY I. BIELEC, Ed.D.,
Assistant Professor of Education
Exceptional Child Education
Florida Atlantic University
Boca Raton, Florida

"In any case, this is probably the only book in the world dedicated to the production of a genius. It's provoking - and refreshing. . ."

RICHARD POTHIER
The Herald's Science Writer
The Miami Herald

"The book provides principles of his Total Educational Submersion Method which signifies a revolutionary breakthrough in Behavioral Sciences. . ."

HERBERT BERGER, Ph.D.
Executive Director
Central Agency for Jewish Education
Miami, Florida

"In this easy to read book Aaron Stern has effectively and beautifully dispelled the myth of the narrow, one-sided, and somewhat mysterious child genius. Edith's sensitivity of people, her keen sense of justice, and her zest and love of living life at its fullest gives us a new and exciting look into childhood and adolescence. . ."

JOHN W. LORTON, Ph.D.
Associate Professor
Early Childhood Education
Louisiana State University, New Orleans

". . . Growing up in my home is a young child. He is six months old. Your accounts of your child's intellectual development set me to dreaming about the beautiful potentiality for intellectual growth in all children. I found in your 'methods' some excellent ideas to be utilized in stimulating growth in this child. I thank you for this. . ."

PATRICIA F. SPEARS
Social Studies Consultant
State of Florida, Dept. of Education

"All educators ought to read this book since it has much to say to those who are committed to educating young people. . . . The challenge, how can teachers in the public schools incorporate some of the Total Submersion Process. . ."

ABRAHAM FISCHLER, Ph.D.
Dean of Graduate Studies,
Director, Behavioral Sciences Center
Nova University, Fort Lauderdale, Florida
Former Assistant Professor, Harvard
University and Professor, University
of California, Berkeley

309

". . .I believe your work is as important - if not more important - than the work of your old friend Einstein."

DAVID ELLER
Menlo Park, California

"Your life and your work are truly remarkable and encouraging. You are one of the few flickers of hope in what I find a generally dismal human prospect."

JESS KLEINERT
Milwaukee, Wisconsin

"This is such an amazing world with all its problems. Individuals such as yourself have served as light-bearers for searching students as myself."

HOWARD KILBY
Honolulu, Hawaii

"I have found your book delightful, moving, and enlightening. I wish to thank you for the book in the name of those of us who strive for the fulfillment of mankind; and to let you know that your words and efforts do not go entirely unheeded."

CHRISTINE ANDERSON
Miami Lakes, Florida

"I am a high school world history teacher and have come to the conclusion that our public school system is almost a total waste of time. I hope some day to set up a private school for my daughters and others, using methods such as yours."

BRUCE MOSIER
Edinburg, Texas

"We are all acutely aware of the education turmoil existing today and knowing you are making an effort to effect changes gives me the assurance there is hope for the future."

DEBBIE ANGELO
Davie, Florida

Index

311

About the Author

Aaron Stern authored 4 other books and many scientific articles. Fluent in 10 languages, he lectured on his theories at over 100 U.S. and European Universities.

In 1974 Stern conducted a landmark study of the Head Start Program for the U.S. Department of Health Education and Welfare. From it emerged proposals for significant reforms, which if implemented "could eradicate the predestined failure of the culturally deprived child".

Stern, alumnus of 4 Universities, is married, the father of 2 and resides in North Miami Beach, Florida.